CONCISE COLLEGE TEXTS
CONSTRUCTION LAW

D0994005

AUSTRALIA
The Law Book Company Ltd.
Sydney : Melbourne : Brisbane

CANADA AND U.S.A.
The Carswell Company Ltd.
Agincourt, Ontario

INDIA
N. M. Tripathi Private Ltd.
Bombay
and
Eastern Law House Private Ltd.
Calcutta
M.P.P. House
Bangalore

ISRAEL
Steimatzky's Agency Ltd.
Jerusalem : Tel Aviv : Haifa

MALAYSIA : SINGAPORE : BRUNEI
Malayan Law Journal (Pte) Ltd.
Singapore

NEW ZEALAND
Sweet and Maxwell (N.Z.) Ltd.
Wellington

PAKISTAN
Pakistan Law House
Karachi

CONCISE COLLEGE TEXTS

CONSTRUCTION LAW

An outline of law and practice relating to the
construction industry

By

JOHN UFF

PhD., B.Sc.(Eng.), C.Eng., M.I.C.E.

of Gray's Inn, Barrister

LONDON
SWEET & MAXWELL
1978

First Edition 1974
Second Edition 1978

Published in 1978 by
Sweet & Maxwell Limited of
11 New Fetter Lane, London,
and printed in Great Britain
by the Northumberland Press Ltd.,
Gateshead, Tyne & Wear

ISBN   *Hardback* 0 421 25090 9
       Paperback 0 421 22430 4

For
DIANA

PREFACE

This book is written chiefly for people in the construction industry. Its aim is to give an overall view of branches of law which impinge on construction projects, particularly when disputes arise. At the same time it descends into detail where this is thought of practical use. My aim has been to make the result readable as well as useful. The chapters devoted to building and engineering contracts may also be of use to members of the legal profession needing a concise introduction to the mysteries of building law.

This edition contains three new chapters. The outline commentaries on the JCT and ICE forms of contract have each been enlarged into separate chapters. In addition to a more detailed treatment, these chapters print relevant parts of the documents. The aim here has been to show the basic working of each form together with the more important detailed provisions. The chapter on standard forms of contract has been enlarged to present a brief review of other important forms likely to be met, including the GC/Works/1 (Government) Contract and the FIDIC (International) Conditions. A further chapter is added dealing with vicarious performance of building contracts and the effects of insolvency. Other additional material includes a section in the special contracts chapter on the sale of new or recently built dwellings, a subject which has created much legal activity of late.

Several developments or changes in the law have made substantial amendment necessary. Among these are the Unfair Contract Terms Act 1977, the Health and Safety at Work, etc. Act 1974 and the new industrial code including the Trade Union and Labour Relations Act 1974. New cases in the building field include *Sutcliffe* v. *Thackrah* (1974), *Anns* v. *London Borough of Merton* (1977) and *Greaves* v. *Baynham Meikle* (1975). The construction industry is now part of a consumer-oriented society. It is therefore no coincidence that each of these statutes and cases represents a shift towards wider liability of suppliers of goods and services to their clients, and of employers to their employees.

In preparing this edition I have been conscious of the great benefit of working within a set of chambers. I am grateful to my colleagues for many helpful discussions and especially to Donald Keating Q.C. whose enthusiasm for this lively subject has always been an inspiration. I am also indebted to my wife Diana Graveson, LL.M. for invaluable assistance on legal and other topics, and for preparing the index.

Extracts from the standard form of building contract are reproduced with kind permission of RIBA Publications Ltd, Publishers and Distributors to the Joint Contracts Tribunal.

Extracts from the ICE Conditions of Contract, 5th edition, are reproduced with kind permission of the Institution of Civil Engineers.

11, KING'S BENCH WALK,   JOHN UFF
TEMPLE
E.C.4

CONTENTS

TABLE OF CASES

TABLE OF STATUTES

CHAPTER 1

THE ENGLISH LEGAL SYSTEM

'CONSTRUCTION law' is neither a legal term of art nor a technical one. It is used to cover the whole field of law which, in one way or another, affects the construction industry. This book is an attempt to cover that field.

Most of the book is concerned with substantive law, that is, law which lays down rights and duties of individuals. The concern of most people is to keep well within the bounds of the law, and to avoid becoming involved in legal action unless it is unavoidable. Therefore substantive law is all that concerns the majority of persons. But the construction industry is a peculiar case. As presently constituted its methods and its structure seem inevitably to lead the parties frequently to the brink of legal action and not infrequently beyond it.

Many individuals in the construction industry will at some time in their careers become professionally involved in litigation or arbitration. And there can be few people who do not have some dealings with contractors' claims, which may be a prelude to litigation. For these reasons the contents of this book extend beyond substantive law, to give some account of the system of English law which lies behind the rights and duties. In this chapter the sources and categories of law are described.

THE NATURE OF LAW

Different types of law create different kinds of rights and duties. Some law applies only between individuals; if A behaves in a way which causes loss to B, then the civil law may allow B to recover his loss from A. Much of the law of contract and tort applies in this way, B's legal remedy being the only sanction against A. In other types of law the state may be involved: if A drives his motor car negligently he may be liable not only for B's resulting loss (through injury to him or his property) but also to criminal prosecution. Some areas of law concern only the rights or duties of the individual against the state; for example planning law or tax law. Most of the principles discussed in this work relate to civil law.

The factor which connects various types of law is that they all exist in order to allow persons to regulate their lives with reasonable certainty, and in a manner which our society presently considers to be just. The law is often accused of unwarranted delay, and of being old-fashioned and too complicated. All these things are at times true. But law is made by and for human beings, who today lead lives of unprecedented complexity. The fact that the law will, if called upon, provide a solution to any type of human problem is in no small degree remarkable.

Law and technology

Most readers will be well versed in scientific or technical pursuits. It may therefore be informative to describe the nature of law by examining examples of ways in which law differs from technology.

First, in technical fields there are always some problems which, for the time being perhaps, cannot be solved. Until recent years engineers considered that tall buildings could not be built in London because of the compressible clay sub-soil. In law such a situation never arises. No matter how complex may be the facts of a case or how confused the law, a judge must always decide which of the parties wins. This does not mean that the judge is always right. There may be an appeal against his decision; but the same problem then confronts a higher court.

The way in which the courts solve a difficult problem may be illustrated by a judicial example. In the case of *S.C.M.* v. *Whittal* (1970) the Court of Appeal had to decide whether the plaintiff's loss was excluded by a rule of law which prevents recovery of purely economic loss in tort. The precise extent of the rule is a matter of uncertainty. In giving judgment, Lord Denning said: "Where is the line to be drawn? Lawyers are continually asking that question. But the judges are never defeated by it. We may not be able to draw the line with precision, but we can always say on which side of it any particular case falls."

Secondly, in engineering and building practice approximation and simplification play a large part: small light structures may be safely designed using approximate methods, while on large structures many more factors have to be taken into account. In law there is (or should be) no such scale effect. The law applied to a claim for £100 in the county court is the same as that applied to a claim for £10 million in the High Court. This view of the law perhaps explains the old adage that a lawyer will never give a simple answer to a simple question. Simplification of the facts of a case does not simplify the law involved, and one may need to know every factual detail before even a guess can be made at the probable legal result. There are many examples in the law reports of leading cases, often going to the House of Lords, where the sum in issue between the parties was very modest.

Thirdly, while technology proceeds upon logical induction and deduction, the development of the common law is different. General principles of law must be arrived at by induction. But when a judge seeks to extend an established principle of law he may do it in a way which does not amount to logical deduction. The common law in its practical application is more the embodiment of common sense than reason. The point may be expressed judicially with a quotation cited in the *S.C.M.* case above: "In the varied web of human affairs the law must abstract some consequences as relevant not perhaps on the grounds of pure logic, but simply for practical reasons."

Fourthly, although technology advances with increasing rapidity not everyone uses the latest theories and methods. Indeed, one could today build a perfectly satisfactory bridge using a design by Brunel. A modern bridge would simply be much cheaper. In law the situation is quite different. Legal rights and duties depend only upon what the law says at the relevant time.

A change in statute law can mean that a man may do an act one day with impunity but on the next at his peril. Common law, or case precedent, is rather different. In theory the judge states what the law is and has always been, so that a restatement applies retrospectively. The practical effect as to the future is, however, the same as a change in the law. Thus, when considering the law on some point, the very latest sources must be consulted; and possible future changes may need to be considered. It is by no means unknown for a court to come to a wrong decision because a recent change in the law was not brought to its attention.

CATEGORIES OF LAW

English law may be categorised in three principal ways. First it may be divided into substantive law and procedure. Substantive law refers to all the branches of law which define persons' rights and duties, such as contract, tort and crime. The substantive law determines in a particular case what facts must be proved to achieve a certain result, such as to establish that a contract has been concluded. These may be called the facts in issue, and in the example given, a fact in issue might be whether the defendant withdrew his offer before the plaintiff accepted it (see p. 44).

Procedure deals with the often complex rules through which the process of law is set in motion to enforce some substantive right or remedy. Procedure properly arises only when there is resort to legal action, but nevertheless it can be as important in practice as the substantive law.

The second division of law is into common law and statute law; that is, into judge-made law and legislation. Thirdly, there is another type of division between common law (used in a rather different sense) and equity, which is a distinction based upon the two great independent roots of English law. These latter two divisions are discussed separately in the following sections because they are fundamentally concerned with the sources of our law. While considering each of the divisions it should be borne in mind that they are not mutually exclusive. Thus statute law deals with procedure and substantive law; judge-made law comprises equity as well as common law, and so on.

Since 1972 a further category of law has applied throughout Great Britain. As a result of joining the European Economic Community (the Common Market) English law became subject to the instruments of the law-making institutions of the EEC. European law is beyond the scope of this book. However, an early example of the effect of the EEC occurred in *Bulmer* v. *Bollinger S.A.* (1974), which became known as the "Champagne" case. The defendant French company claimed that use of the word champagne to describe an English beverage contravened community law. The court was asked to refer the issue to the European Court of Justice under Art. 177 of the Treaty of Rome. Lord Denning said that in matters containing a European element "we must speak and think of Community law, of Community rights and obligations, and we must give effect to them."

The common law

English law is based upon the common law system. The common law means literally the law which was applied in common over all parts of the realm. It was created in the twelfth and thirteenth centuries by the King's judges and has been developed and handed down to the present day.

One remarkable effect of the spread of the English-speaking peoples from the sixteenth century onwards, was that they took with them their laws. In the result, by the nineteenth century there was established literally throughout the world, a greater common law (subject, of course to the effect of statute law in any particular state). Within the British Empire, and later the Commonwealth, this law was maintained as a truly common system by establishing the Privy Council (composed largely of members of the judicial committee of the House of Lords) as the final court of appeal. Today this still applies to a limited number of countries including New Zealand and some states of Australia. Countries which have abolished the right of appeal to the Privy Council such as Canada and South Africa tend inevitably to diverge from English law with the passage of time. The United States, which has developed its own law for 200 years has adopted some notable differences from English law, such as much stricter liability under the law of negligence. The remarkable fact remains however that English courts take note of and guidance from decisions from any common law country, and vice versa. Like the constitution, the common law is not written down in an objective sense. Instead, it is stated by the judge at the end of a case when he gives reasons for the legal rules embodied in his decision. In practice, therefore, the common law is to be found in the reports of judgments, and the law on any topic is to be discovered by reading all the cases which turn on related facts. In some areas there will be only one or two cases, but in others there will be many dozens, perhaps going back several centuries. Building and engineering law is one field where authorities are often sparse, and much assistance can be gained from foreign decisions.

Not every case before the courts makes new law. It is only cases which involve a point of law which can do so; that is, when the law is uncertain in its application to the particular facts. Many cases in the lower courts and in the field of crime depend simply upon conflicting versions of the facts; and when the court has come to a decision on the facts the application of the law is clear. Of the cases which lay down new law the important ones are published in reports. A law report contains verbatim the essential points of the judge's decision. Subsequently, writers of textbooks and articles, and judges in later cases, will comment upon the judgments and mould them into propositions of law. This is an essential process to make the law manageable. But when a point of law arises the lawyer must go back to the reports to discover the words in which the judges have previously stated the law.

It is curious that in England there has never been an official organisation to produce law reports. Until the last century all law reporting was carried on by private enterprise and the quality of reports was not always very high. Today there is a semi-official body which produces a series called "The Law Reports," which are completely authoritative. There are also still a number of commercially produced series. Two of these, which often include important building and engineering cases, are the Local Government Reports (L.G.R.) and Lloyds Reports (Lloyd's Rep.). Two well-known series which contain most cases of general interest are the Weekly Law

Reports (W.L.R.) and the All England Law Reports (All E.R.). Building cases in the Law Reports will appear in Queen's Bench reports (Q.B.) or Chancery (Ch.) or Appeal Cases (A.C.). The abbreviation in brackets is the citation for a particular series (the year, volume and page also being given). Frequently, cases will be reported in more than one series.

The common law is what is said by the judge, not merely what is reported. If, therefore, a case fails to get into the reports it may still be relied upon provided it can be vouched for by a member of the Bar who was present when judgment was given. In the field of building contracts there are sometimes fairly important cases which go unreported. Fortunately many of these are noted in textbooks, such as *Hudson's Building and Engineering Contracts*, and *Keating's Building Contracts*.

A notable disadvantage of case law is that the law can only be altered or restated when a case comes before the court. Thus, if a decision is made which is thought to be wrong, this remains as the law until a similar case comes before that or a higher court, when the law can be reconsidered. Furthermore the judges are concerned solely with stating what the common law is, and not what it should be, so that the courts' capacity for legal development is somewhat limited. Both these disadvantages are overcome by augmenting the common law with statute law.

Statute law

While the judges declare and apply the common law, Parliament in its legislative capacity passes enactments to change the law. Since the seventeenth century Parliament has had supreme authority so that in theory it can make or unmake any law. The passage of Bills through Parliament and the argument over what each Bill should contain can be followed in the news media. The end result is an officially printed document which states, in the words chosen by Parliament, the law on some topic or group of topics.

Once enacted, and in force, the words of the statute are themselves law. But there naturally arise situations where the words call for interpretation, and this is done by the courts. The courts' declarations on the interpretation of statutes thus become a sub-branch of the common law, with which the statutes must be read to decide their meaning.

In addition to statute law proper there has, principally during this century, grown up a great body of delegated or sub-legislation which is written not by Parliament itself but by some other body or official to whom Parliament has given specific authority. The sub-legislators range from ministers of the government to bodies such as local authorities. The delegated legislation, which goes under such names as rules, regulations or by-laws, takes effect as though it were contained in the parent Act which sets out the delegated power. As an example of this, the Public Health Acts contain authority under which the Building Regulations are made. A great deal of day-to-day activity in industry, including the construction industry, is covered by delegated legislation. In general this lays down more stringent and specific duties than those which are to be found in the common law (see Chapter 14).

Much of European Community law consists of delegated legislation. This is made, not under direct English statutory authority, but under powers in the European Treaties to which the United Kingdom has acceded. Rights and obligations so created are given effect to in English law by the surprisingly simple device of providing, by section 2 of the European Communities Act 1972, that such rights and obligations "are without further enactment to be given legal effect."

Equity

In the division between common law and equity each branch comprises both judge-made law (found in case reports) and statute law. The difference arises because before 1873, when the systems began to be jointly administered, there were two separate legal systems which operated in different courts. Equity was applied in the old Court of Chancery, which is still to be found in Lincoln's Inn. Dickens found much to criticise in the courts of early nineteenth-century England; but he reserved the most biting condemnation for the interminable delays of Chancery in *Bleak House*. Happily, the delays in the Chancery Division are today no more nor less than in the rest of the High Court.

The differences between law and equity are still of importance. One essential distinction is that a common law remedy is a right whereas a remedy in equity is, theoretically, discretionary and dependent upon the justice of the cause. The distinction may be illustrated by the consequences of a breach of contract. The common law remedy is damages, which will be awarded however unjustly the plaintiff may have acted, or whether or not damages will make good the loss suffered. Alternatively, in equity the plaintiff can ask for the remedy of specific performance, that is, that the defendant be compelled to fulfil his obligation. But this will be available only under certain conditions, *inter alia*, that the plaintiff has acted fairly and has not delayed in seeking his remedy, and that damages would not adequately compensate the plaintiff (see further p. 59).

Where to find the law

From the foregoing it may be said that the law proper is to be found only in law reports and in statutes, regulations, and the like. However, textbooks and articles by academics, practitioners and judges play an important part in stating the law. Their role is not only to present the source material in a convenient form, but to analyse, comment and speculate upon gaps in the law. In some fields, of which building and engineering contracts are a good example, what is said in the established textbooks can often be a valuable guide to the court in deciding a point of law. Sometimes the court cites, with approval, a particular passage from a textbook as being an accurate statement of the law. The status of any book depends, of course, on the standing of its author and current editor. As a general rule, it is said that the courts pay less attention to the views of an author while he is still alive.

THE COURTS

There are a number of different courts in which civil actions may be tried. A case will be heard at first instance in the High Court (or in small cases in the county court). Appeals may then be brought to the Court of Appeal and finally to the House of Lords. As an alternative, technical cases are often heard at first instance in an Official Referee's court, from which an appeal may be brought to the Court of Appeal and to the House of Lords.

Courts of first instance

The High Court is divided into three divisions: the Queen's Bench, the Chancery and the Family Division. Although each division administers the common law and equity and could theoretically deal with any matter, in practice a particular case will be heard only in one division. Matters concerning the construction industry come usually before the Queen's Bench Division, but occasionally before the Chancery Division. The Queen's Bench Division deals with most common law work, such as contract and tort. The Chancery Division deals with matters such as trusts, contracts relating to land and company and partnership disputes. Formerly some important civil cases were tried on Assize. Under the Courts Act 1971 the Assizes were abolished, and such cases are now tried by the High Court sitting out of London.

County courts can hear almost all civil actions. Their jurisdiction in most common law matters is limited to £2,000, but claims in excess of this figure can be heard by consent of the parties. The main advantages of county courts are said to be their lower costs and shorter delays before coming on for trial. The same is often said of arbitration (see p. 22). But building disputes tend to be costly however they are tried, and the most material consideration is usually to obtain the speediest means of reaching a decision.

An alternative tribunal for cases at first instance is the official referee's court (see p. 17). This is a part of the High Court, but is presided over by circuit judges who are experienced in trying technical matters. In practice such a case will start in the High Court and be assigned to an official referee, usually at the close of pleadings. A further alternative, much used in building and engineering disputes, is arbitration. This type of tribunal is considered later (see p. 22).

Appeals

After the hearing of a case at first instance either party may consider an appeal. From the High Court there is a general right of appeal in civil cases to the Court of Appeal, subject to some cases where leave is necessary and to some exceptions where appeal is excluded. One important exception is that there is no appeal from a finding of fact in an official referee's case, except for facts relating to fraud or to professional negligence.

After appealing to the Court of Appeal, a further appeal may be brought to the House of Lords. But leave is always necessary and is sparingly given. House of Lord's appeals are almost always on a point of law. Where both the High Court and the Court of Appeal are bound by previous decisions it is possible to appeal direct from the High Court to the House of Lords.

Every court must apply statute law. However, with case law, courts are generally bound only by the decisions of higher courts, and to some extent by their own decisions. It is therefore usually necessary to take a case to a higher court if it is sought to avoid an adverse case precedent. It is theoretically possible for the House of Lords to reverse its own previous decisions. But in practice the law laid down by the House of Lords is likely to be changed only by Parliament.

Further Reading

Glanville Williams, *Learning the Law* (9th ed., 1973).
Kiralfy, *The English Legal System* (6th ed., 1978).
Newton, *General Principles of Law* (2nd ed., 1977), (Concise College
    Texts).

CHAPTER 2

LITIGATION AND ARBITRATION

SOME disputes in the construction industry must be determined in the courts by litigation; others may be tried either in the courts or by arbitration. This chapter deals with the ways in which both types of tribunal function in terms of procedure and the rules of evidence. To a large extent what is said about litigation applies to arbitration, with the proviso that arbitration arises out of an agreement, so that what takes place at a hearing is less predictable and less standardised than in litigation. The procedure in a court action will be described and the ways in which arbitrations differ will be indicated.

PROCEDURE IN LITIGATION

Procedure is a general term which covers all the various steps necessary to turn a legal right into a satisfied judgment. It might appear that procedure is mostly concerned with the rituals of trial and is the concern only of lawyers. But this is far from the case. In many actions, particularly larger civil actions, the trial is only a small part of the whole case. What goes on before the trial can often have a great effect on the course of the action and may make the trial unnecessary. The pre-trial proceedings will usually extend over months, or even years. Matters such as appeals and the enforcement of judgments may prolong the matter further after the trial. Procedure covers all these different stages in an action.

The basic steps involved in a civil action in the Queen's Bench Division, where most cases concerning the construction industry will be brought, are as follows. The action is begun by issuing and serving a writ; the defendant must enter an appearance to the writ and then an exchange of pleadings takes place so that the parties will know the area of contention. The next stage is the preparation for trial which includes discovery and inspection of documents. Finally comes the trial itself which results in a judgment. If there is no appeal the matter is concluded by enforcement of the judgment. The principal steps are enlarged upon below.

Very few actions proceed in such an apparently straightforward manner. At every stage there are alternative courses, and in fact the great majority of High Court actions (well in excess of 90 per cent) are disposed of before reaching trial. The preparatory stages between the issue of the writ and trial are known as interlocutory proceedings. Where any decision may be given by the court at an interlocutory stage it is usually given by a master of the court. He is an official who has most of the powers of a judge, and is responsible for giving judgment in a great number of cases which for various reasons do not come to trial, *e.g.* because there is no defence to the action.

Commencement of proceedings

A typical action is begun by issuing a writ, which places the matter on the official record. A copy of the writ must be served on each defendant, either by delivering it to him personally, or by other means such as service on his solicitor. The general rule is that the defendant must be made aware of the proceedings against him. But there is an important exception in respect of limited companies. The Companies Act 1948 provides, by section 437 that a company may be served by leaving the writ at the registered office, or sending it there by post. A company which does not trade from its registered office must therefore make arrangements to collect the post.

Some actions must be begun by a different type of document such as an originating summons or a petition; *e.g.* a petition is appropriate to wind up a company (and a marriage). After he has been served with a writ the defendant must formally show his intention to defend the action by entering an appearance, after which the parties, through their counsel or solicitors, exchange pleadings.

Pleading

The object of pleadings is to define the areas of dispute between the parties before the action comes to trial. A party will not normally be allowed to raise a matter at the trial unless he has pleaded it. A pleading should contain a concise statement of the facts relied upon, but not the evidence by which they will be proved; and matters of law should not normally be pleaded. The first pleading is called the statement of claim, from the plaintiff; the defendant answers with a defence; and if the plaintiff wishes, he may answer the defence with a reply. In larger cases there may be pleadings subsequent to the reply. In arbitrations, pleadings are subject to the arbitrator's directions; but usually they follow High Court practice, and are called points of claim, points of defence, etc.

With his defence, the defendant may raise any matter of complaint which he has against the plaintiff. When the complaint is in the nature of a cross-action, it is called a counterclaim. A common form of counterclaim in building disputes is that the work, for which the plaintiff claims payment, is defective. If the counterclaim has a sufficiently close connection with the claim (it need not always arise out of the same contract) it may operate as a set-off or defence to the action. This may have important consequences in costs. If a counterclaim is raised, the plaintiff must serve a defence to it with his reply.

The statement of claim, and any counterclaim, must claim the remedy sought. In contract and tort actions the remedy is usually damages, that is, the payment of a sum of money by way of compensation. But there are several other remedies, which may be more appropriate in different circumstances, such as an injunction, or specific performance, or rectification of the contract. The damages claimed may be either general or special. General damages are claimed where the plaintiff has suffered loss which cannot be quantified, in terms of money, e.g., damages for pain and suffering or for loss of use of a building by the plaintiff himself. General damages must be assessed by the judge and no specific sum is claimed in the pleading. This is contrary to the position in the United States, where one reads of specific and substantial sums being claimed as damages, e.g. for personal injury. Special damages are those which can be calculated in money as an actual or prospective loss. Special damages are sometimes referred to as "liquidated" sums which should not be confused with "liquidated or ascertained" damages which may be specified in a building (or other) contract at £x per week for delay. Provided the amount of x is not wholly unreasonable, the employer (if it was for his benefit) may recover the sum without proof as to his actual loss.

The form of pleadings is illustrated by some examples (see overleaf) concerning a dispute over delay and defective work. Note that the disputes emerging from the pleadings are two in number; first, whether the engineer's instructions justify a further extension of time and a monetary claim; secondly, who is responsible for the wearing course (if defective). This case is typical of many, brought either in the High Court or in arbitration. Often the question, which party is to be plaintiff, is a matter of chance. Had the contractor been paid in full (in the example) the employer would be more likely to initiate the proceedings. The courts attach no significance to the order of parties, save that the task of pursuing the case rests with the plaintiff.

In the High Court of Justice
Queen's Bench Division

Between

AB CONTRACTORS LTD.   *Plaintiff*

and

CD DISTRICT COUNCIL   *Defendant*

STATEMENT OF CLAIM

1. By a contract dated 1st January 1977 incorporating the ICE conditions of contract the Plaintiff (as contractor) agreed to carry out road works for the Defendant (as employer).
2. The Plaintiff has carried out and completed the works but the Defendant has failed to pay the balance of the Plaintiff's final account namely £10,000, which sum has been certified by the engineer, one EF.
3. It was an implied term of the contract that the Defendant would not interrupt the regular and economic progress of the Plaintiff's work.
4. In breach of contract—the Defendant, through the said EF, issued instructions in excessive and unreasonable numbers and at unreasonable times, whereby the Plaintiff has suffered loss and damage in the sum of £20,000. Particulars of the instructions relied on appear in Schedule I; particulars of the Plaintiff's loss appear in Schedule II.

AND THE PLAINTIFF CLAIMS

   (1) Under paragraph 2 £10,000
   (2) Under paragraph 4 £20,000
   (3) Interest under statute.

In the High Court, etc.

DEFENCE AND COUNTERCLAIM

1. The Defendant admits paragraphs 1 and 2 of the Statement of claim. Paragraphs 3 and 4 are denied. The Plaintiff's final account includes all sums to which they are entitled under the contract.
2. The contract required the Plaintiff to complete the works by 31st December 1977 and provided for liquidated damages at £1,000 per week. The Plaintiff failed to complete until 25th March 1978, *i.e.* 12 weeks late. EF has granted an extension of time of 2 weeks. The Defendant is, therefore, entitled to withhold the sum of £10,000.

3. In breach of contract, the wearing course laid by the Plaintiff did not comply with the specification. In consequence, it became fluid at a temperature of 25°C. The Defendant has incurred expense in replacing the wearing course in the sum of £30,000. Particulars of breaches of the specification are contained in Schedule III: particulars of the Defendants' expense are contained in Schedule IV.
4. The Defendant will set off the counterclaim against any sum due to the Plaintiff.

AND THE DEFENDANT COUNTERCLAIMS

(1) Under paragraph 2 £10,000
(2) Under paragraph 3 £30,000

In the High Court etc.

REPLY AND DEFENCE TO COUNTERCLAIM

1. The Plaintiff admits paragraph 2 of the Defence and Counterclaim, save that EF should have granted a further extension of 10 weeks in respect of the matters particularised in Schedule I. The Defendant is therefore not entitled to liquidated damages.
2. Paragraph 3 is not admitted. EF orally instructed the Plaintiff to vary the specification for the weaving course, but wrongfully failed to confirm this in writing.
3. If (which is denied) the wearing course behaves as alleged, it did not require to be replaced.

If either party needs more information than his opponent's pleadings give he may ask for further and better particulars of specific matters. If such particulars are not given voluntarily the court may order the information to be given. Requests for further particulars are very common. This should not be so, since the pleading should contain all necessary information. In the above examples, a request for further particulars of the engineer's instruction, relied on in paragraph 3 of the reply, would be justified.

If, in the course of the case, either party thinks that a third party should be liable to him for any part of the claim which is made by his opponent, he may serve a notice on the third party which has the effect of bringing him into the action. There will usually be an exchange of pleadings between the third party and the party who joined him. There may be more than one third party (called first, second third party, etc.). If a third party wishes to join a further party himself, that party becomes a fourth party. The court must give directions as to the mode of trial; and where third and subsequent parties are joined, the trial of certain issues (*e.g.* whether materials are defective) may be ordered between the plaintiff and one of the subsequent parties.

Interlocutory judgments

In certain circumstances the plaintiff may obtain judgment on his action without going to trial. He may do so if the defendant fails to enter an appearance to the writ or if he fails to serve a defence within the periods laid down by the rules of court. In these cases the judgment is called a default judgment. The defendant may apply to the master to have it set aside, but will usually have to pay the costs thrown away. Another form of pre-trial judgment is summary judgment. The plaintiff may apply to the master for summary judgment on the ground that there is no defence to the action. If the master is not satisfied that there is an issue which ought to be tried, he may give judgment for the plaintiff. Frequently the only dispute on an application for summary judgment is whether or not the defendant has a counterclaim which he is entitled to set-off against the sum due to the plaintiff.

In disputes arising from construction contracts, the procedure for summary judgment is often invoked by the contractor seeking payment of sums certified by the engineer or architect. In such a case, the employer may set up a triable issue, and seek leave to defend the action, by disputing the certificate, *e.g.* on the basis that it is not given in accordance with the contract. If the certificate is admitted, the employer may establish a counterclaim and set-off, *e.g.* based on delay or defective work. In the example pleadings above, an application for summary judgment on the claim would clearly have failed.

While default or summary judgment disposes of many actions, many others reach settlement. Sometimes this is because one party lacks confidence in his case. But a more common reason is that the sums of money in issue and the inevitable risks of litigation do not justify the heavy expenditure on legal costs. Construction disputes, because of their technical complexity, tend to be more costly than most litigation.

Proceedings up to trial

After the close of pleadings, if an action is to continue, there follows the work of preparing for trial which will be done mainly by solicitors. One important step is discovery and inspection of documents, when each side must disclose to the other all documents which relate to the matter in dispute. The rules of court require a party to disclose all documents which are *or have been* in his custody or power. This includes documents which have been destroyed or which are in the physical custody of some other person. All relevant documents must be disclosed except those for which privilege is claimed. Privileged documents include letters between the party and his solicitor, and documents which came into existence as a result of the dispute, such as experts' reports. The mere fact that documents were intended to be private, personal or confidential, does not permit a party to withhold them. Documents which come to light on discovery may have a profound effect upon the course of the action.

Another task for the solicitors is to interview witnesses and to take proofs of the evidence which they will give at the trial. The proof should be directed towards the issues remaining between the parties after the exchange of pleadings. A proof begins *"John Brown will state . . ."* and at the trial counsel will use the proof to help his examination of the witness, who must usually give his evidence from memory. It is not uncommon for a witness to say one thing in his proof but something less helpful in his evidence at trial. Lawyers speak of such a witness as being not up to proof.

In cases with a technical or scientific element it is common for one or both sides to produce expert witnesses. These are persons, usually unconnected with the case, who are called to give their professional opinion on the matters in issue, *e.g.* as to whether certain material is defective. While an ordinary witness of fact is paid only his expenses, an expert must be paid a proper fee for his work. It is curious that experts called in support of opposing cases tend often to disagree. While some divergence of opinion is inevitable in any dispute, experts should be wary of seeking to support the party by whom they are employed. An expert who over-states his case rarely benefits his client.

Judges and Referees

The great majority of actions in the Queen's Bench Division take place before a single judge who decides all matters of fact and law. Civil jury cases are extremely rare and are practically confined to actions in defamation and fraud. Cases which involve prolonged investigation into technical matters, such as building disputes, are mostly tried in an official referee's court. The judges in these courts were, before the Courts Act 1971, known as official referees. Now they are designated circuit judges appointed to deal with official referees' business. But the original term continues to be used. An official referee has practically the same powers as a High Court judge and sits in a special court in the Law Courts in London, although he may also sit elsewhere.

In official referees' cases the rules of evidence and procedure generally follow High Court practice and include pleadings and discovery of documents. There are, however, some distinctive features. In official referees' business, experts' reports, which technically are privileged documents, are usually ordered to be disclosed to the other side before the start of the case. This can assist greatly in narrowing the area of dispute and therefore in saving costs. The practice does not apply to arbitration proceedings, although it is always open to the parties to waive privilege in respect of specific documents.

The official referees' practice has recently been extended to all divisions of the High Court by new rules of court. These require a party to obtain leave before calling expert evidence; such leave is usually granted only on terms that the experts' report is disclosed in advance of the trial.

A further feature of official referees' business is the use of schedules as a method of collecting into a convenient form all relevant particulars from each side. Detailed particulars are not usually given in the pleadings and instead the official referee will order a schedule, to be completed by each side. Where there is a dispute, *e.g.* over rates for work the schedule might show, for each item, the plaintiff's rate and comments and the defendant's rate and comments. This will avoid many folios of legal prolixity. Such documents are known as official referee's, or Scott schedules.

Trial and enforcement

English law is based on the adversary system. The court has no duty and very little power itself to investigate the issues. It is limited to making a decision on the basis of the case presented by the parties. Consequently, unless a party is an individual who can represent himself, the parties must have their cases presented by an advocate. In the High Court barristers have exclusive right of audience. In arbitration however, any person may act as advocate. It is usually found of advantage to engage an advocate who has not been concerned personally in the dispute.

The proceedings at a trial usually start with the plaintiff's counsel opening the case by outlining the issues involved. If there is a counter-claim, the plaintiff will usually open his case as to this. In the course of opening, the pleadings and relevant documents will be read or referred to. After opening, the plaintiff calls his witnesses, including experts, to give evidence about the matters in dispute. The defendant's counsel then opens his case and calls evidence for the defence. After this there are the closing speeches and submissions on the law, first from the defendant's and then from the plaintiff's counsel. In addressing the court it is the duty of counsel to put forward all the relevant facts and law, not just those favourable to his client, although he will endeavour to present the matters in the most favourable light. This is particularly important when legally qualified advocates appear before a lay arbitrator.

Finally, the judge must come to his decision on the facts (if there is no jury) and on the law. He gives his decision in the form of a reasoned judgment, which may be delivered immediately the case is concluded, or reserved to a later date if the judge wishes to consider the case. The successful party is entitled to judgment and his costs are usually ordered to be paid by the loser, although the award of costs is discretionary. An award of "costs" or "taxed costs" means that the successful party will recover such of his outlay in costs as were strictly necessary, and subject to fixed scales of allowable charges. In practice, a successful party is likely to recover not more than about two-thirds of what he must pay to his solicitor. This is a further reason why cases tend to settle before trial.

The award of costs becomes less clear when, in addition to (or in lieu of) a defence, the defendant has a counterclaim. If both claim and counterclaim succeed then each party is prima facie entitled to costs on his claim. To save the laborious process of taxing items of cost as between claim and counterclaim, the court will often make a more rough and ready order, such as one side to pay a proportion of the costs of the other. However, when the counterclaim is sufficiently connected with the claim to operate as a set-off and defence, if the counterclaim exceeds and extinguishes the claim, the defendant is entitled to ask for his costs of the action.

A further matter which should be dealt with in a judgment is interest. The court is empowered to give interest on a judgment for debt or damages under the Law Reform (Miscellaneous Provisions) Act 1934. The amount awarded should normally represent a realistic rate for the time which the successful party has been wrongfully deprived of the sum awarded.

Frequently the parties, having started an action, make attempts to settle it before trial. This disposes of a great number of actions. If the case is not settled, but nevertheless the defendant considers he is likely to be found liable in some degree, he may protect himself against costs by making a payment into court. The plaintiff will be notified of the payment in, and may within a limited period of time accept the money in settlement of his claim, together with his costs on the claim. If the plaintiff chooses not to accept the payment in and fails to obtain judgment for more than that sum, he must pay the defendant's costs after the date of notification of the payment, even though he has won the action. The judge must not be told of the payment in until he has determined how much money the plaintiff is to recover. The calculation of how much to pay into court and the decision as to whether or not to accept the payment may require very careful consideration in view of the large sums for costs which may be at risk. Where there is a counterclaim the plaintiff may pay into court, but any payment in must state whether it takes into account the claim of the party making the payment. This has further important consequences as to costs.

The final stage in the action is enforcement of the judgment. If the judgment debtor does not pay, there are a number of methods available to the judgment creditor by which he may obtain at least some payment from the debtor. The most important of these are that the sheriff, who is a court officer, may seize and sell the debtor's goods; the debtor's land may be charged for the payment or a receiver may be appointed to receive the rents and profits; if the debtor has a bank account or has debts owed to him, his banker or debtors (if they can be identified) may be ordered to pay over the sums owed to satisfy the judgment.

A further weapon available to the judgment creditor, where the debtor is a limited company, is winding up. The Companies Act 1948 section 422 allows the creditor to petition for winding up, *inter alia*, if a debt for more than £50 has not been paid within three weeks of demand. However, if the threat does not produce payment, winding up is unlikely to improve the judgment creditor's position, since he will then rank equally with other unsecured creditors (see further Chapter 8).

INTERNATIONAL CASES

Many activities in the construction industy contain some foreign element, particularly since for legal purposes Scotland is a foreign country. Such activities may be the design of works abroad by architects or engineers based in England, or construction work abroad by an English company. Disputes arising out of such projects may entail procedural problems above those encountered in domestic actions. Whenever a dispute exists which has a foreign element, two preliminary questions must be answered before any court can determine the matter. First, which national court has jurisdiction to determine the dispute? secondly, what law will that court apply? A third question which may arise after the dispute has been determined is how the judgment can be enforced. The resolution of these questions forms a separate branch of English law which is called conflict of laws or private international law. The first title is preferred because there is in fact no international law relating to private suits, but only national laws for solving international conflicts.

In the construction industry the international problems most likely to be encountered are those involving contract or tort. In this section the problems of jurisdiction, procedure and enforcement of judgments in the English courts are discussed; the question of which law the English courts will apply is dealt with in the general chapters on contract and tort (see pp. 60 and 186).

The English courts normally assume jurisdiction to hear actions in contract and tort in three cases. First, if the defendant is served with a writ while he is present in England: a foreign company is regarded as being present in England if it carries on business here. Secondly, if a defendant submits to the jurisdiction, *e.g.* by bringing an action himself in the English courts. Thirdly, the English courts may in certain cases allow a writ to be served abroad so that the action can proceed, if necessary, in the absence of the defendant. The principal grounds on which this is allowed are: that the defendant is normally resident in England; or that the dispute arises from a tort committed in England; or that the dispute arises from a contract which was made or broken in England, or agreed to be governed by English law. But in the latter cases, relating to actions in contract, the rules of court provide exceptions where the defendant is ordinarily resident in Scotland. Actions in contract against Scottish defendants must generally be brought in Scotland.

Where there is a conflict of laws involving an arbitration clause in a contract, the validity and effect of the clause is to be determined by the proper law of the contract (see p. 60), unless the contract provides otherwise. But the arbitration is not necessarily governed by the same law as the contract. The leading case of *Whitworth* v. *Miller* (1970) held that the procedure in an arbitration was governed prima facie by the law of the country in which the proceedings were conducted.

If the English courts have jurisdiction to try a case it may proceed to trial in the same way as a similar case with no foreign element, and generally English rules of procedure and evidence are applied. After establishing the facts in a case, it is necessary to decide which country's law is to be applied. If this should be

English law, then the judge will treat it as an ordinary domestic case and decide upon the law himself. If the law to be applied is a foreign law, then the relevant provisions of that law must be proved to the court, usually by an expert legal witness.

An ancillary problem in international cases may be the enforcement of a judgment in a country other than that which gave the judgment. In every country enforcement depends solely on the internal laws. In England a foreign judgment for damages is enforceable only if it complies with certain conditions. These require that the foreign court had proper jurisdiction; that the judgment is final and for a fixed sum; and was properly obtained.

If these conditions are satisfied the judgment may be enforced in one of two ways. First, there are reciprocal statutory arrangements between England and a number of foreign countries by which a judgment may be reigistered in England and enforced as an English judgment. Such arrangements exist, *inter alia*, with Scotland, Northern Ireland, and most western European countries. Secondly, a judgment from a country with which there is no statutory arrangement is treated as a simple contract debt which may be enforced by suing in the English courts.

ARBITRATION

Arbitration is an alternative to litigation which is much used for settling disputes which involve technical or commercial elements. The essence of arbitration is that disputes are determined by a tribunal of the parties' own choosing. The right to arbitrate and the powers of the arbitrator depend largely upon agreement between the parties. An arbitration agreement is often to be found as one of the clauses of a standard form of contract, *e.g.*, clause 35 of the JCT form and clause 66 of the ICE form. In such clauses the parties agree to submit specified future disputes to arbitration. There may also be an agreement to arbitrate made after the dispute has arisen. Either type of agreement, provided that it is in writing, is governed by the Arbitration Act 1950. This provides that the arbitrator's authority is irrevocable except through the court (section 1) and that the arbitrator's award is final and binding (section 16) unless the parties agree otherwise. The Act also contains important provisions governing the conduct of the proceedings.

The Act provides that a reference to arbitration is deemed to be to a single arbitrator unless the contrary is expressed (section 6). Many commercial arbitrations (*e.g.* in shipping disputes) employ three arbitrators who sit as a court of two arbitrators (one appointed by each side) with an umpire to settle any disagreement. This mode of trial has never been favoured in building and engineering disputes. The JCT and the ICE forms of contract refer specifically to one arbitrator; the international (FIDIC) conditions contemplate that there may be more than one arbitrator.

It is unnecessary for the arbitrator to be named in the arbitration agreement (section 32). Written agreements usually provide for the arbitrator to be agreed by the parties or appointed by a specified person or body. The JCT and ICE forms provide for appointment, in default of agreement by the presidents of the RIBA or ICE respectively. Where the parties cannot agree and there is no mechanism for the appointment, the court has power to appoint an arbitrator (section 10).

Connection with the courts

Although arbitration is a private alternative to litigation, arbitration proceedings are closely connected with the courts. The connection arises in two ways. First, arbitrations are usually conducted in a manner analogous to proceedings in the High Court. Thus, the arbitrator must follow the ordinary law and not his own concept of fairness. Interlocutory proceedings, such as pleadings and discovery of documents, usually (though not necessarily) follow the same course as in litigation. The procedure at the hearing will usually follow High Court practice, and in matters of any substance the parties will be represented by counsel or solicitors. However there are essential differences of procedure: the Arbitration Act makes no provision for joining two or more defendants or for third parties. Thus if a dispute necessarily involves more than two parties, the matter should be taken to court, or a special arbitration agreement drawn up. The alternative is to have two tribunals try the same issue, with the possibility of inconsistent findings.

The rules of evidence apply to arbitration, although in practice they are applied somewhat less rigidly than in the courts. Where a technically qualified arbitrator is appointed (which is usually the case in building and engineering disputes) he is entitled to use his own knowledge, *e.g.* as to whether particular material is defective. This does not, however, preclude calling expert witnesses to try to influence the arbitrator's opinion.

Secondly, the courts exercise various controls over arbitrations, and have wide powers to make orders relating to the proceedings. Under section 12 of the Arbitration Act, the court has power, *inter alia*, to issue subpoenas to compel the attendance of witnesses at an arbitration, and to make orders in relation to security for costs, discovery of documents, preservation and inspection of goods or property and to issue interim injunctions.

If a point of law arises in the reference there is machinery to have the point decided by the High Court, although the arbitrator himself may decide it and must do so if there is no application to the court. Under section 21 the arbitrator may state any question of law arising in the course of the reference as a special case for the decision of the High Court. This method is usually referred to as a consultative case and is appropriate where the point of law is fundamental to the reference or concerns the powers or jurisdiction of the arbitrator. Alternatively he may state the award or part of the award in the form of a special case, usually referred to as an award case. This is appropriate where only the final decision depends on the point of law.

The decision whether to state a case is discretionary. If the arbitrator refuses the court has a discretion to order him to state a case. Normally the arbitrator should accede to the request unless, for example, he has made a decision on the facts which makes the point of law irrelevant to the outcome. The special case should be drafted by the party applying for it. The case must formulate precisely the issue for the opinion of the court and should also request all relevant findings of fact.

The courts can also exercise controls over the conduct of an arbitration and over the award. Under section 23 of the Arbitration Act the court has power to remove an arbitrator who has misconducted himself or the proceedings, or to set aside his award. Misconduct covers a wide range of factors such as refusing to hear one party or deciding the wrong issues. But not every irregularity amounts to misconduct. The popular belief that an arbitrator must guard against any expression of opinion during the reference is unjustifiable.

An alternative, less drastic remedy lies under section 22, by which the court has power to remit matters to the arbitrator for reconsideration. An example of remission is where an award deals wrongly with the question of costs, *e.g.* by awarding them to the unsuccessful party. The court has no power to substitute its own decision for that of the arbitrator. If satisfied that the award cannot stand, the court will remit the matter to the arbitrator with directions as to the courts opinion. The overall function of the courts in all such matters is to ensure that the parties to an arbitration obtain a fair and proper decision.

Arbitration agreements

Since arbitration is a matter of private agreement, the arbitrator's authority depends upon the scope of that agreement. This may be completely general, such as an agreement to refer "any dispute or difference arising under or in connection with the contract"; or it may be limited to specified areas of dispute *e.g.* an agreement in a lease that disputes as to rent increases are to be settled by arbitration. Building and engineering contracts usually contain wide arbitration clauses, but the clauses in the JCT and ICE forms are expressed to be subject to certain time limits. Also, arbitration under these forms cannot, in respect of most disputes, usually be opened until after completion of the works (see pp. 147 and 169).

Although parties may agree that future disputes will be settled by arbitration, this does not prevent either party from litigating. Any clause purporting to exclude the right to action in the courts is void. However, there is a form of agreement which makes the arbitrator's award a condition precedent to litigation. This will be enforced by the courts and means that no action may be brought until the amount of liability has been determined by arbitration. This form of agreement is known as a Scott v. Avery clause, after the case in which it first came before the courts. Neither the JCT nor the ICE arbitration clause is in this form, so that under these conditions of contract, arbitration and litigation are alternatives.

If one party to an ordinary arbitration agreement starts an action in the courts he is technically in breach of contract. The courts will not, however, order specific performance of an arbitration agreement. Instead, the usual remedy is to apply for a stay of the court proceedings, thus leaving arbitration as the only remedy. If a stay is not granted the arbitration cannot proceed because only one tribunal can determine the parties' rights in the same matter and the courts must prevail.

The court's power to order a stay of proceedings and thus indirectly to enforce the arbitration agreement is discretionary; but the court leans in favour of granting a stay so that the burden of persuasion falls on the party wishing to litigate. There are several grounds on which the court may refuse a stay. For example, if there are more than two parties involved in the dispute a stay will usually be refused since the Arbitration Act makes no provision for two defendants or for third party proceedings. To grant a stay of litigation in this case might result in two different tribunals trying the same matters with the danger of inconsistent findings.

The award

Unlike a judgment of the court, an arbitrator's award does not usually give reasons or make findings other than of the overall result, *e.g.* that the Respondent pay the Claimant £x, or that the claim be dismissed. The award must decide all the disputes submitted, and must be clear and certain. Unless it contains errors on its face, no appeal may be brought, unless the procedure for case stated has been invoked. If the award contains an error, the procedure for setting aside (section 23) or remission (section 22) may be invoked.

The arbitrator is bound to make a final award, unless the dispute is compromised. In addition, section 14 of the Arbitration Act gives power to make an interim award. In practice this is much more restricted than the power of the court to give summary judgment. However, an interim award is a convenient remedy when liability is not seriously in issue but quantum cannot be proved, for example, without waiting until remedial work has been completed.

An arbitration award does not of itself compel the losing party to comply with its terms. The aid of the court must be invoked, and this may be done in two ways. First, under section 26 of the Arbitration Act, the award may, by leave of the High Court, be enforced as a judgment. For the purpose of obtaining leave, an originating summons is issued in the High Court. Secondly the award may be enforced by action, not relying on the Arbitration Act. If the award is for a sum of money, the claimant may seek to enter summary judgment for the amount awarded. In either case the losing party is entitled to object to enforcement, *e.g.* on the ground that the arbitrator had no jurisdiction.

Two final matters which must be dealt with by an award are costs and interest. As to costs, the arbitrator should adhere to the principles of the courts, *i.e.* the successful party should have his costs unless there are proper reasons for not so awarding. An award which deprives the successful party of costs without reason may be remitted by the court. As to interest, the arbitrator has an implied power to include this in his award. He should normally do so, interest being awarded at a realistic rate for the time during which the successful party has been wrongfully deprived of the sum awarded.

From the foregoing it may be apparent that arbitration has both advantages and disadvantages over litigation in the courts. Among the attributes are said to be speed and cheapness, but this is not always the case. Arbitrations are, however, conducted in private. Among the disadvantages, not necessarily to both parties, may be noted the arbitrator's lack of many of the powers possessed by judges, for example, to penalise defaults; and that judges and courts are provided by the taxpayer, while the parties must pay for their own arbitrator and court facilities.

EVIDENCE

Every fact in dispute which is necessary to establish a claim must be proved to the judge or to the arbitrator by admissible evidence whether oral, documentary or of other kind. Oral evidence must normally be given from memory by a person who heard or saw what took place.

In a civil action the facts in dispute must be proved on a balance of probabilities, unlike criminal cases where proof beyond reasonable doubt is required. The burden of proving a fact usually lies upon the party asserting the fact. When deciding how much evidence must be adduced in a case, it must be considered that a judge, unlike an arbitrator, cannot draw upon his own knowledge, except in very obvious matters, and therefore every fact relied on must be proved. However, in practice some of the facts in the case will usually be admitted by the other side and they will not then need to be proved. Admissions may be made in the pleadings, or in any other appropriate manner, *e.g.* in open correspondence between solicitors. If party A refuses to admit some fact which, while likely to be true would be expensive to prove formally (*e.g.* that the clerk of works signed hundreds of day-work sheets purporting to bear his signature), party B may serve him with a "notice to admit facts." If the facts are not then admitted, the court may order party A to pay the costs of proof, whoever wins the action.

The main body of the law of evidence is concerned with which matters are admissible as evidence; that is, which matters a party is entitled to try to prove in order to establish his case. For example, matters which are subject to privilege are not admissible; also, a party may be prevented (or "estopped") from denying a fact which he has previously led the other party to believe to be true or where he has acted as though the fact were true. Normally a witness may relate only what he himself has perceived. Facts which another person has told him are hearsay and are admissible only under special circumstances. Further, a witness may not normally give his opinion; although an expert may do so, and is usually introduced solely to give his professional opinion on matters in dispute. In almost every case there is in addition to oral testimony, documentary evidence. The documents, if admissible, must either be admitted as authentic by the other side, for example, on discovery; or if they are not admitted they must be proved.

The law of evidence also deals with the way in which oral testimony may be given. A witness at a trial or arbitration is subjected first to examination-in-chief by his own advocate, then to cross-examination by the opposing advocate and then if necessary he is re-examined. Evidence is adduced by the witness answering questions put by the advocates and sometimes by the judge or arbitrator. In examination-in-chief there is a fairly strict rule that an advocate must not "lead" the witness by asking questions which suggest the answer. There is good practical sense behind this rule, because if the advocate misunderstands the case, a witness who is trying to be helpful may succeed in giving misleading evidence. In cross-examination however, an advocate may, and indeed should, lead the witness in order to put to him the opposing version of the case. Thus, if Mr. Jones is suing his employer as a result of an accident at work, his own advocate may say "What happened on 3rd April?" but not "Did you fall from a scaffold because no toe boards were provided?" On the other hand, the opposing advocate may properly say "Come, come, Mr. Jones, you were larking about and it was all your fault, wasn't it?"

A party may compel the attendance at the trial of any person whom he wishes to give evidence for him. Attendance is enforced by serving a subpoena on the witness and paying his expenses. In an arbitration the High Court has a specific power under the Arbitration Act 1950, section 12, to issue subpoenas. Witnesses may be compelled to attend either to give oral evidence or to produce relevant documents in their possession. Discovery cannot normally be ordered against a person who is not a party to the action.

There is no right or property in witnesses. Any person may be called by either side. The potential witness is, however, entitled to refuse to give a statement in advance to one side (or both). A party may even compel his opponent to give evidence. But it is unwise to call a person who may be hostile because he cannot be cross-examined by the party calling him. There is therefore no means of challenging what such a witness says in evidence.

Further Reading

Odgers' Principles of Pleading and Practice (21st ed., 1975) Casson and Dennis.

Graveson, *The Conflict of Laws* (7th ed., 1974).

Russell on Arbitration (18th ed., 1970), Walton.

Cross and Wilkins, *Outline of the Law of Evidence* (4th ed., 1975).

CHAPTER 3

SPECIAL PARTIES

THE principles of substantive law as set out in this volume apply to an individual of full age and legal capacity. While most persons involved in the construction industry will have attained the age of majority (now 18) they will usually be involved only as employees or representatives of some larger body whose legal capacity and liability is limited. In this chapter the position and status of the different parties who make up the construction industry is examined. Then the legal capacities and liabilities of those bodies most commonly encountered is discussed.

PARTIES IN THE CONSTRUCTION INDUSTRY

The first and most essential person is the client, who is to pay for the new building or works. He may be referred to as the building owner or promoter, but the term employer is preferred since this is used in both the JCT and ICE standard forms of contract. The employer may have practically any status; he may be a private individual, a partnership, a limited liability company, a part of local or central government, or anything else.

The person who carries out the works is the contractor, who is sometimes called the builder, building contractor, civil engineering contractor, etc. The employer and the contractor are the two parties to the main contract, which may also be called the building contract or engineering contract according to the nature of the works. Although there are other persons connected with the main contract, who may even be named in it, such as the architect, these are not parties to the main contract. Their relationship is by separate contract either with the employer (as in the case of the architect or engineer) or with the contractor (as in the case of a sub-contractor) or even with both as when the sub-contractor gives a direct warranty to the employer before entering into the sub-contract (see p. 97).

The contractor, in all but the smallest jobs, usually sub-contracts (or sub-lets) parts of the work to one or more sub-contractors. Main contracts commonly provide for certain sub-contractors to be chosen by the employer. They may then be called "nominated" sub-contractors. Main contracts usually contain special provisions governing the rights of the parties in regard to nominated sub-contract work (see JCT form clause 27, ICE form clause 59A, B). Sub-contractors who are not nominated are sometimes called domestic sub-contractors. Both the contractor and the sub-contractor will usually be a limited liability company although small concerns may be partnerships or even sole traders.

The task of designing and of supervising the construction of the works is usually carried out by the same person or body. Under a building contract he is the architect, and under a civil engineering contract the engineer. The title "architect" is, in England, reserved by statute for those professionally entitled to it (under the Architects Registration Act 1938). Unfortunately the same is not true for engineers, although in some countries, such as Italy and West Germany, the title is protected. Usually a specific person or firm is designated as the architect or the engineer under the main contract. The person so designated will be given certain powers and duties by the contract which he must exercise as the construction work proceeds.

The architect or engineer is not a party to the main contract or to any sub-contract, but is engaged under his own contract with the employer. Engineers (who professionally call themselves Consulting or Chartered Engineers, to avoid confusion with engine drivers) and architects practise mostly in partnerships, but occasionally as individuals.

A quantity surveyor is often found on larger contracts. His principal function is to take off quantities from the drawings and other technical descriptions of the work and to prepare from them bills of quantities; and to carry out measurements and valuations. In the JCT form a quantity surveyor is named and given certain duties. He does not appear in the ICE form. His duties there are placed on the engineer (see p. 163), but are usually carried out by a surveyor. The surveyor may be engaged by the employer or by the architect or engineer under a separate contract. He will practise either in a partnership or as an individual.

In his capacity under the main contract, the architect or engineer is required to carry out functions as the employer's agent (see p. 69) when he must represent the interest of his employer. In addition the architect or engineer is usually required to carry out certain duties in an independent capacity, such as certification. In such cases while he remains the employer's agent, he is under a duty to hold the scales fairly between the two parties.

In addition to the major participants there is a group of persons who appear in building and engineering contracts with certain functions and powers, such as the engineer's representative, the clerk of works, the agent and the foreman. All these persons are individuals who represent one or other of the major parties; *e.g.* the engineer's representative and the agent represent on site, respectively, the engineer and the contractor.

Finally, the construction industry, perhaps more than any other, depends largely upon manual labour, albeit with mechanical assistance. Most men employed will be members of a trade union and therefore the contractor and through him the employer is likely to be affected by the peculiar status of trade unions in law, particularly having regard to recent legislation. The existence of trade unions is often expressly recognised in building and engineering contracts.

In the following sections the differing legal capacities and liabilities of those bodies most often encountered in the construction industry are discussed. It will be seen that the most common is perhaps the limited company, while most of the professional bodies will be partnerships. As an illustration of the practical importance of the legal status of the parties, consider a building owner who has a claim against his contractor (a limited company) for bad workmanship, and alternatively against his architect (a partnership) for bad design. If the contractor is insolvent or nearly so, the claim may force the company into liquidation, and so effectively defeat the claim, even though the directors may personally be well off. The architect's firm however will have no such protection. Even if the firm as such is insolvent, the partners may be liable to the limit of their personal possessions (see further Chapter 8).

LIMITED COMPANIES

The word company embraces any body of persons combined for a common object, whether incorporated or not. But it can also be used, as it is here, in the narrower sense of an incorporated company, as opposed to a partnership. A company may be limited by shares or by guarantee or it may be unlimited. This section is concerned only with companies limited by shares, and this will include practically all incorporated companies likely to be connected with the construction industry.

The essential feature of a limited share company is that it exists as a separate entity, distinct from its shareholders (members). The assets of such a company are contributed by the members who buy the shares, and their liability on behalf of the company is limited to the nominal value of their shares. The assets and debts belong to the company, which has perpetual existence until it is dissolved. Changes of the directors or the members do not change the company. When a company contracts only the company can sue or be sued on the contract. If a wrong is done by or to a company, the proper party in any action is the company itself. A member is generally not entitled to conduct an action even if he is the majority shareholder.

The principal governing legislation is the Companies Act 1948, under which there are two types of company limited by shares. These are known as public and private companies. Private companies are usually much the smaller and are often family businesses, although they comprise by far the greater number of registered companies. In a private company the number of members is limited to 50, and the shares cannot be freely transferred. But a private company enjoys certain privileges which make its operation simpler. In a public company the membership is unlimited; shares are quoted on the Stock Exchange and are freely transferable. However, both private and public companies must file annual accounts which are open to public inspection. Only unlimited companies are not required to file accounts.

Generally any legal person, including another company, can buy shares, but a company cannot buy its own shares or those of its holding company. The capital of a company has a nominal or authorised limit, which in a small private company is often £100. Some or all of this will be sold or "issued" by dividing it into shares of, say, £1 each. The proceeds of sale become the initial assets. Thereafter the company, according to its fortunes, may prosper so that its assets go up in value, or founder so that they go down. This rise or fall is reflected in the price for which the shares would sell. Thus the initial value of the shares and the value of the issued capital may bear no relation at all to the financial state of the company. A £100 company may have assets worth many thousands of pounds so that a £1 share is worth perhaps £100; whereas a company with issued capital of £1 million might be insolvent so that its shares are worthless. Shareholders are paid an annual dividend out of the company's profits. Additional capital can be raised by selling unissued shares or, more usually, by a fresh issue of shares for some specified new venture. Companies may also borrow money; this may be done by issuing a debenture as security.

On the formation of a company two important documents called the articles and the memorandum of association, must be drawn up. The articles regulate the internal management of the company, for example, the appointment and powers of directors. The memorandum sets out, *inter alia*, the objects for which the company was formed. A company is entitled to do only those things set out in the memorandum, and anything reasonably incidental to them. An act outside the company's object is *ultra vires* and void. Thus, where the objects of a company included making and selling railway carriages, plant and fittings, and carrying on the business of mechanical engineers and general contractors, it was held to be *ultra vires* to finance the construction of a railway line. The company was therefore not liable for breach of this contract: *Ashbury Rwy. Co. v. Riche* (1875).

The effect of the *ultra vires* rule on a person dealing with a company is substantially amended by the European Communities Act 1972 section 9. This provides that in favour of a person dealing with a company in good faith, a transaction is deemed to be one which is within the capacity of the company to enter into. Such a person is not bound to inquire into the capacity of the company to contract.

The modern practice is to draft the objects clauses of commercial companies very widely so that, for example, a building company may if it wishes carry on business in property development or plant hire or financing. There will, however, always be some activities which are *ultra vires* such as (in one reported case), pig breeding.

Management of companies

A company is run jointly by its board of directors and by the members in general meeting. The directors are usually appointed at an annual general meeting and must usually hold shares in the company. Prima facie only the board has power to act for the company, but subject to the articles it may delegate powers to a managing director and to other directors, who frequently hold paid employment in the company. Subject to the *ultra vires* rule a company can contract in the same way as an individual and will be equally bound by written or oral contracts provided they are entered into by an agent with authority (see p. 68). A company may also be liable in the ordinary way for torts, although they must necessarily be committed through its servants. The only question which arises is whether the company is vicariously liable for the particular act of its servant (see p. 182).

In carrying out his office, a director's primary duty is to the company and not to the shareholders. He must act in the best interests of the company, and must disclose his personal interest in any contract made by the company; *e.g.* if he stands to make a personal profit from a contract. A director must act with reasonable skill and care, although he may delegate his duties to employees of the company. Although the liability of members is limited, a director may become personally liable, *e.g.* for breach of duty, or for fraud. A company must have a secretary who is responsible for putting into effect the decisions of the board and for keeping records.

The members exercise their powers by voting in general meeting. It is obligatory to hold an annual general meeting at which the usual business includes dividends, accounts and reports, and the election of directors. Any other meeting is called an extraordinary general meeting and may be held to consider business such as the removal of a director or amalgamation with another company. Meetings must be conducted strictly in accordance with statutory procedure.

Winding up

When a company is wound up all its business is concluded by a liquidator who takes over the powers of the board. He collects in the debts which are owed to the company and, so far as he is able, pays off the creditors. He may have to decide whether an alleged liability shoud be settled, such as a pending action for damages against the company. When the debts are paid, any money left is distributed among the members. Finally the company is dissolved and ceases to exist.

Winding up may be compulsory or voluntary. Compulsory winding up is by order of the court, for which a petition may be presented by, *inter alia*, a creditor or a member. In most cases the grounds for winding up will be that the company is unable to pay its debts; and this is deemed to be so if a debt for more than £50 has not been paid within three weeks of demand. This provision is an incentive to a solvent company to pay its debts promptly or to risk a winding up petition from a creditor with its attendant adverse publicity. A company may be wound up voluntarily for any reason by the passing of a resolution in general meeting. This may be done, *e.g.* to amalgamate with another company, or because its liabilities prevent it from carrying on business. If the company is insolvent the creditors control the winding up. For the consequences of insolvency, see Chapter 8.

If a company is found to be insolvent the assets are distributed according to the bankruptcy rules, under which the creditors' interests are divided into classes which are paid in the following order: winding up costs; preferential debts; debentures; ordinary debts; and member's capital. Preferential debts include taxes and employee's wages; ordinary debts include an unsatisfied judgment against the company. Thus, if a creditor is owed an undisputed ordinary debt, a judgment for the debt is of no advantage if the company goes into liquidation before it can be executed. The situation on final distribution of assets of an insolvent company is usually that the first three classes are paid in full, the ordinary debtors are paid so much in the pound, and the shareholders are left with nothing.

PARTNERSHIPS

As opposed to a limited company, a partnership or firm is an unincorporated body of persons combined for a common object. While the incorporation or dissolution of a company is an unequivocal act, it can be difficult to determine whether or not a partnership exists. There is often a written partnership agreement or articles of association which may be in the form of a deed. Professional firms such as architects or consulting engineers will invariably have their constitution set out in such a document. However, a partnership agreement may be oral or even inferred from the course of dealing between the parties. The essential feature which distinguishes a partnership is the carrying on of a business in common with a view to profit. There must be a sharing of net profits, although the shares need not be equal and it is unnecessary for all the partners to take part in running the firm. They may make whatever arrangements they wish among themselves.

A partnership is not a separate legal entity. It is owned by the partners in common, and each partner, except a limited partner, is liable for the firm's debts. The capital of the firm is contributed by the partners in any proportions on which they agree, so that one partner may contribute only capital and another only his expertise. They may agree to share profits in any proportions and prima facie losses must be shared in the same proportions. The question whether a partnership exists or not may have important consequences, e.g., in relation to loans. If A lends £100 to B to help to finance B's business, then depending on the circumstances, a partnership agreement could be inferred between A and B so that A might not only lose his £100 but could also liable for B's debts.

In the absence of a special agreement, a partnership ceases on the death, bankruptcy or retirement of a partner and must be dissolved. A partnership agreement therefore usually provides for the firm to be carried on by the surviving or remaining partners. The true names of the actual partners must always appear on correspondence. The number of partners in a firm is, in most cases, limited to twenty. Much of modern partnership law is codified in the Partnership Act 1890.

A partnership may be formed for any legal purpose. A partnership agreement usually specifies the nature of the business so as to limit the partners' powers to bind each other. But they are always free to vary the agreement so that the *ultra vires* principle has no application (see p. 33). Neither the partnership agreement nor the accounts are ever open to public inspection. A partnership agreement may specify the duration of the firm, but if no time is stipulated it lasts during the will of the partners. A partnership created to carry out a specific project is sometimes called a syndicate.

Partnerships are particularly suitable for associations of professional persons, such as consulting engineers, architects and solicitors. Partners are liable to income tax but not to corporation tax.

Management of a firm

The relationship of partners between themselves must be that of the utmost good faith, and no partner may make a private profit from the firm's business. Subject to agreement to the contrary, every partner may take part in the management of the partnership. Ordinary business matters are decided by a majority of partners, but changes in the constitution of the firm, such as taking in a new partner, must be agreed unanimously. Every partner is prima facie the agent of the firm and can make binding contracts on its behalf. If a partner commits a tort in the course of the firm's business, the firm will be liable.

When a firm is liable in contract or debt the partners are jointly liable so that they should all be sued, either in their own names or in the name of the firm. A judgment may be enforced against any of the partners sued, but if they cannot satisfy the judgment and another partner is discovered who was not joined in the action he cannot subsequently be sued. It is therefore important to sue all the partners in contract. In tort, however, partners are jointly *and* severally liable so that they may all be sued together, or sued separately until a judgment is satisifed.

Dissolution

Partnerships, like marriages, are made until death or dissolution. But partnerships have the added advantage that they may be dissolved with or without the help of the courts. A partnership may be dissolved automatically by, *inter alia*, expiry of a fixed term for which it was formed, or if it was formed for an indefinite period by one partner merely giving notice to the others of his intention to dissolve it. If the partnership is for a fixed and unexpired term it can only be dissolved by a decree of the court on the grounds, *e.g.* that one of the partners is guilty of prejudicial conduct, or that the business can only be carried on at a loss.

Unlike the dissolution of a company, which can take place only after winding up and distribution of assets, dissolution of a partnership is the first act. This is followed by the winding up of the firms's affairs, for which purpose the partners' authority continues but may be limited by the appointment of a receiver. After winding up a final account is produced and the assets are distributed in the following order: firm's debts to creditors; firm's debts to partners; and partners' capital. Any residue is divided amongst the partners.

OTHER CORPORATE BODIES

Local authorities

Local authorities are corporate bodies whose consitution and powers derive directly or indirectly from statutes. Constitutional and general matters are found principally in the Local Government Act 1972. The powers and duties of local authorities are laid down in many statutes; examples of particular importance are the Public Health Acts 1936 and 1961, the Education Act 1944, the Highways Act 1959 and the Town and Country Planning Act 1971. Every part of the country is within the jurisdiction of one or more authorities. The distribution of functions between the different local authorities and between the authorities and central government varies according to district and according to the service in question. Different local authorities may combine to provide certain services by setting up joint committees or a permanent joint board.

The Local Government Act 1972, which came into operation in April 1974, brought about a massive reorganisation of local government. In addition to the re-drawing of boundaries, the Act created a uniform two-tier structure of local government throughout England and Wales. In any area, the primary local authority is now either a county or a metropolitan county council. Below this are district councils, many of which have as their base the former county boroughs or boroughs.

London has always been in a special position and its present local authority system was laid down in the London Government Act 1963. It consists of 32 London Borough Councils, including the City, presided over by the Greater London Council. This system replaced the old London County Council and Metropolitan Boroughs and in doing so transferred much more power to the boroughs.

The powers of a local authority to enter into contracts are similar to those of an incorporated company. A local authority will be bound by a contract whether written or oral, provided it is made by an agent acting with authority. However, since the powers of all local authorities derive directly or indirectly from statute, their capacity to contract is limited by these powers in the same way that an incorporated company is limited by its objects. Any contract which a local authority purports to make for a purpose beyond such powers is *ultra vires* and void.

In entering into a contract a local authority must also comply with its own standing orders, unless such orders are suspended. In one case a council attempted to make a contract without complying with its standing orders as to invitation of tenders. It was held that this action could be restrained by a group of local contractors who considered themselves prejudiced, but only in the capacity of ratepayers: *R. v. Hereford Corporation, ex p. Harrower* (1970). However, a contract once entered into is valid despite any breach of standing orders. Any member of a local authority having an interest in a contract made or proposed must disclose the fact in the same way as a director of a company. Such a member may not, however, take part in discussion or voting connected with the contract.

The Crown

The word "Crown" has several different meanings. It is here used to denote the sum total of governmental powers exercised through the civil service, that is, central government as opposed to local government. It is not synonymous with the monarch, but historically governments have found it convenient to invest themselves and their executive departments with the privileges and immunities attaching personally to the monarch, and so the term "Crown" is an apt metaphor. Formerly the Crown enjoyed general immunity in tort and could only be sued in contract by a special process. The situation was radically changed by the Crown Proceedings Act 1947, which now allows the appropriate government department, or the Attorney-General, to be sued by ordinary process of law.

In contract the Crown is bound by any agreement made on its behalf by an agent having authority. But if a contract provides for funds to be voted by Parliament, an affirmative vote is a condition precedent to liability. With some exceptions, principally relating to the armed forces, the Crown is liable in tort as if it were a private person of full age and capacity, and it can be made liable for the acts of its servants or agents. By virtue of its residuary immunities the Crown cannot be restrained by injunction, nor can it be deprived of property. The Crown also has a far reaching privilege to restrain disclosure of documents in legal proceedings, whether or not it is a party to the proceedings.

One distinguishing feature of the Crown in building and engineering contracts is that the main contract is often subject to a standard form known as GC/Works/1. This gives the Crown (or "the authority") very wide powers of control (see p. 181). However, some departments favour the use of the standard forms used in the private sector, such as the ICE form.

The above discussion concerns the position of British government departments being sued in England and Wales. Where it is sought to bring an action against a foreign government, whether the action is brought here or abroad, the position may be very different. As a general rule a foreign sovereign state is immune from action brought in this country, whether in civil or criminal law. Further, if there is no local equivalent to the Crown Proceedings Act, it may not be possible to bring proceedings in the country in question. Parties contracting with foreign states should therefore give serious consideration to the question of guarantees or performance bonds.

Public corporations

Public corporations, which operate the nationalised industries, are essentially companies which are owned by and run for the benefit of the state. They have almost all been created by statute since 1945. Most of the corporations have a complete monopoly, although there are exceptions, *e.g.* British Airways. There is no fixed pattern for the constitution of a public corporation, but each constituent Act provides for a minister to be answerable to Parliament for the industry, and he will have powers to appoint and dismiss members of the board and to give general directives in the national interest. Some nationalised industries function principally through centralised control, *e.g.* the National Coal Board, while others such as the Gas Board have regional units which are relatively free from central control.

The powers of a public corporation to make contracts and to conduct legal proceedings are substantially the same as those of an incorporated company. A public corporation could theoretically be restrained from an *ultra vires* act, but the objects set out in the constituent Acts are expressed in such general terms that in practice it is unlikely. The corporations do not in general enjoy the privileges and immunities of the Crown, and their employees are not classed as civil servants.

TRADE UNIONS

A trade union is never to be found directly engaged in a building or engineering contract unless, perhaps, in the incongruous role of employer. However, the existence and importance of trade unions is often expressly recognised in building contracts; *e.g.* the "fair wages" provisions, clause 34 of the ICE form and clause 17A of the JCT form. Since the last century, trade unions have occupied a special position in law which has from time to time been modified by statute. The latest and most radical modifications were introduced by the Trade Union and Labour Relations Act 1974, which was itself amended in 1976, and by the Employment Protection Act 1975. These Acts are generally abbreviated as T.U.L.R.A. and E.P.A. But the Acts were partly inspired by the Industrial Relations Act 1971, now repealed. A brief review of the 1971 Act assists in placing the current legislation in perspective.

The Industrial Relations Act 1971 introduced many new concepts, some of which are now incorporated in the present Acts. Thus the 1971 Act created the concept of unfair dismissal and set up the Industrial Tribunals and the National Industrial Relations Court to deal with industrial disputes. The Tribunals continue to exist and the Court's functions are now carried out by the Employment Appeal Tribunal. Among the features of the 1971 Act which have not been re-enacted may be noted the provision for ordering a "cooling-off" period in industrial disputes involving the national interest; and the statutory right not to belong to a trade union. The 1971 Act also gave certain privileges to unions which registered under the Act (few did).

T.U.L.R.A. introduced a new definition of a trade union as an organisation (whether permanent or temporary) consisting wholly or mainly of workers whose principal purposes include the regulation of relations between workers and employers (section 28). A body such as a site organising committee may therefore be a trade union. There is now maintained, instead of a register, a list of trade unions; the inclusion of an organisation on the list is evidence that it is a trade union (section 8). A trade union is not a corporate body, *i.e.* it does not have a legal existence distinct from its members. However, T.U.L.R.A. (section 2) allows a union to make contracts, to hold property through trustees, to sue and be sued in its own name, and allows a judgment to be enforced against it.

T.U.L.R.A. grants certain immunities under the law of tort to trade unions and to members and officials (sections 13, 14). No court is to compel an employee to do any work (section 16); collective agreements are to be unenforceable unless stated to be enforceable. Under the 1971 Act the closed shop was prohibited. The law now permits both a pre-entry (where a prospective employee must be a union member) and a post-entry closed shop (where a new employee is required to join the union). The setting up of a closed shop is a matter for agreement, but industrial action to influence the employer's decision is lawful. An employee who is dismissed because he is not a union member in a closed shop is not unfairly dismissed and has no right to compensation from his employer (nor from the union if their refusal of membership lead to his dismissal). The only permitted reason for non-membership is on the ground of religious belief. Then the employee will be compensated for his dismissal (see T.U.L.R.A. Schedule I).

The new Acts draw a distinction between unions which are independent and those which are not. An independent union is one not under the control of employers. It enjoys certain exclusive rights particularly under the E.P.A. Section 17 of this Act imposes on employers a duty to disclose certain information to an independent trade union engaged in collective bargaining. The E.P.A. also sets up the Advisory Conciliation and Arbitration Service (ACAS) which has the general duty of promoting the improvement of industrial relations. Note, however, that an arbitration conducted by ACAS is not subject to part I of the Arbitration Act 1950 (this covers sections 1 to 34; see Chapter 2). This means that the arbitration is not subject to any control by the courts, nor is any award enforceable or binding.

Further Reading

Underhill on Partnership (9th ed., 1971).
Wade and Phillips' Constitutional Law (8th ed.,), Wade and Bradley.
Charlesworth and Cain, *Company Law* (11th ed., 1977).

Chapter 4

CONTRACT: GENERAL PRINCIPLES

ENGLISH law of contract is contained principally in case law. It is only during the present century that statutes have begun to play any significant part. Historically the law of contract has been built up by the judges as a coherent whole so that there exists a body of principles which apply generally to all contracts including building and engineering contracts. In this chapter the general principles are discussed under three headings: first, the formation of a contract; secondly, contracts which though validly formed may not be binding; thirdly, the discharge of contracts. In later chapters there are considered some particular types of contract including building and engineering contracts. These particular contracts, in addition to the general principles set out in this chapter, have their own characteristics, and some are governed by individual statutes.

The law of contract is based on the concept of bargain, in that each side must contribute something to the agreement to make it binding. The only exception to this principle is a contract under seal; such a contract binds its maker without need of any bargain. Contracts other than those under seal are called simple contracts, whether made orally or in writing. It is with simple contracts that this section of the work is concerned. Although the practice is not universal, some lawyers use the term *agreement* to denote a mutual understanding between the parties and reserve the term *contract* for an agreement which is binding in law. In such terms there can be an agreement without a contract, but every contract must embody an agreement, except perhaps a contract under seal. This terminology will be used in the following pages.

In general the parties to a contract are free to make any terms they choose, but certain limits may be placed upon them by the common law and by statute. For example, terms may be implied into a contract which will mitigate the severity of an agreement; or one party may have relief against the other for a misrepresentation outside the terms of the contract itself. Apart from such limits, the courts will attempt to implement contracts according to the terms agreed. However unjust the terms are, or however unjust they may become the courts have no power to rewrite the terms of an agreement. Thus, if a contractor has contracted to carry out works at such prices that he is bound to make a loss, he must still carry out the works or pay damages for breach of contract.

FORMATION OF CONTRACT

If a simple contract is to be legally binding, there must be an offer from one party which is accepted by the other, and each party must contribute something to the bargain. The contribution is called consideration. If a contract exists the courts will determine what are its terms, *e.g.* when part of the agreement is in writing and part oral, or when there are implied terms. These points are considered in order.

Offer and acceptance

An offer must consist of a definite promise to be bound on specified terms, and it may be made to a particular person or class of persons, or even to the public at large. The exhibition of goods for sale is not an offer but an invitation to make an offer. Thus, a shopkeeper may accept or reject an offer from a customer to buy; he is not bound to sell the goods at the price shown. The same rule applies to an invitation to tender for the construction of building works. The invitation to tender, whether to the public or to an individual builder is no more than an offer to negotiate. The contractor's tender constitutes an offer which the client may accept or not, and once accepted it forms a binding contract. This is so despite any provisions as to subsequent execution of formal documents (see ICE form, clause 9).

A proviso that the client is not bound to accept the lowest or any tender is generally unnecessary as the contractor, whether the successful tenderer or not, must bear the costs of tendering. However where the contractor at the employer's request does work outside the normal scope of tendering (*e.g.* design work) there may be an implied promise to pay a reasonable sum for such work. Thus, where a contractor was led to believe he would get the work and prepared calculations and other particulars which the employer used for obtaining a war damage claim, it was held that the employer must pay a reasonable sum for the work done: *William Lacey* v. *Davis* (1957).

The offer and the acceptance may be in writing or oral, or may even be inferred from the parties' conduct. Thus, a person who goes into a barber's shop and sits down in the chair is bound to pay for the ensuing haircut. However, if a particular method for communicating acceptance is prescribed, it must be adopted; although an equally expeditious method may be sufficient. For example, if an offer requires acceptance by return of post, a telegram would be sufficient. When the post is used the rule is that the acceptance is effective and the contract made at the moment of posting. Generally silence cannot constitute acceptance. If an offerer says "I will consider my offer accepted unless I hear to the contrary by Friday," the offeree is not bound if he refrains from replying, unless he has agreed to be bound by his silence. But there is an exception when goods are taken on a sale or return basis. There will be an implied acceptance if they are not returned within a reasonable time.

An acceptance must be unqualified, and a conditional acceptance or a counter offer may simply destroy the original offer. The traditional form of acceptance "subject to contract" is not binding at all. Acceptance of a contract may have retrospective effect if this is the intention of the parties. Thus where a contractor was instructed to proceed and started work while the contract for the works was still under negotiation, it was held that the parties had intended such work to be governed by the contract as eventually made: *Trollope & Colls* v. *Atomic Power Construction* (1963).

In some types of building contract (and many other commercial transactions) the principles of implied or retrospective acceptance need often to be applied to discover the legal basis of contracts which neither party has ever doubted were binding. A problem which frequently occurs is where the parties enter into correspondence as to the precise terms on which they are to contract. This happens often between main contractor and sub-contractor: the contractor places an "order" on his standard terms and the sub-contractor "accepts" on his standard terms, which are inconsistent with the order. Correspondence follows in which some terms are agreed and others not. At some point (often without interrupting the negotiation) the sub-contractor starts the work. The principles to be applied to such problems are that the last letter is deemed to be accepted if the recipient then starts or continues the work (or permits the other party to do so). The courts will endeavour to find a concluded agreement. But if the parties are clearly not agreed as to important terms there will be no contract, and the party who has carried out work at the request of the other will be entitled to payment of a reasonable sum.

Revocation of an offer is effective only when it reaches the offeree. A promise to keep an offer open for a certain period does not prevent the offer from being revoked prematurely, unless the promise is itself a binding contract, *e.g.* an option to purchase shares in a company. An agreement for the periodic supply of goods to order has the legal effect of a standing offer from the supplier which creates a binding contract each time goods are ordered. The offer may accordingly be revoked by the supplier except in respect of orders already placed. If there is no period fixed an unaccepted offer may lapse after a reasonable time.

Consideration

Each party to a contract not under seal must give consideration if the contract is to be binding. The most common forms of consideration are payment of money, provision of goods, or performance of work. But it may also consist in any benefit accruing to one party or detriment to the other. For example, A may promise to release B from a debt if he will dig A's garden. The courts are not concerned with whether the bargain was a good one: if B's debt was £1,000 and the garden takes ten minutes to dig, there is still good consideration.

There are, however, certain acts and promises which constitute no consideration at all. Anything which has already been done is no consideration, so that if B voluntarily dug A's garden yesterday, today's promise of reward is not binding because B gives no fresh consideration. Further, if a party promises to do nothing more than he is already bound to do he provides no consideration; so that if B is A's gardener, A's promise of additional reward is not binding.

Intention to be legally bound

Sometimes, despite the undoubted existence of offer, acceptance and consideration, one party alleges that the contract is not binding because there was no intention to create legal relations. This is not uncommon, *e.g.* in family arrangements and it is presumed that domestic agreements are not intended to create legal relations. It is therefore up to the party seeking to enforce such a contract to rebut the presumption. But even where there is no enforceable contract at law, equity may affect the situation. In *Hussey* v. *Palmer* (1972) a mother-in-law who lived with the family paid for building work to the house. Although there was no enforceable loan, it was held that the value of the work done was held on trust for the mother-in-law.

In commercial agreements there is naturally a strong presumption that there was an intention to create legal relations. Nevertheless, the intention may be rebutted. This was done in a case where a trade union had entered into a collective agreement for wage negotiations with a motor company: *Ford* v. *AEF* (1969) (the position is now governed by statute: see p. 41). The parties may go further and make it an express condition that the contract is not to be binding in law. This is invariably a condition under which football pool companies accept entries, and the effect is that no enforceable contract exists. A similar result is achieved by a clause purporting to exclude the parties' rights to bring actions in the courts upon the contract. Such a clause will be treated as of no effect by the courts, and may make the contract void and unenforceable.

Terms of a contract

The final step in the formation of a contract is the identification of the terms and their effect. If the contract is wholly in writing, then the problem is one of construction. But often there are additional terms: statements made by the parties during their negotiations may have contractual effect, and there may also be terms implied into the contract. An express term purporting to exclude or limit liability may raise special problems of interpretation. These points are discussed below.

A statement made during the negotiation of a contract may be a mere representation (see below p. 51) or it may become a term and have full contractual effect, There is no decisive test, but a statement is more likely to become a binding term if it is made immediately before agreement is reached, or if the maker of the statement had special knowledge as against the other party, or if the agreement was not reduced to writing.

In addition to the express terms there may be other terms implied into a contract which, although not specified by the parties either in writing or orally, are nevertheless as binding as express terms. Implied terms may arise in three ways. First the parties are presumed to have contracted with reference to any prevailing trade or local custom unless they show a contrary intention in the contract. Secondly, there are certain types of contract into which terms are implied by statute, such as under the Sale of Goods Act 1893 (see *post* p. 63).

Thirdly, where there is no customary or statutory authority for an implied term the courts may imply a term which is necessary to make the contract workable or, in legal parlance, to give the contract business efficacy. But note that the courts will not add implied terms which appear necessary to make better sense of the agreement. If the parties have agreed clear terms, then the court's function is limited to enforcing those terms, however unreasonable they may be. Terms which have been implied in decided cases may act as precedents for similar contracts and therefore give rise to what is sometimes called a common law contractual duty, beyond the express terms of the contract.

There are some important terms which may be implied into building and engineering contracts. Such terms require that the building owner shall give possession of the site within a reasonable time, and also give instructions and information at reasonable times. Similarly the contractor must carry out his work with all proper skill and care or, as sometimes expressed, in a workmanlike manner. Goods and materials must normally be of good quality and reasonably fit for their purpose (as to the effect of subcontracts, see p. 105). However, there will be no implied term where the matter in question is dealt with by express terms. The matters just mentioned are often covered by express provisions in building contracts, so that there may be no case for further implication. There are some notable terms which are normally not to be implied into building and engineering contracts. The employer gives no implied warranty of the nature or suitability of the site or subsoil, or as to the practicability of the design. Thus where a contractor agreed to build a new bridge over the Thames using caissons, it was found they could not be used and the work proved much more expensive. There was held to be no implied warranty that the bridge could be built according to the engineer's design: *Thorn* v. *London Corporation* (1876). Further, where a contractor builds according to detailed plans and specification, there is no implied warranty of fitness. Thus, where a builder constructed, as specified, a solid brick wall without rendering which allowed rain to enter the house, it was held that the builder was not liable for the defect: *Lynch* v. *Thorne* (1956). However, in such circumstances, even if the contractor is not in breach of contract, the work is likely to contravene the Building Regulations. This may render the builder liable to the purchaser of the house (see p. 175) and will also make the work unlawful (as to which see p. 52).

It is common practice, particularly in standard form contracts, for one party to insert a term excluding or limiting his liability to the other. This is often done by suppliers of goods or services in an attempt to exclude or limit liability for defective materials or work. Such clauses may be wholly or partly unenforceable by virtue of recent statutes. However the courts have always been ready to find grounds on which exclusion clauses could be avoided. It is therefore necessary to consider first the position at common law. The effect of statute law is considered below.

An exclusion clause must be carefully drafted since it will be construed against the party seeking to rely upon it (see p. 82). General words are unlikely to exclude specific liability. If the term is contained in a document forming part of the contract then the party assenting to such a document is bound by its terms, whether or not he reads them and whether or not he signs the document. An exclusion clause may be over-ridden by a representation. Thus, where a customer took a dress to be dry cleaned, she was asked to sign a document excluding all liability; the assistant, however, said that the exclusion covered only damage to buttons. It was held that the cleaners could not rely on the clause to exclude all liability: *Curtis* v. *Chemical Cleaning Co.* (1951).

Where an exclusion clause is exhibited, *e.g.* in an hotel or a garage stating "The management accepts no responsibility ..." the term is not binding unless the party must be taken to have known of, and agreed to it, before entering into the contract. Even when such a term is effective it protects only the parties to the contract, so that while a party may exclude his own liability for negligently performing the contract, his servants or sub-contractors cannot rely on the contract and they may be sued in tort for their own negligence. It should be noted that while liability may be limited or excluded, it can generally be done only by contract or in situations akin to that of contract. The exhibition on a motor car of a sign saying "no liability for negligent driving" would not prejudice the rights of the public at large. But where liability in tort would arise, *e.g.* from free advice which is given negligently, such liability may be excluded or limited by an appropriate written or oral statement (see further p. 177).

Statutory alteration of contract terms

The above represents the common law position on exclusion and limitation clauses. The fundamental principle of freedom and enforceability of contract terms has recently been the subject of statutory intervention. The Sale of Goods (Implied Terms) Act 1973 provided that clauses excluding or restricting the implied rights of the buyer of goods in regard to their conformity with description or sample, quality or fitness, should be void in a consumer sale; and in a non-consumer sale, *i.e.* one between commercial parties, such terms are enforceable only so far as is fair and reasonable (see further p. 64).

By the Unfair Contract Terms Act 1977 these provisions have been substantially re-enacted (section 6) and extended in their application to other contracts involving the provision of goods (section 7) which will include building contracts. The Act contains other far-reaching provisions governing exclusion clauses and notices. Liability for death or personal injury may not be excluded where resulting from negligence, which includes an obligation to exercise care or skill in contract or tort (section 2(1)). Liability for other loss resulting from negligence may be excluded only so far as fair and reasonable (section 2(2)). Any contractual term excluding or restricting liability for breach of contract is enforceable only so far as is fair and reasonable provided the innocent party deals as a consumer or on the other party's written standard terms of business (section 3). A private employer under a building contract may deal as a consumer, and therefore be entitled to the protection of section 3. It is not clear to what extent other employers under building contracts would be regarded as dealing on the contractor's standard terms where, for example these are the JCT or ICE conditions.

Where an exclusion clause is required to be fair and reasonable, it is to be given effect even when the contract has been terminated by acceptance of repudiation (section 9). This alters the common law position in favour of the party in breach (see p. 57). The application of the Act is restricted in regard to certain types of contract, including contracts of insurance, and contracts having a foreign element. The Act is not to apply where English law applies merely as a choice of proper law in a foreign contract (see p. 60). However the Act cannot be excluded by stipulating a foreign proper law in an otherwise English contract. The Act applies to contracts made after 1st February 1978.

Form of contract

Simple contracts may in general be in any form and are enforceable despite a complete absence of documentation. But a few special types of contract are unenforceable unless evidenced in writing. These are principally contracts for the sale or disposition of land or an interest in land, and some others such as a contract of guarantee. Such a contract need not be made in writing, but some written evidence is necessary which must be signed by or on behalf of the defendant and which states the material terms. However, a contract which does not comply with these requirements may sometimes be enforceable in equity if there has been a part performance of the contract by the person seeking to enforce it, such as a buyer who has entered into possession of a house.

CONTRACTS WHICH ARE NOT BINDING

The law recognises a number of situations where although a contract has been formed one or both parties are unable to enforce the agreement. The most common of these situations are: when one or both parties make a mistake of fact; and when the contract is induced by misrepresentation. Other contracts which may not bind the parties include those which involve illegality, and contracts where one party is under some legal incapacity. These various categories are discussed below.

Mistake

There are two distinct legal categories of mistake. First, where both parties make the same common mistake the existence of agreement is undisputed, but one party may say that the mistake has deprived the contract of its efficacy. Where the mistake relates to the existence of the subject matter the contract is void, as in the case of a sale of goods which have perished at the time of sale, or which never existed; but less fundamental mistakes may not be sufficient. Thus, the sale of a painting by Constable was held not to be void when the picture turned out to be by a lesser artist: *Leaf* v. *International Galleries* (1950).

The second category of mistake arises when the parties have different intentions. Whether they are both mistaken or whether the mistake is unilateral (one party merely acquiescing in the other's mistake) the law considers this as a question of offer and acceptance. The contract is void only if the mistake prevents one party from appreciating the fundamental character of what he is offering or accepting. A mistake which affects only motives, as when one party thinks he had a much better bargain than was the case, cannot affect the validity of the contract.

If the parties had different intentions the court will if possible ascertain the true meaning of the contract; if this cannot be done the contract is void. Thus, where the parties contracted for the sale of cotton *ex Peerless* from Bombay, there were two such ships called Peerless; the buyer intended one and the seller the other. It was held there was no binding contract: *Raffles* v. *Wichelhaus* (1864). Where one party only was mistaken the question is whether there was an acceptance of what was offered. If there was such acceptance the contract is not void, but may still be voidable for misrepresentation (see below).

In addition to common law remedies for mistake, other relief may be available in equity. Principally, if both parties, or even one party, intended something different from what the documents record, the contract may be rectified (see p. 83).

Misrepresentation

A representation is a statement made in relation to a contract by one party which is not a term of the contract. If it is untrue, whether fraudulent or innocent, it is a misrepresentation and the general effect is to render the contract voidable. A voidable contract may be renounced by the injured party, but until such time it is valid. Only when a misrepresentation has induced mistake can the contract be automatically void.

In order to constitute a representation, the statement must be made before or at the time of contracting; and it must be a statement of fact, not opinion or mere "puff." An estate agent's description of a second-rate house as a "desirable residence" is not to be taken as a statement of fact. Silence may amount to a misrepresentation, as when a previous statement becomes false before the contract is concluded. Further, a misrepresentation does not make a contract voidable unless it induced the contract. Thus, the injured party must have relied on the statement and it must have been a material cause of his entering into the contract.

The rights and remedies which flow from a misrepresentation depend upon whether it was fraudulent or innocent. If the person who made the representation did not honestly believe it to be true then, whatever his motive, it is fraudulent. This gives the other party a right in tort to damages for deceit, and a further right to elect either to affirm the contract (when it will continue for both parties) or to rescind it. Rescission involves cancellation of the contract and restoration of the parties to the state they were in before the contract was made.

A misrepresentation is innocent if the maker honestly, although perhaps carelessly, believed it to be true. The principal remedy for the other party is then under the Misrepresentation Act 1967 whereby damages can be recovered unless the maker proves that he had reasonable grounds for believing that the facts represented were true. The person to whom the innocent misrepresentation is made may also sue for rescission, as well as for damages. However, under the Misrepresentation Act the court may in its discretion award damages in lieu of rescission.

The right to rescind a contract for misrepresentation, innocent or fraudulent, is available only if restoration of the parties to their former positions is possible, and if no innocent third party would suffer. A party who affirms the contract loses the right to rescind. An alternative remedy for misrepresentation may be available under the law of tort for negligent misstatement (see p. 177). Further, a representation which has become a term of the contract will give rise to the usual remedies for breach of contract if it proves untrue (see p. 58).

Illegal contracts

Contracts which contravene the law are in general void and no action may be brought upon them. The illegality may involve doing an act prohibited by statute, such as building contrary to the Building Regulations; or it may consist in a project not as such prohibited, *e.g.* an agreement to commit a crime or a tort or some immoral act. Such contracts cannot be enforced by either party.

The law draws a distinction between a contract which is illegal in its inception and one which is merely performed in an unlawful way. A contract illegal in its inception is totally void and no action can be brought by either party. Property transferred under the contract cannot generally be recovered. But when a contract is illegal only as performed, the effect depends upon the extent of the illegality. If this goes to the core of the contract then a guilty party will have no remedy, while an innocent party may have the usual contractual remedies. If however the illegality is not essential to the performance of the contract, both parties may have their normal remedies. Thus, where a ship was illegally overloaded in the course of a voyage it was held that the owners could still recover the freight charges since the overloading was not an essential incident of the contract: *St John Shipping* v. *Rank* (1957).

Where building work is carried out in contravention of statutory provisions, such as the Building Regulations or Planning Acts, the above principles apply in determining whether the builder can recover the price of the work (apart from the question of statutory powers as to enforcement and penalties). Thus where on the face of the contract the work must contravene the law, the contractor cannot recover payment. In *Townsend* v. *Cinema News* (1959) building work which was specified so as to comply with the law was carried out in contravention of a building by-law. It was held that the contractor could recover payment for the work since there was no fundamental illegality. But in such circumstances the building owner will usually be entitled to set off a counterclaim in respect of any work necessary to make the original work comply with statutory requirements. Difficulties arise, *e.g.* where the fault lies in the foundations, which can be cured only by demolition and re-building of parts which are properly built. Such problems depend upon whether the local authority seek to enforce compliance, whether the building owner has acquiesced in the breach and also on the express terms of the contract.

Incapacity of parties

Certain parties are restricted in their contractual capacity and liability. The most important of these are corporate bodies and infants. A corporate body (such as a limited company or a local authority) can make contracts only within its specific powers; any contract outside these powers is void (see pp. 33 and 38).

An infant occupies a privileged position under the law of contract. He is in general bound only by contract which are substantially for his benefit. Thus, if an infant contracts to purchase goods, he is only liable to pay for them if they are necessary and suitable for his requirements, and he is liable to pay only a reasonable price. An acquisition of property such as land or shares is binding, but may be avoided by an infant before or within a reasonable time after reaching majority (*i.e.* 18 years). The fact that the infant himself may not be bound does not mean that he cannot take advantage of the contract, *e.g.* by suing the supplier of defective (though nonnecessary) goods. It has also been held that a guarantee by an adult of an infant's unenforceable contract was itself void. Contracts with infants should therefore be approached with caution. For even greater privileges which may be enjoyed by government, particularly a foreign government, see p. 39.

Privity

The common law rule of privity is that a contract cannot be enforced by or against a person who is not a party to that contract. For example, a clause in a building contract enabling the employer to pay money direct to a sub-contractor may be used by the employer, but cannot be enforced by the sub-contractor, who is not a party to the main contract. There are, however, exceptions both general and specific. The law of agency is a general exception, for the principal may sue and be sued on contracts made by his agent (see p. 66). Specific contracts on which a stranger may sue include (by statute) a contract under seal respecting land or other property, and a third party insurance policy (see p. 76). Contracts which can be enforced against a stranger are practically limited to restrictive covenants over land, which on certain conditions are enforceable against a person who subsequently acquires the land (see p. 191).

DISCHARGE OF CONTRACTS

Discharge of contract is a general term for release of contractual obligations, when the contract ceases to exist. This must generally be brought about by some act of the parties. Contracts do not end automatically, unless perhaps by becoming statute barred (see p. 60).

Once a contract is discharged neither party can rely on its terms but can only enforce whatever rights may arise from the discharge. It is therefore important to know whether or not a contract is discharged (although this may well be an issue between the parties). For example, determination of the contractor's employment under a provision in a building contract does not generally determine the contract, so that the parties remain bound by all its terms (see ICE clause 63, JCT clauses 25 and 26).

Discharge of a contract may be brought about in four ways. First, if the parties perform all their obligations the contract is said to be discharged by performance. Secondly, if an event during the course of the contract renders performance impossible or sterile it may be frustrated. Thirdly, in certain circumstances a breach by one party may render the contract discharged; and whether or not the contract is discharged by a breach, the innocent party can always sue for damages. These methods of discharge and also the wider topic of recovery of damages for breach of contract are discussed below. The fourth category of discharge is by express agreement; this is discussed elsewhere under variation of contracts (see p. 84).

Performance

In general only exact and complete performance of contractual obligations can discharge the contract and a party who has only partially performed his obligations cannot recover payment. This rule is mitigated in a number of cases. Where a contract has been substantially performed payment may be due with an allowance for deficiencies. Further, when a contract is divisible, either expressly or impliedly, payment will be due for parts which have been completed (as to performance of building contracts, see p. 87).

A building or engineering contract will be discharged by performance when the contractor has completed all the work, including his obligations as to maintenance, the architect or engineer has issued all requisite certificates and the employer has paid all sums due. If undisclosed defects are later discovered it is sometimes suggested that the contractor is not liable since the contract has been discharged by performance. However, the contract has not been performed if there are hidden defects. The employer will retain his right to sue for breach during the period of limitation, subject to the effect of any certificates (*e.g.* the JCT final certificate) under the contract.

Frustration

As a general rule contractual obligations are absolute in that a party is not absolved merely because performance becomes more expensive or even proves to be impossible (a party who contracts to do the impossible is liable for failing to do it, unless he excludes such liability: see for example ICE clause 13). If, however, without default of either party, the circumstances change so that performance of a contractual obligation becomes radically different from that undertaken, the contract may be frustrated and thereby automatically discharged.

Examples of situations which have constituted frustration are: where a building in which one party is to carry out work for the other is accidentally destroyed by fire; where seats are sold to view a public event which does not take place; and where government action prohibits performance of contract for a substantial period. If a term of the contract provides for the contingency which has occurred, it is a question of construction whether it covers the particular circumstances, and thus keeps the contract in being. In *Metropolitan Water Board* v. *Dick Kerr* (1918) the contractor had agreed in 1914 to construct a reservoir in six years, with a provision for extensions of time for various delays. In 1916, due to the war, the Ministry ordered work to cease. It was held that the interruption was likely to be so long that the contract would be radically different, and the extension of time provision did not prevent frustration.

Examples of building or engineering contracts being frustrated are extremely rare. It may be stated with some certainty that such contracts are not frustrated by the work proving more difficult than could have been anticipated, in any degree, unless the difficulty arises from some change of circumstance or supervening event. In the case of *Thorn* v. *London Corporation* (1876), the contract was not frustrated when the engineer's design for a new bridge over the Thames, with piers constructed inside caissons, proved impossible to construct. The contractor had taken the risk as to the method of construction and remained liable to carry out the work by whatever means were necessary, at no extra cost.

The legal effect of frustration is that the contract is discharged as to the future. Money paid before frustration is recoverable and money payable ceases to be payable. But the court may permit a party to retain or recover a sum to compensate him for any expense incurred, or for any benefit to the other party before the time of frustration. A contractor whose contract becomes frustrated may therefore be unable to recover any payment if the employer gets no benefit from what work has been completed. These rules are, however, subject to the provisions of the contract, and will usually be mitigated by insurances.

Breach of contract

Breach of contract occurs when a party fails to perform some obligation under the contract, for example, when goods are not delivered on the date fixed, or when materials or workmanship do not conform to contractual requirements. Under normal building and engineering contracts defective work will not necessarily be a breach of contract if the contractor is not bound to execute particular work at a specified time. A breach would, however, occur if the contractor refused to obey a proper instruction to remove defective work or if work were not completed according to the contract by the date when it should have been completed.

It is important, particularly in dealing with claims under a building or engineering contract, to appreciate the distinction between a claim for *breach* of contract and a claim *under* the contract. A claim under the contract arises when some event occurs (which may or may not be a breach of contract) for which the contract provides some remedy. The remedy is usually the payment of a sum of money to or by the contractor, or it may be some other benefit such as an extension of time. Often the same event will give rise to claims both under and in breach of contract. But the consequences of the two heads of claim are different. For example, consequential damages may be recovered for a breach; but under the contract only such remedies as are provided can be recovered. A claim under a contract is a way of enforcing its provisions. This section is concerned only with breach.

A breach of contract may have two principal consequences. First, every breach entitles the innocent party to sue for damages. Secondly, if the breach is sufficiently serious it gives the innocent party an option to treat the party in breach as having repudiated the whole contract. In such a case the innocent party may bring the contract to an end by accepting the repudiation; or he may at his option treat the contract as still subsisting, when it will continue to bind both parties.

A repudiation may consist in an express or an implied refusal by one party to perform the contract; or it may be a serious breach which goes to the root of the contract. The latter type of breach may be called a fundamental breach, or breach of a fundamental obligation. Fundamental breach of a building contract might consist in building a house without foundations, or perhaps constructing a bridge in the wrong place. But in each case the question whether the breach is to be taken as a repudiation depends upon the importance of the breach in relation to the contract as a whole. In practice, breaches such as those given as examples above are very unlikely to occur if the works are properly specified and supervised. In other words, such errors are likely to be discovered and rectified before the work is so far advanced that they become fundamental breaches.

One type of repudiation which may occur in a building contract is where a contractor carries out defective work and fails or refuses to comply with a proper instruction to rectify it. This constitutes a refusal to perform the contract, rather than a fundamental breach. In such circumstances the employer has various remedies available including the right to refuse to pay for the work and to claim damages for delay until the work is properly completed. But he has, in addition, an option to accept the contractor's repudiation as terminating the contract, and expel the contractor from the site. The employer will then be entitled to sue the contractor for all loss arising from the original breach and from the termination, including the additional costs of completing the contract works. In addition to the above remedies most building contracts provide, in such a situation, for determination of the contractor's employment *under* the contract. In such a case the contract is not determined and the parties remain bound by its provisions.

One method of describing the relative importance and effect of the obligations under a contract is to call a particular term a *condition* if a breach will amount to repudiation, and a *warranty* if a breach will give a right to damages only. This sharp distinction is inadequate for complex contractual terms and it would be impossible to distinguish the terms of a building contract in this way. But under the Sale of Goods Act the terms of contracts of sale are so classified (see p. 66). Thus the delivery of goods which do not correspond to a sample amounts to repudiation of the contract of sale, and gives the buyer a right to terminate the contract.

Where the innocent party elects to treat the contract as discharged he must expressly or impliedly tell the other party. His choice is binding and will terminate the contract as from the election. Alternatively, if the innocent party chooses to treat the contract as subsisting, it will continue to bind both parties.

At common law, when a contract is terminated by acceptance of repudiation, the party in breach generally cannot rely on an exclusion or limitation clause in the contract to avoid or reduce his liability. However where, under the Unfair Contract Terms Act 1977, an exclusion clause is required to be fair and reasonable, such clause is to given effect even when the contract is terminated by acceptance of repudiation (see above p. 48).

Remedies for breach

If the innocent party has the right to treat the contract as discharged, and does so, he is relieved from further liability. He may then sue for damages which may include both loss flowing from the breach and loss flowing from the termination of the contract The latter will usually include the additional cost of completing the contract. If the contract is not discharged, either because the innocent party elects to treat it as still subsisting or because the breach was not one which could discharge the contract, the innocent party has two possible remedies. First he may recover damages and secondly he may sometimes obtain an order for specific performance, which compels the other party to perform his obligation.

Damages

Not every loss which stems from a breach of contract is recoverable in damages; a claim can succeed only in respect of damage which is, in law, not too remote. Further, the innocent party must take all reasonable steps to mitigate his loss.

Damage is not too remote if the parties must reasonably have contemplated it at the time the contract was entered into. Damage is recoverable if it results *either* from the natural consequences of the breach, *or* from special circumstances of which the parties had actual knowledge and which caused the breach to result in exceptional loss. In *Victoria Laundry* v. *Newman* (1949) the plaintiff ordered a new boiler from the defendant for the purpose of taking on new work of an exceptionally profitable nature. The boiler was not delivered and the work was lost. It was held that the plaintiff could recover only the normal profit to be expected, since the defendant had no actual knowledge, at the time the contract was entered into, of the proposed new work.

The rules of remoteness have no application to a claim under a contract as opposed to a claim for breach. Thus if a dealer warrants that a motor car is in good condition and it breaks down, the purchaser may recover as damages for *breach* of contract the cost of repairs and the cost of hiring an alternative vehicle. If, however, the dealer promises only to replace defective parts, the purchaser's entitlement *under* the contract is to the cost of repairs, and no question of consequential damage arises. In contracts of sale, an undertaking to replace defective items is often given in lieu of any warranty as to quality or fitness, so that the supplier is not in *breach* if the article is defective. In building contracts the position may be different. Defects liability clauses, which oblige the builder to put right defects, do not normally prevent the builder also being in *breach* so that consequentional loss may be recoverable even though the builder has repaired the work (see also p. 102).

As to the measure of damages to be awarded, this is usually the actual monetary loss. The principle is that the innocent party should be restored to the position he would have been in had the other party performed his obligation. Thus where the plaintiff's factory was burnt down as a result of the defendant's breach and there was no reasonable alternative to rebuilding the factory, the plaintiff recovered the full cost of rebuilding, without any allowance for getting new for old: *Harbutts Plasticine* v. *Wayne Tank* (1970). Where a contractor in breach of contract puts up defective work, the normal measure of damages is the actual or estimated cost of re-instatement; and where the breach consists of not doing work the damages will normally be the extra cost of completing the work at the earliest reasonable time. Additional damages such as loss of rents or profits will depend upon the rules of remoteness set out above.

There is an apparent exception to the rule of reinstatement of the plaintiff, where a surveyor gives an erroneous report on the condition of a property. The purchaser relying on the report can recover not the cost of repairing the undisclosed defects, but the difference in value between the property as reported and as it actually was: *Phillips* v. *Ward* (1956). This case is not a true exception to the rule, however. The purchaser's position, had the surveyor performed his contract properly, would be that he knew the true value of the property, and would not pay more than this figure.

Specific performance

Specific performance is an equitable remedy and is discretionary. It is not normally awarded if damages would be an adequate remedy, or if performance would require supervision by the court. Therefore, as a general rule, specific performance will not be ordered of a contract to build. The remedy may be available, however, in exceptional circumstances as when the plaintiff sells or leases land to be built upon. Specific performance may be ordered if the following conditions are satisfied: the plaintiff has a substantial interest such that damages would not compensate him; the defendant is in possession of the land so that the plaintiff cannot do the work without committing trespass; and the work is sufficiently particularised. Specific performance may be granted of a landlord's repairing covenant in a lease, when the tenant himself has no right to carry out the work.

Limitation periods

One final condition which must be satisfied before any claim in contract can be pursued is that the action must not be statute barred. Under the Limitation Act 1939, 2, claims in simple contract must generally be brought within 6 years and claims on a contract under seal within 12 years. A claim in respect of personal injuries for breach of duty must normally be brought within 3 years. In each case time runs from the date when the cause of action arose, that is, from the time the breach of contract occurred. The fact that actual damage is not suffered until a later time does not affect the limitation period. The position in tort may be quite different so that an action in negligence may be pursued long after an alternative claim in contract is statute barred; see below, Chapter 9. A liquidated claim (such as a debt) is revived, and time begins to run anew, if there is a signed acknowledgment or part payment by the debtor. The effect of the Limitation Acts is to bar the remedy, but not the original right.

An exception is contained in section 26 of the Limitation Act which provides that where the right of action is concealed by fraud, the period of limitation does not begin to run until the plaintiff discovers or should discover it. "Fraud" under the Act has a wide meaning and includes concealing a breach of contract. In the case of *King* v. *Victor Parsons* (1973) a developer knew that he was building over an old rubbish tip and that a reinforced concrete raft was required on which to found the building. A raft was constructed but it was too thin and without reinforcement. After the normal period of limitation had run the owner brought an action in respect of serious cracking due to subsidence. It was held that the defendants' actual knowledge of the breach was sufficient to prevent limitation running until the plaintiff discovered the defects.

INTERNATIONAL CASES

In Chapter 2 (see p. 20) the effect of a foreign element was considered upon the procedure in a case. In this section it is assumed that the English courts are proceeding to hear a case in contract containing a foreign element. The question then arising is which national law to apply.

The law to be applied in determining a dispute arising out of a contract depends upon the nature of the dispute. But most aspects are governed by one particular national law, known as the proper law of the contract. This can be chosen by the parties, expressly or impliedly; or if there is no choice the courts will determine it.

The parties to a contract are generally free to choose as the proper law, the law of any nation, even if it has no connection with the contract (subject now to the Unfair Contract Terms Act 1977: see above p. 49). Thus, if a Scottish company contracts in England to build a pipeline in Iran for an American company the parties may, if they wish, stipulate that the contract is to be governed by French law. In the event of a dispute an English court, if it accepted jurisdiction, would determine the dispute according to the law of France. The choice of French law does not mean that the dispute must be taken to a French court. If an English court has jurisdiction even an express choice of a foreign tribunal to settle disputes cannot oust that jurisdiction. A stipulation that disputes were to be settled in Paris would, however, probably take effect as an implied choice of French law as the proper law of the contract. The International Conditions of Contract for civil engineering work (FIDIC) contain a clause in which the national law to be applied to the contract is to be specified. Before agreeing to a foreign law a party should, of course, ascertain the effects of that law, *e.g.* as to whether clauses in the contract for his benefit will be enforceable.

Where there is no express or implied choice of law, the proper law is determined by the court as the law of the country having the closest connection with the contract. This may be decided by considering, *inter alia*, in which country the contract was made, where it was performed and the place and currency of the payment, although none of these factors is conclusive.

When the proper law has been identified it will determine such matters as whether a binding contract has been made, how the provisions of the contract are to be construed, what is the effect of a misrepresentation, and whether a clause excluding liability is valid. If a contract is illegal by the proper law it is unenforceable in England. However, there are some topics which are governed by a different law. For example, a transfer of land is governed generally by the law of the place where the land is situated. Further, in a recent building case a Scottish company contracted in the standard JCT form to carry out works in Scotland for an English company. The House of Lords held that the proper law of the contract was English, but the arbitration proceedings should be governed by Scottish law: *Whitworth* v. *Miller* (1970).

Further Reading

Chitty on Contracts, Vol. 1 (24th ed., 1977), Guest *et al.*
Cheshire and Fifoot's *Law of Contract* (9th ed., 1976), Cheshire, Fifoot and Furmston.
Davies *Contract* (3rd ed., 1977), (Concise College Texts).

Chapter 5

SPECIAL CONTRACTS

This chapter deals with some special types of contract which are likely to be encountered in the construction industry, and which are governed by their own special rules in addition to the general principles set out in Chapter 4.

This chapter covers the sale of goods, which is perhaps the most universal form of legal transaction; the law of agency, which defines the position of architects and many other persons who act on behalf of another; contracts of employment, which affect most persons in the industry either as employer or as employee; and contracts of insurance, which are an incident to most building and engineering contracts. Finally, the section on sale of dwellings covers a combination of contractual and other relationships which may be encountered when a recently built house or flat is acquired.

In addition to the matters covered in this chapter, reference should be made to Chapter 3, which deals with the legal status of parties involved in the construction industry. These may also embody a special type of contract; *e.g.* that between a company and its members or directors, and between the partners of a firm. Chapter 7 should be consulted for the special features of building and engineering contracts.

Sale of Goods

Contracts for the sale of goods are governed by the Sale of Goods Act 1893. This field covers a multitude of transactions ranging from retail purchases in shops to the sale of articles of great value or rarity, and may include contracts under which the goods are to be specially made. The Act does not apply, *inter alia*, to contracts which are in substance to carry out work or which relate to hire-purchase, or the sale of land or "things in action" such as shares or debts.

The Act does not displace the ordinary principles of the law of contract except where they are inconsistent with its provisions. Thus, *e.g.* the formation of contract and the effects of misrepresentation and mistake are the same as for any other contract. The Sale of Goods Act is a codification of the common law, so that its principles can apply outside the limited sphere to which the Act strictly applies. For example, the supply of materials under a building contract may be governed by the same principles as a sale (see p. 47). The most important part of the Sale of Goods Act lays down a series of terms which, unless excluded or modified, are to be implied into all contracts to which the Act applies. These consist of four terms relating to description and quality and one relating to title; they are considered in turn. The Act is substantially amended by the Supply of Goods (Implied Terms) Act 1973.

Implied terms

Where goods are sold by description, the goods must *correspond with the description*. And if the sale is by sample as well as by description, it is not sufficient if the goods correspond only with the sample; they must also correspond with the description (section 13). Even a small deviation from description (providing it is not absolutely trifling) will constitute a breach of the term, so that where a variation can be permitted it is in the interests of the seller to stipulate a specific tolerance or margin. Description may extend not only to the goods but also to their packing. Thus, where a contract of sale stipulated for tins to be packed in cartons of 30, the buyer was held to be entitled to reject a delivery in which some of the cartons contained 24 tins: *Re Moore and Landauer* (1921).

Where there is a sale by sample, the goods must *correspond with the sample in quality*, and the buyer must be given a reasonable opportunity for comparison. Further, despite correspondence with the sample, the goods must also be free from latent defects rendering them unmerchantable (section 15). The use of a sample does not therefore protect the seller from hidden defects in the goods. Sections 13 and 15 apply to all contracts of sale, but section 14 (considered below) applies only to sales which are made in the normal course of business by a dealer. Thus, in private sales, the only terms to be implied are those relating to correspondence with description and with sample. Dealers are additionally bound by two important terms which relate to fitness for purpose and to merchantability (or quality).

If a dealer is expressly or impliedly informed of any particular purpose for which the goods are being bought, the goods must be *reasonably fit for that purpose*. However, such an obligation is not to be implied where the circumstances show that the buyer does not rely, or that it is unreasonable for him to rely, on the seller's skill and judgment (section 14(3)). Fitness for purpose may extend to the container as well as the goods. Where the condition applies, the dealer's liability is strict, so that it is no defence that all reasonable care was taken if the goods are still unfit.

In addition to being fit for their purpose, goods purchased from a dealer must be *of merchantable quality*. The buyer is under no duty to examine the goods but if he does so, however superficially, the dealer is not liable for defects which examination ought to have revealed; nor is he liable for defects drawn to the buyer's attention before the contract is made (section 14(2)). Goods are of merchantable quality if they are reasonably fit for the purpose or purposes for which such goods are commonly bought, having regard, *inter alia*, to their description and price (s. 62(1A)).

The type of defect which can render goods unmerchantable or unfit for their purpose will generally be a much more substantial defect than is necessary for a breach of section 13 or 15. However the fact that goods are substantially defective does not mean there must be a breach of both sections 14(3) and 14(2). In the *Hardwick Game Farm* case (1969), feeding stuff was supplied to the plaintiffs who breed pheasants. It contained a substance which killed the pheasants. When the supplier sought an indemnity from his supplier it was held that there was a breach of section 14(3) as the goods were unfit for their particular purpose. But there was no breach of section 14(2) since the goods could be used for some purpose, and were consequently not unmerchantable.

In any sale, unless a different intention is shown, the seller must always have *a right to sell the goods* at the time of sale (section 12). This applies principally to the seller's right to pass title to the goods. But where goods could not be sold because of a trade mark infringement it was held that there was a breach of section 12: *Niblett* v. *Confectioners' Materials* (1921). The effect is that if the seller cannot pass title, for example, because he holds the goods on hire-purchase, the buyer can recover the whole price even though he may have used the goods.

Until 1973, all the implied conditions described above could in principle be excluded from the contract of sale by an appropriately worded clause (see p. 47), and subject to the question of fundamental breach (see p. 56). This situation was radically altered by the Supply of Goods (Implied Terms) Act 1973, which provided that any clause excluding or restricting the operation of sections 13, 14 or 15 of the Sale of Goods Act is void in the case of a consumer sale, and in any other case is unenforceable so far as it is not fair or reasonable to allow reliance upon it. Further, any exclusion or restriction of section 12 is void. These provisions are now substantially re-enacted by the Unfair Contract Terms Act 1977, which also applies the same principles to other types of contract (see p. 48).

Other rights and remedies

Much may depend upon precisely when the property in goods passes from the seller to the buyer if, *e.g.* the goods are damaged or one party becomes insolvent before physical delivery of the goods. No property can pass until the goods are ascertained, *e.g.* by separating the number to be sold from a bulk. Once the goods are ascertained or specified the property passes when the parties intend it to pass. But if no intention is expressed or to be implied, the Sale of Goods Act defines when the property is to pass. In the simplest case where the sale is unconditional and the goods are in a deliverable state, property passes when the contract is made (sections 17, 18). Unless otherwise agreed risk passes with the property. Thus if a contract is made to sell specific goods, delivery to be suspended until payment, the risk passes to the buyer on making the contract. If the goods are damaged or destroyed before delivery, the buyer remains liable for the price.

Remedies of the buyer under the Sale of Goods Act for breach of contract depend on whether the term broken is to be construed as a condition or as a warranty (see p. 57). Breach of a condition gives the buyer a right to treat the contract as repudiated (as well as the right to sue for damages). Breach of a warranty gives only a right to damages, and the buyer remains liable for the price. The buyer may at his option treat the breach of a condition as a breach of a warranty. If he has accepted the goods the buyer must so treat the breach, so that he cannot reject the goods after accepting them and can only sue for damages. The five implied terms set out above are stated in the Act to be conditions so that a breach of any one of them, subject to the effect of any exclusion clause (see above), gives the buyer a right to refuse to accept the goods. Which of the other terms are conditions and which are warranties depends on the construction of the contract. In normal commercial transactions, time of delivery is a condition, so that the buyer can reject goods for late delivery.

AGENCY

Agency is a broad term describing the relationship between two parties whereby one, the agent, acts on behalf of the other, the principal. Common situations when this arises are when a person is appointed to buy or sell goods, or to conduct business on behalf of the principal. Examples of agents are brokers, auctioneers, architects and engineers. An agency may be either special, that is limited to a particular transaction, or it may be general. An agent may represent his principal in many different ways. He may conduct legal proceedings, or even commit a tort on behalf of his principal. But this section is concerned only with the ways in which an agent may affect the contractual position of his principal.

An agency may arise under a contract, whereby the agent is appointed by his principal to carry out certain duties. Engineers and architects are frequently so appointed to act for promoters of building schemes. An agency may also arise not under contract but because of the relationship between the principal and the agent. A director of a company or a partner of a firm may hold such an agency. This section applies generally to both types of agency.

When an agent acting on behalf of his principal makes a contract with a third party the usual result is that the agent drops out, leaving the contract enforceable only between the principal and the third party. Agency is thus a substantial exception to the rule of privity of contract (see p. 53). There may be two or three distinct contracts involved in an agency transaction. First, there is the relationship between principal and agent creating the agency. Secondly, there is the contract with the third party which the agent makes on behalf of the principal. There may also be an implied promise by the agent to the third party that he has authority to contract for the principal; this is referred to as a warranty of authority.

Formation of agency

Agency can arise in a number of ways. The most common is by an agreement under which the principal expressly authorises an agent to perform certain duties for him usually in return for a fee or other payment. The agent will have, in addition to his express authority, the implied authority to do things reasonably incidental to his express powers. Implied authority depends upon the circumstances of the agency and is discussed below in relation to architects and engineers.

Alternatively there are three ways in which an agency may arise without actual authority. First, if the principal acts so as to clothe a person with ostensible authority, the principal will be bound by acts within such authority. For example, an estate agent instructed to find a purchaser may have ostensible authority to accept a deposit. If this is so and the agent defaults, the principal will be liable for repayment. Secondly, an agency may arise when it becomes an urgent necessity to perform some action on behalf of another person whose instructions cannot be obtained; *e.g.*, where a person is in charge of goods in transit which are in danger of perishing. In such a situation the person in charge of the goods may lawfully sell them on behalf of the owner. Thirdly, if a person without authority purports to act as agent for an identified principal, that principal may within a reasonable time ratify the agent's act and become bound by it. Ratification of a contract relates back to the date when the agent purported to make it. But the principal must be competent to make the contract both at the date of the agent's act and at the date of ratification. Thus a fire insurance policy made by a broker without the owner's authority could not be ratified by the owner after his premises had been burnt down: *Grover* v. *Matthews* (1910).

Rights of parties

The position of the third party, that is, the person with whom the agent makes the contract, depends upon whether the third party knows that he is dealing with an agent. If an agent with authority discloses his agency, the third party can in general sue and be sued only by the principal. But if an agent with authority does not disclose his agency, in general either the agent or the undisclosed principal can sue on the contract. The third party after discovering the principal may choose whether to sue the principal or the agent on the contract. But his choice is binding, and if a judgment obtained against one is unsatisfied, he cannot then sue the other.

Where an agent purports to act as agent but acts without authority, or in excess of his actual authority, the principal will be bound only if he has clothed the agent with ostensible authority or if he ratifies the contract. Otherwise the agent himself will be liable to the third party, not on the contract which he has purported to make (which is of no effect) but for breach of warranty of authority. The agent is so liable whether he has acted fraudulently or innocently.

The relationship arising out of contract of agency is akin to that of employment in that an agent has certain legal rights and duties. His rights are: to an indemnity against all liabilities properly incurred; to a lien over the principal's goods in his possession; and to payment. If the contract of agency makes no express provision for payment, an agent is entitled to receive what is customary or reasonable. Disputes may arise as to when payment becomes due. This is a matter of construction of the contract of agency, but in the case of an estate agent there is a presumption that his commission is payable out of the purchase money, so that it is not normally due unless and until the property is sold.

The duties of an agent are to act honestly and obediently, and to exercise reasonable skill and care. The agent must generally himself carry out the duties entrusted to him. However, there are circumstances in which an agent may delegate his duties. These arise when there is an express or implied agreement to permit delegation, or where it is necessary for the proper performance of the work. In the construction industry, an architect has no power to delegate his duty without express authority. If, *e.g.* an architect agrees to design a building but is unable to perform the structural design work, there are two courses open to him. He may request the client to employ a specialist; or he may, while remaining liable to the client, himself seek advice and assistance (see p. 97). In either event the client will have a remedy for negligent design work.

An agent must not take any secret profit from his transactions, nor must his own interest conflict with his duty. Thus, where a supplier of coal paid to the buyer's agent a secret commission of one shilling per ton, it was held that in addition to recovering the commission from the agent (and dismissing him) the buyer could recover damages from the supplier for fraud: *Salford* v. *Lever* (1891). The duties of the architect and engineer are considered below.

Termination

A contract of agency may be brought to an end by the parties themselves, or by operation of law. Architects and engineers are normally employed, expressly or impliedly, until the completion of the works, although such an appointment may be limited to separate stages of the work. An agency may at any time be terminated by agreement, and there is frequently a provision for termination upon reasonable notice. A contract of agency may be terminated automatically by the death of either party (not being a corporate body) or by the bankruptcy of the principal. It may also be terminated by frustration, *e.g.* by destruction of the subject-matter, or by the contract becoming illegal.

Architects and engineers as agents

An agency between the promotor of a building scheme and his architect or engineer arises when it is proposed to construct the works. Such an agency does not normally embrace entering into contracts on behalf of the promoter. Building contracts are almost invariably made directly between the contractor and the promoter. The role of the architect or engineer is usually to represent the interests of the promotor during the course of the works, in addition to his duties as independent certifier under the building contract (see p. 91).

The authority of the architect or engineer is invariably expressly given, and there will often be standard conditions of engagement which extend to supervision of the works, such as those of the RIBA or The Association of Consulting Engineers (see further Chapter 9). However, such appointments rarely deal fully with the authority of the agent, and it is necessary to consider what implied or ostensible authority will exist, where not expressly given.

An express duty to certify payments to the contractor will usually carry with it an implied authority to supervise the works. There is no implied authority to vary the terms of the contract nor to warrant the accuracy of information in the contract documents. There is further no implied authority to order variations or extra works. However, standard building contracts invariably give many express powers to the architect or engineer. He will always have an ostensible authority to exercise such powers under the building contract, unless the contractor has been expressly informed of any limitation of authority. Thus, the employer or promotor will not be able to deny the architect's or engineer's authority when sued by the contractor. Where the architect or engineer is an employee of the promotor, his ostensible (or actual) authority is likely to be more extensive and may cover negotiation of the contract terms with the builder. This applies particularly to local government officers, *e.g.* the Borough Engineer. This may allow the contractor, *e.g.* to sue the employer directly on an oral variation order, if the contract requires an order to be in writing.

As an exception to the normal position, when an architect or engineer negotiates with a nominated sub-contractor he is no longer the agent of the employer, who is not a party to the sub-contract. He must therefore exercise caution when conducting such negotiations, especially before the appointment of the main contractor, since he may become personally liable for breach of warranty of authority.

The remuneration due to an architect or engineer under standard conditions of engagement is usually based upon a percentage of the cost of the works. Where there is no express agreement he will be entitled to be paid a reasonable sum, and this may be calculated with reference to the standard conditions, among other factors. The documents prepared for the building project become the property of the promotor. The architect or engineer has a lien over such documents in his possession, in respect of any unpaid fees. Copyright in the designs remain vested in the architect or engineer. The employer has an implied right to use the designs for the project in question; but if it is desired to repeat the work a further fee must be paid.

EMPLOYMENT

A contract of employment involves the provision of services to an employer. Such contracts are subject to statute and to case law, which lays down rights and duties of the parties beyond their express agreement. Under a contract of employment one person places his services at the disposal of another. A person who contracts to carry out specific works is an independent contractor, as opposed to an employee or servant; but the distinction is not always easy to draw. Persons who work in the building industry as labour-only sub-contractors are generally independent contractors and their contracts are not contracts of employment.

The contract of employment

A contract of employment may be in writing or oral. If is is oral, the Contracts of Employment Act 1972 requires that a written notice must be given by the employer specifying terms of the contract. These must cover the rate of pay, the hours, requirements as to notice, and any provisions as to holidays, sick pay and pensions. Notice is not required in special cases such as part-time employment.

Under the Contracts of Employment Act minimum periods of notice are provided, to which the employer and employee are entitled. There periods apply where the employee has worked for 13 weeks or more. The employee must give a minimum of one week's notice. The minimum notice required from the employer depends upon the length of service and varies from one week to eight weeks where the employee has worked for over 15 years.

The statutory minimum period may be extended in any particular case by the common law rule that where no period of notice is ageed, notice must be reasonable. This applies particularly to professional employment and depends upon the circumstances of each case. For example, a person employed in a managerial position may be entitled to between three and twelve months' notice. However, the above rules as to notice are subject to the law on unfair dismissal, which applies when an employee has worked for 26 weeks (see below).

It is always open to the parties to waive their rights, and it is common for employees to accept payment in lieu of notice. Further, where there is a right of summary dismissal neither notice nor payment in lieu is required, on the ground that the employer is accepting the employee's implied repudiation of the contract (see p. 56).

Duties of employee

The employee must use reasonable care and skill in carrying out his duties. He must obey lawful instructions from his superiors. He must act in good faith; for example he must not misuse confidential information. Generally the employee must conduct himself in a reasonably proper manner.

Where the employee behaves in such a way as to show an intention to flout some essential condition of his employment he is liable to summary dismissal without notice or payment in lieu. This is usually a matter of degree; an act of insolence or disobedience may be insufficient. But dishonesty by an employee in a position of trust will be sufficient. The question is whether the employee is to be taken to have repudiated his employment. Thus, where a gardener who had previously been insolent replied to his employer's inquiry "I couldn't care less about your bloody greenhouse or your sodding garden" and walked off, the employer was held to be entitled to dismiss the gardener without notice: *Pepper* v. *Webb* (1969).

Duties of employer

The employer must keep his side of the bargain by paying the wages agreed upon. In the nineteenth century a practice developed of paying workmen's wages in kind, *e.g.* by giving them tokens which could only be exchanged for goods at shops run by the employer. This practice reached such scandalous proportions that it was very severely restricted by a series of statutes known as the Truck Acts 1831 to 1940. Wages must now generally be paid in cash. The employer may, however, deduct from wages the proper value of certain items supplied to the workman (such as housing) provided there is a written agreement to this effect signed by the workman.

The employer is under a strict duty at common law and under statute to take reasonable care for the safety of his employees (see p. 179). In many industries, and particularly in construction, this general duty is enlarged by detailed statutory provisions (see p. 207).

Unfair dismissal

An employee who has worked for less than 26 weeks may be dismissed without reason. He must be given proper notice or payment in lieu, unless he is liable to summary dismissal. However an employee who has worked for 26 weeks or more is entitled not to be unfairly dismissed. If he is dismissed unfairly he is entitled to compensation, which may be substantial, and to ask for an order of reinstatement. These provisions, which create a right of property in employment, were introduced by the Industrial Relations Act 1971. Since the repeal of this Act they are contained substantially in Schedule I to the Trade Union and Labour Relations Act 1974. A complaint of unfair dismissal must be brought to an Industrial Tribunal, which has its own rules of procedure. An appeal on a point of law may be brought to the Employment Appeal Tribunal.

On a complaint of unfair dismissal the employer generally assumes the burden of proving that the dismissal was not unfair. He may do this by showing (*inter alia*) that the principal reason for dismissal related to the employee's capability or conduct or was that the employee was redundant. The employer must also satisfy the tribunal that he acted reasonably in treating the reason shown as sufficient to justify dismissal. If the employer shows no reason for the dismissal or a reason outside those specified or fails to satisfy the tribunal that he acted reasonably, the dismissal will be found unfair. The employee will then be entitled to compensation, principally in respect of actual and prospective loss of earnings and other benefits. There is a limit of £5200 on compensation. Alternatively the tribunal has a discretionary power to recommend reinstatement of the employee.

Since its inception in 1971, unfair dismissal has become a "growth area" of litigation. By their rules of procdure, tribunals are normally precluded from awarding costs to either party. This does not prevent the frequent appearance of solicitors and counsel, often on each side of a dispute. In contrast, court actions arising from dismissals are practically confined to cases where a fixed term contract has been terminated (*e.g.* a director's service contract) where the damages will exceed those recoverable in a tribunal.

INSURANCE

The nature of a contract of insurance is that one party (the insurer) undertakes to make payments to or for the benefit of the other party (the assured) on the happening of some event. The contract may generally be in any form, even oral; but it is usually contained in a document called a policy. The consideration provided by the assured is referred to as the premium.

There are essentially two different types of insurance. The more common is where the insurer agrees to compensate for losses which the assured may suffer in certain events. This type is called an indemnity insurance. The other type provides for the payment of a specified sum on the happening of some event, such as the death of the assured. This may be referred to as non-indemnity insurance, or sometimes as assurance. In many ways the two types are governed by the same rules. But there is one essential difference. On an indemnity insurance the insurer pays out only the actual financial loss. The essence of a non-indemnity policy is that the fixed sum should be paid when the event occurs. Common examples of indemnity policies are fire, motor, and third party liability insurance. Non-indemnity policies include life and personal accident insurances.

Formation of contracts

An essential feature of practically every insurance contract is that the assured must have an *insurable interest*. This usually means a foreseeable financial loss or liability resulting from the event insured against. But there is no complete definition. A person has an insurable interest in his own life even though his loss will hardly be a financial one.

A person need not own the thing he seeks to insure in order to have an insurable interest. For example a carrier or custodian of goods has a sufficient interest to insure them himself. A creditor may insure the life of his debtor to secure the debt; and a judge's life may be insured against the costs of the action he is trying. But in *Macaura* v. *Northern Assurance Co.* (1925) the plaintiff, who owned almost all the shares in a timber company, insured the timber in his own name. When the timber was destroyed by fire it was held he could not recover under the policy since as a shareholder he had no insurable interest in the company's assets.

Insurance is often effected through an agent or broker. Generally, such a person has no authority to make a binding contract on behalf of the insurer. His duties are limited to issuing and receiving proposals, although a broker may be authorised to issue temporary cover as a separate contract. The broker is, in law, the agent of the assured.

Any insurance contract is said to be *uberrimae fidei*, that is, based upon utmost good faith. Thus, the assured must make full disclosure of every material fact known to him. A fact is material if it would influence the judgment of a prudent insurer. The duty of disclosure continues after filling in the proposal form, up to the making of the contract. Non-disclosure of a material fact makes the policy voidable by the insurer. Thus, where diamond merchants insured their diamonds without disclosing that their sales manager had a previous conviction for diamond smuggling, it was held this was a material fact and the policy was therefore voidable: *Roselodge* v. *Castle* (1966). The policy may even make every stated fact a condition of the contract, so that the policy may be avoided if any fact is untrue, whether material or not. Where a policy is void or voidable the assured may be entitled to recover the premiums paid. This is generally possible only where the insurer has never been at risk.

Insurance policies are usually printed on standard forms, each company issuing its own terms. There are, however, certain provisions which are found in most forms. There must be a definition of the events upon which the insurer agrees to pay, and this may be accompanied by certain exclusions of liability. In an indemnity policy, *e.g.* a house insurance policy, the right to payment will be defined by specifying the property or item insured (the house and contents) and the risks insured against (such as fire, flood, subsidence, etc.). There may be a term requiring notice of an event which may lead to a claim. Some policies, especially motor insurances, contain an "excess clause" requiring the assured to bear the first £x of any claim. Such a term does not, however, prevent the assured himself suing the third party to recover the excess. If goods are insured for a sum less than their full value, an "average clause" may be inserted to reduce the sum payable by the proportion of their under-insurance. Where there is more than one indemnity policy covering the same risk there may be provisions which prevent full recovery, or even any recovery, on one or other of the policies.

Rights of parties

Upon the happening of an event insured against, the assured has a right to sue for payment under the policy irrespective of any rights which may exist against a third party. But under an indemnity policy the sum payable is limited to the actual loss, and subject to any excess clause. The right of the assured is a claim *under* the contract, and accordingly there can be no claim for losses consequential to the insured risk, such as delay in building works occasioned by an insured accident on the site. Consequential loss may itself be insured by a suitable policy.

When the insurer pays out on the policy a right of subrogation arises. This is a right to sue, in the name of the assured, any person who could have been sued by the assured in respect of the loss. Thus, in the above example, a house insurer who has paid on the policy in respect of a subsidence claim may, in the name of the insured, sue the builder or architect in respect of defective foundations, to recover the sum paid. On a professional indemnity policy, *e.g.* one insuring an architect against negligence, the insurer will usually have the right to conduct the defence to any disputed claim. If the insured is found liable, the insurer will then pay the damages awarded direct to the plaintiff. Where the loss insured arises from negligence of the insured person there will be no question of subrogation unless, *e.g.* the negligence was that of a sub-contractor.

The assured is under a duty not to prejudice the insurer's right. Thus, he must not release a third party from any liability he may be under in respect of the insured loss. If the insurer pays out a sum on the policy less than the actual loss, and the assured then receives some other payment in respect of the loss, the assured must repay to the insurer anything received in excess of the actual loss. The assured may not recoup more than he has lost.

There are statutory provisions which enable a third party, who is not a party to the insurance contract, to obtain the benefit of the policy despite the common law rule of privity of contract (see p. 53). The Third Parties (Rights against Insurers) Act 1930 applies when the insured person or company becomes insolvent. If liability is incurred to a third party, either before or after the insolvency, the right against the insurer vests in the third party. The Act also imposes duties on the insured person and on the insurer to give information to the third party. Apart from these provisions, either the insurer would escape liability or the insurance money would go to the creditors and not to the injured party. Under a motor insurance policy a third party, having obtained judgment against the assured, may claim against the insurer irrespective of the solvency of the assured.

SALE OF DWELLINGS

The term "dwelling" is used to cover any form of residential accommodation. The purchase of a dwelling often forms the most important economic transaction which many individuals enter into during their lives. It may involve complex problems relating to the title of the property sold, and to the means of raising finance. This section is concerned solely with problems relating to the quality of the building and the rights of parties where there is a dispute. It is further limited to the sale of new or recently built dwellings, where the sale is of the land and building together. When builders are employed directly to build a house, the rights of the owner will be governed primarily by the building contract.

The term "sale" is here used loosely. The essential feature of the transaction is that the property should be transferred or conveyed form vendor to purchaser. In the case of a house this is usually done by a conveyance by which the title of the land is vested in the purchaser. In the case of flats and maisonettes, and sometimes houses also, the vesting of title may be by a lease, usually for a fixed (but long) period. In either case all that needs to be transferred is the physical *space* in which the building stands (or is to stand, if not completed). The law automatically transfers with the land everything attached to it, including buildings, paths, walls, trees, etc. The conveyance or lease may therefore create no rights in the building itself.

The conveyance or lease is, however, almost invariably preceded by a contract of sale. This needs to be in writing or at least evidenced in writing (see p. 49). The contract may contain (in addition to the agreement of sale) terms relating to the building, *e.g.* that the work has been or will be carried out in accordance with an identified plan or specification, or in a good and workmanlike manner. But contracts of sale are sometimes entirely silent as to the building itself. In the absence of contractual terms, and until certain recent developments, the law was expressed by the maxim *caveat emptor*: let the buyer beware. He had no redress if the building proved to be defective.

Substantially, this remains the law in respect of the sale of old houses. Where the building is new or of recent construction, a number of developments in the law have changed the position radically. In 1966 the Court of Appeal held in *Hancock* v. *Brazier* that where a dwelling was sold in course of erection there were implied, in the contract of sale, warranties that the dwelling would be fit for habitation, and properly constructed of good and suitable materials. However, this did not protect the purchaser of a completed house, nor subsequent purchasers of newly built houses. An important further measure of protection was introduced by a private body now known as the National House Building Council (the NHBC).

The NHBC publish forms of agreement relating to the quality of the building (see p. 121 for a review of the principal features of the forms). They operate a scheme of registration for builders under which any company who wishes to become registered must undertake to offer to enter into an NHBC agreement with purchasers of dwellings. The agreement gives a wide measure of protection to the first purchaser, which may, in general, be transferred to subsequent purchasers. The scheme is backed by extensive insurance provisions so that purchasers will have a considerable degree of protection in the event of the vendor's insolvency. However, there remains the possibility of purchasers being unprotected because the vendor was not a registered house-builder, or because an NHBC agreement is not in fact entered into, or because a subsequent purchaser fails to acquire the right to enforce the agreement. In such cases the purchaser may have further rights under statute.

In 1972 Parliament passed an Act to impose duties on all persons taking on work for or in connection with the provision of dwellings. The Defective Premises Act, which came into force 1st January 1974, creates a general duty on such persons to see that the work is done in a workmanlike or professional manner, with proper materials and so that the dwelling will be fit for habitation (section 1). The duty applies to builders and to professional persons such as architects. It may be enforced independently of any contract which may exist, by any person acquiring an interest in the dwelling. Purchasers' rights under the Act cannot be excluded by contract (section 6(3)). But the operation of section 1 may be excluded if there is an approved scheme conferring rights in respect of defects (section 2). The NHBC scheme is approved under the Act, so that rights under the Defective Premises Act or under an NHBC agreement are alternative remedies.

In addition to the foregoing remedies, the courts have developed rights under the law of negligence (see p. 175) which may override the general common law principle *caveat emptor*. In *Dutton* v. *Bognor Regis U.D.C.* (1972) the Court of Appeal found a local authority liable for the failure of a building inspector to exercise reasonable care when inspecting foundations, pursuant to powers under the Public Health Acts. This case was reviewed by the House of Lords in *Anns* v. *London Borough of Merton* (1976) when it was held that since the Public Health Acts created a power but not a duty to inspect, it would usually be necessary to prove that an inspection was actually made.

Anns case further dealt with the period of limitation in respect of actions in negligence. It was held that the right of action did not arise, in respect of defective foundations, until defects in the superstructure were apparent. Where the defect remained undisclosed for many years, therefore, the owner of the property would not lose his rights (nor would the liability of the local authority be extinguished). This gave the house-owner rights which are potentially much wider than those under the Defective Premises Act. Section 1(5) of the Act provides that the cause of action is deemed to accrue when the work is completed. Therefore, if defects, for example, in foundations come to light more than six years after completion of the building, the right under the Act is likely to be extinguished. Note that the period of protection under an NHBC agreement in respect of a major defect in the structure is 10 years. In negligence, however, it appears that the liability of a local authority may be virtually unlimited.

A further principle arising from *Dutton* and *Anns'* case is that there may be a general liability in negligence arising from the construction of dwellings, which may create a right of action in any person who may acquire an interest in the dwelling. In *Anns'* case it was stated that a builder could be liable for breach of duty in failing to comply with the Building Regulations. Although further consideration by the courts is inevitable, it may be that builders and architects (as well as building inspectors) now owe a further duty to the ultimate occupier of a dwelling to perform their work carefully. If so the maxim *caveat emptor* will virtually cease to apply to a sale of any recently built house. It is to be hoped these develpments in the law will lead, not to an increase in litigation but to better standards of building.

Further Reading

Chitty on Contracts, Vol. II (24th ed., 1977), Guest *et al.*
Charlesworth's Mercantile Law (13th ed., 1977), Schmitthoff and Sarre.
Robert Lowe, *Commercial Law* (5th ed., 1976).

CHAPTER 6

DOCUMENTS

ALTHOUGH in most cases an oral contract is as good in law as a written contract there are obvious practical differences: when the parties to an oral contract are in dispute they often disagree over the terms of the contract. It is therefore an advantage to put agreements into writing. This is almost invariably done with building and engineering contracts. The principal problem which then arises is to construe the contract, that is, to decide the meaning of the words used. This can be difficult where the circumstances which have arisen were not foreseen by the draftsman, or when the full implications of the terms were not properly considered.

In addition to their construction, written documents can give rise to other problems. One of the parties may claim that a document does not record what was agreed. If this is so he may, in certain circumstances, obtain rectification of the contract through the courts. If the parties agree that they intended something different from the written agreement, or if they subsequently change their intentions, they may themselves alter the contract. It may then be necessary to determine the legal effect of the alterations. These problems and some of their solutions are discussed in this chapter.

CONSTRUCTION

As a general rule a written document is interpreted as the sole declaration of the parties' intention and it is from the words used that the intention must be discovered. It is therefore important to ensure that what is written truly records what the parties have agreed. One way to do this is to use words and phrases which have acquired accepted meanings through precedent. These may make a contract sound archaic but they are more likely to cover an unexpected situation. This is one advantage of using a standard form of contract. A contract will generally be construed as a whole so that no words can have an absolute meaning out of context. But the meaning of similar words in another document is often a guide to construction, and previous decisions of the courts on the meaning of the standard forms of contract are treated as binding precedents.

The general rule that intention is to be inferred from the words alone has several exceptions, when extrinsic evidence (that is, evidence outside the document) is admissible to interpret the terms. The principal exceptions are: to explain the meaning of technical terms; to prove a trade usage; and to show the surrounding circumstances of the contract. Technical terms are frequently found in building and engineering contracts, particularly in bills or specifications. It is unnecessary to define such terms in the contract, unless there is likely to be uncertainty. Trade usage can be invoked to give special meanings to words (*e.g.* the proverbial baker's dozen) and also to annex implied terms to a contract (see p. 46). Evidence of the surrounding circumstances is admissible to resolve a patent or obvious ambiguity in the document. For example, if A contracts to repair B's house without specifying where B lives, the meaning is uncertain and evidence of B's address would be admissible to resolve the doubt. There is another type of ambiguity which is called latent because the meaning appears to be clear on the face of the document, but is in fact ambiguous. In this case, evidence of intention is admissible. Thus if A contracts to repair B's house, and B owns two houses, there is a latent ambiguity. Evidence of intention is allowed to explain which house was meant.

Sometimes the body or operative part of the document is preceed by a recital relating what has led up to executing the document. For example, the JCT forms of contract commence with a number of recitals beginning "Whereas ..." which give a brief description of the works with the name of the architect, and a list of contract drawings. In the absence of doubt as to construction, the body of the document alone is effective. But where there is an ambiguity in the body, the recital, if clear, may give the true meaning.

Where a contract is partly in a printed standard form and partly in terms specially written, the latter will usually prevail in the event of an inconsistency on the basis that they represent the parties' true intention, rather than a document which was prepared by others. Thus provisions of a standard form may be over-ridden by an inserted clause, or by a contrary provision in the specification or bill of quantities. This is subject, however, to the terms of the contract itself: see, *e.g.* JCT form clause 12(1) and ICE clause 5.

Maxims of construction

Where doubt as to the precise meaning of a document remains after allowing for such extrinsic evidence as may be admissible, and after giving due weight to the different parts of the document, there are a number of maxims of construction which may assist in arriving at a definite meaning. They are often quoted in Latin but, for the most part, an English rendering is offered here:

(i) *The law prefers a reasonable to an unreasonable meaning.* This is part of a wider legal principle by which many things are judged against an objective standard of reasonableness. Thus, if a document can be read as having a sensible meaning or an absurd meaning, it is taken to have the sensible meaning. Further, if there is either a lawful or unlawful meaning, the lawful meaning will be adopted.

(ii) *An erroneous description can be given effect as it should have been stated, provided it is clear what was meant.* This maxim can be used to correct an obvious error in a document. It may apply for example to the statement of a price in pounds when pence was obviously meant, and vice versa. If there is genuine doubt, however, the contract will be enforced as written.

(iii) *Where there is express mention of some things, others of the same class not mentioned will be excluded.* This may assist where it is not clear what is to be included in a list of items. Thus, a contract to sell a house and a factory with the fixtures of the house will be taken to exclude the fixtures of the factory. Further, a contract to supply and lay bricks and to supply paving slabs would not include laying the paving slabs. In most building and engineering contracts such matters are put beyond doubt by the contract documents.

(iv) *The words of a document are to be construed against the person seeking to rely on them.* This is known as the *contra proferentem* rule. Thus, a clause excluding liability must be drafted precisely, because any loophole will be interpreted in favour of the party against whom it applies. For example, a clause stating "No responsibility is accepted for loss to customers" can be construed as an exclusion of liability in the absence of negligence, so that the person seeking to rely on the clause may still be liable if he has been negligent (he might however exclude such liability by adding at the end "howsoever caused"). In building and engineering contracts an extension of time clause is regarded as benefiting the employer since it protects the liquidated damages provision. It is therefore to be construed against the employer (see p. 100).

(v) *The meaning of a doubtful word may be ascertained from the words associated with it.* For example, the term "general contractors" might include almost any commercial activity; but in the context "engineers and general contractors" it must be limited to the field of engineering. This is part of a wider rule that words are to be construed in their context, which may include looking at the whole document.

(vi) *Where a series of words comprise a class and is followed by general words, the general words cover only things of that class.* This is known as the *ejusdem generis* rule, and an example is probably simpler than a statement of the rule. Thus, the words "iron, steel, brass, lead and other materials" could include copper since the class is one of metals; but stone or wood could not be included. However, if the words had been "... and other materials of whatsoever kind" they would preclude the operation of the rule and include any other materials. Further, a list reading "steel, bricks, plywood and other materials" forms no particular class, so that again the rule is excluded.

In conclusion it may be added that building and engineering contracts (particularly the latter) are not noted for their clarity and consistency of drafting. Problems often arise because "the contract" is contained in several long and complex documents often written by different persons at different times. It may be necessary to apply any or all of the above rules and then to balance the competing results. The disadvantage of this is that the parties may not be able to ascertain their legal rights (even when the facts are undisputed) without recourse to the courts.

RECTIFICATION

If, by mistake, a document does not record the true agreement between the parties, the courts have power to rectify or alter the documents so as to give effect to the true agreement. There can be no rectification of a mistake in the transaction (see p. 50), but only of the way in which the transaction was put into writing. Rectification is an equitable remedy, and it is therefore not available as of right, but is discretionary. One consequence of this is that rectification will not be granted if relief can be obtained by other means. The court itself will correct an obvious mistake such as a clerical slip or even an erroneous "not," without recourse to formal rectification. It should be added that while rectification may appear to be a universal panacea for badly written contracts, it is a remedy which is rarely granted in practice.

A claim for rectification must establish that the document was intended to carry out the parties' prior agreement, and not to vary it. If the opposing party says that the prior agreement was intended to be varied by the subsequent document, a heavier burden of proof falls upon the claimant. However, it is not necessary to prove that a prior concluded agreement was reached before drawing up the document. It is sufficient to show that the parties had a common intention, and that the written contract failed to conform to that intention. Usually the mistake to be rectified is one of fact, but it may also be as to the legal effect of the words used.

Generally the mistake must be common to both parties, but in a few situations a unilateral mistake may be rectified. These situations include the case where one party is mistaken but the other is fraudulent, and also where one party is mistaken and the other party knows of his mistake. Thus, where a building contractor tendered to build a school in 18 months, the employer after accepting the tender inserted a period of thirty months into the formal contract without the contractor's knowledge. It was held that the employer knew of the contractor's mistaken belief as to the term, and that the contractor was entitled to have the contract rectified by insertion of a completion period of 18 months: *Roberts* v. *Leicestershire C.C.* (1961).

VARIATION OF CONTRACTS

This section refers only to variations of the terms of a contract and not to variations made pursuant to an express power in the contract, such as the usual provisions for variation of the work found in building and engineering contracts.

An agreement to vary a contract is like any other contract in that it requires either to be for consideration or under seal in order to be binding. A variation may take the form of an alteration of some of the terms of the contract, or its replacement by a new contract, or even its complete discharge. If the original contract is one which is not required to be evidenced in writing (see p. 49), it can be varied by an oral agreement even if the original is in writing or under seal. An example of a variation is where each side surrenders some outstanding obligation. Each surrender constitutes consideration and the agreement will be binding. Thus, if the employer (without express power) wishes to omit a piece of work and the contractor agrees to the omission, the variation is binding and no action will lie for breach of contract by either party.

When only one party agrees to waive or not to insist on some right under a contract, the other party gives no consideration for the waiver. Nevertheless, if the other party has acted on a waiver, the court may treat it as binding. Where a waiver is binding, it remains effective until reasonable notice of withdrawal has been given. Waiver is a principle which parties in litigation frequently seek to rely on or to hide behind; its effect may be that where a party has not insisted on his legal rights, he may be unable to claim the benefit retrospectively. Thus, in the case of *Rickards* v. *Oppenheim* (1951) the defendant ordered a Rolls Royce from the plaintiff, to be completed by a certain date. It was not finished on time, but the defendant continued to press for delivery. Eventually the defendant stated that if the car was not completed by a specified date he would not accept it; the car was not finished in the time. It was held that the defendant had waived the original completion date, but was entitled to withdraw his waiver by reasonable notice; the plaintiff was therefore in breach of contract by failing to keep to the final delivery date. There are however certain rights which, once waived, cannot subsequently be relied on. This applies, for example, to the right to written notice of a claim within a specified period. If oral notice is received within the period and is acted on, the recipient cannot, after expiry of the period, insist on written notice.

Where one party has completely performed his obligations under a contract any variation or release of the obligations of the other party will be binding only if made under seal or if the party being released provides some new consideration, since he has no rights under the contract to give up. The consideration may take any form, and what is commonly surrendered is a potential claim. Thus, where a contractor has completed his work and agrees to accept a sum less than the full amount due in return for the surrender by the employer of a claim for bad workmanship, the agreement is binding. Such an arrangement is called an "accord and satisfaction" and the surrender constitutes good consideration provided the claim is bona finde, even though in fact not sustainable.

Further Reading

Odgers' *Construction of Deeds and Statutes* (5th ed., 1967), Dworkin.
Cheshire and Fifoot's Law of Contract (6th ed., 1976), Cheshire,
Fifoot and Furmston.

CHAPTER 7

BUILDING AND CIVIL ENGINEERING CONTRACTS

THE essence of building and civil engineering contracts is that the contractor agrees to supply work and materials for the erection of a building or other works for the benefit of the employer. In legal terms there is no difference between a building and an engineering contract, and for convenience the term building contract will be adopted to cover both. Almost invariably there will be other parties involved in a building contract in addition to the contractor and the employer, such as an architect or engineer, surveyors or sub-contractors. The status and capacity of the various parties involved has been considered in Chapter 3. This chapter deals with those particular areas of the common law which help to define the rights and duties of the parties and which regulate the performance of building contracts.

The number of statutory provisions which directly affect building contracts (as opposed to building operations) is small. Similarly the number of decided cases which apply directly to building contracts is not great compared to the amount of case law in other fields. There are some areas of building contract law in which there is no direct authority. In such a situation assistance may be obtained from the standard textbooks. These are often consulted by, and sometimes expressly approved by the courts in deciding new points of building law.

In Chapter 5 a number of special types of contract are considered. Each of these contracts has its own special features; *e.g.* a sale of goods is largely governed by statutory provisions. The special features of building contracts arise almost entirely from the form which most contracts take and from their various common features, such as the functions assigned to the architect or engineer and the provisions for payment as the work proceeds. These special features are dealt with in this chapter; and the following chapter covers some factors outside the contract itself which may have an important effect on the parties' rights. The particular provisions of common forms of building and engineering contracts are considered in Chapters 9, 10 and 11.

PERFORMANCE AND PAYMENT

In a building contract the contractor agrees to carry out the works; the employer's side of the bargain is a payment of money. Problems may arise in deciding when the contractor's obligation is discharged, and when and what amount of money is payable to the contractor. In each case the answer depends first on construction of the contract, since the parties may make whatever contractual provisions they choose. There are, however, some general principles which may amplify the parties' intentions.

Where the contract is to carry out and complete a specific piece of work, the general rule is that only complete performance can discharge the contractor's obligation and no payment is due until the work is substantially complete. Thus, where a contractor agreed to erect certain machinery for a fixed price and the partially completed work was accidentally destroyed by fire, it was held that the contractor could not recover any part of the agreed price: *Appleby* v. *Meyers* (1867). The contractor in such a situation is not, however, always without a remedy. He may, *e.g.* recover if he can show that completion was prevented by the employer, or that a fresh agreement to pay for the partially completed work is to be implied.

Building contracts usually state a price for which the work is to be completed. This is invariably subject to modification as the work proceeds on account of ordered variations, allowable price fluctuations, re-valuation of prime cost or provisional sums, claims etc. In addition, the original stated price may not itself be fixed. If it is fixed the contract may be called a "lump sum" contract. But if the sum is based on quantities which are to be recalculated when the work is done, the contract is called a "re-measurement" contract. This will be the position when there is an express right to have the work re-measured; or where the bills are stated to be provisional or approximate. The JCT form of contract is a lump sum contract, whether or not it is based on quantities (see Chapter 10). The ICE form creates a re-measurement contract; this is emphasised by the fact that the price of the work is referred to as the "tender total" (see Chapter 11). A further term sometimes used is "fixed price" contract. This is generally taken to mean a contract where the sum payable is not adjustable by reason of price increases (fluctuations).

In most building contracts of any substance there are express provisions for interim payments to be made as the work proceeds. The usual provision is for the contractor to be paid the value of the estimated quantities of work done and materials supplied less a retention which the employer holds as security for completion of the works. In such cases the rule of payment on substantial completion may still apply to the last payment, but subject also to the provisions as to certificates (see p. 91). Even where there is no express provision for interim payments there may be, in the absence of express agreement to the contrary, an implied term for interim payments as the work proceeds. Where a shipwright agreed to repair a ship, he was held to be entitled to demand an interim payment for work done before proceeding with the remainder: *Roberts* v. *Havelock* (1832).

In most cases the sums payable to the contractor are expressly provided in, or to be ascertained from the contract. Where this is not so, the contractor's claim for payment is called a *quantum meruit*. This is a claim for payment of a reasonable sum; the question of what sum is reasonable is for the court to decide if the parties cannot agree. A claim on a *quantum meruit* is appropriate where there is an express agreement to pay a reasonable sum or where such an agreement is to be implied, *e.g.* because no sum was agreed. *Quantum meruit* is also the proper claim where work is done under a contract which proves to be void. A *quantum meruit* claim will not, however, assist a contractor who has not completed work the completion of which was a condition precedent to payment, unless the employer has waived the condition. In assessing what is a reasonable sum for work done the parties may use various means, *e.g.* cost of materials and labour plus profit, or measurement and assessment of reasonable rates. The courts do not lay down rules as to this.

VARIATIONS

One of the most common features of contracts in the construction industry is that the quality and quantity of the work is liable to require variations as the work proceeds. The magnitude of variations tends to be greater in engineering works, reflecting the greater element of the unknown in such operations; but it is still a rare event for even the smallest of building jobs to be completed exactly according to the original contract provisions. Strictly the contractor is not bound, without express provision, to execute more than the contract work; and the employer will be in breach of contract if he omits a part of the work included in the contract without a contractual provision enabling him to do so. Modern building contracts, therefore, invariably provide a clause expressly stating that the employer (or his agent) may require additions or omissions to the contract work and that the contractor is bound to carry them out;

see, *e.g.* clause 11 JCT form and clause 51 ICE form.

When there has been a departure from the work specified in the contract, it is necessary to decide whether there is, in law, a variation under the contract; if there is a variation, whether the contractor is entitled to be paid extra; and if so, the amount of the extra payment. These questions are considered below.

Contractual variations

It is pertinent to state first what is not a contractual variation. Contractors sometimes make claims on the basis that the contract work has cost more than was anticipated. This is not a variation and the contractor is entitled to no extra payment unless he can claim under the contract, *e.g.* under a price fluctuations clause. When the contractor has undertaken to carry out and complete the work for a stated price he is bound to do so, however expensive it may prove to be. Thus, where a contractor undertook to build sewerage works in unknown ground which turned out to be marshy, he abandoned the works when the engineer refused to authorise additional payment. It was held that since there was no express warranty as to the nature of the site, the contractor was not entitled to additional payment: *Bottoms* v. *Mayor of York* (1892). If the work had been easier and less expensive than anticipated, the contractor would not expect to recover a lower price for the work.

Extra work for which the contractor is prima facie entitled to be paid must constitute something additional to what has been contracted for. It is, therefore, necessary to construe the contract to ascertain whether work claimed as extra is covered by the contract price or not. Building contracts may be divided into three broad groups according to the method by which the contract price is arrived at. The first type, which is most common in larger contracts, is where the work is set out in a bill of quantities, each item being priced. In this type of contract, the question whether the amount of contract work is exceeded is a matter of calculation; and whether an item is extra depends on whether it is included in the bill. However, the exact function of the bills of quantities depends upon the contract. The JCT form provides that the contract work is *deemed to be that set out in the contract bills* and errors and omissions are to be treated as variations (clause 12). The ICE form provides that the bills are *the estimated quantities of the work*; the work done is to be re-measured (clauses 55, 56).

The second type of contract is an agreement to produce the finished works for a fixed sum. The contractor's obligation in this case is to do everything necessary to complete; there will be no variation in the contract merely because it is necessary to use different means to achieve the finished works. In *Sharpe* v. *San Paulo Railway* (1873), a contractor agreed to build a railway in Brazil for a fixed sum. During the work redesign was necessary which vastly increased the quantities of excavation required. It was held that the extra cost was not recoverable. This type of contract is rare today, save in cases where the amount of work, and therefore the risk, is small.

The third type of contract falls between the two extremes; in this case the agreement is to do work set out and itemised in a specification for a fixed sum. There are no quantities which can be varied. Unless the specification is itemised in detail (which is often not the case) it may be difficult to decide what items must be taken to be included in the work specified. It will usually be implied that everything indispensably necessary for completion of the items expressly described will be included in the contract. In *Williams* v. *Fitzmaurice* (1858), where the contract was to build a house for a fixed sum, the specification omitted to mention floor boards and the contractor claimed the boards were an extra. It was held that the boards must be taken to be included in the contract and were therefore not an extra.

A further type of contract is the "cost-plus" contract. The essence of this arrangement is that the contractor is to be paid the cost of the work (the means of calculating this may or may not be specified) plus a further sum which may be called profit or overheads or a fee. There is no contract price as such, and the question whether work is a variation is usually of little significance. Cost-plus contracts sometimes take sophisticated forms. One example is the RIBA fixed fee form of prime cost contract; another is the "target" contract under which the contractor's fee or profit varies according to how near to the target is the final cost.

Payment for extras

If the contractor carries out work which is an extra to the contract, he will be able to recover payment for that work only if he can show that the employer is bound under a contract to pay. The mere doing of extra work, or doing work in a way different from that specified, does not, without more, bind the employer to pay for extras. If the building contract provides for the ordering of and payment for extras, the contractor may claim payment under the contract provided that any condition precedent to payment is satisfied. Most contracts provide that a written order is necessary; however, there may be an implied promise to pay if an appropriate order is refused. Thus, where a building contract provided that no payment for extras would be made without a written order, the contractor contended that certain work was extra. The employer denied this and refused to give a written order. It was held that there was an implied promise to pay for the works as extras if they were extras: *Molloy* v. *Leibe* (1910). Alternatively, the decision whether the work should have been ordered as a variation may be open to arbitration.

If a promise is made to pay for extra works, that promise may be enforceable as a separate contract whether or not the extras are claimable under the building contract. However, this will not avail the contractor if the "extras" are in fact no more than he was bound to do under the building contract, since the promise is then unsupported by consideration (see p. 45). Most contracts which make provision for extras also lay down means of valuation and these will determine what the contractor is entitled to be paid. In the absence of such provision, extra work will be paid for at the contract rates or at reasonable rates. In addition, it is common for building contracts to provide for some additional payment (or a "claim") if the ordering of variations causes expense beyond the payments allowed. The JCT form allows recovery of loss or expense not recoverable elsewhere in the contract (clause 11(6)). The ICE form permits a refixing of the rates for any items of work in addition to those varied (clause 52(2)). The International (FIDIC) form allows the contractor to recover additional payment if variations exceed 10 per cent of the net contract sum.

Contracts do not usually place any limit on the permissible extent of variations. The usual provision that no variation is to vitiate or invalidate the contract, make it difficult to imply any particular limit. However, it is thought there will always be some limit to what may be added to a contract. If work exceeding such limit is ordered, the contractor may be entitled to be paid for the whole of the works on a *quantum meruit* (that is, at reasonable rates) on the basis that the original contract has ceased to bind the parties.

CERTIFICATES

A very common feature of building contracts is a provision that the architect or engineer is to issue certificates. This is such a well established practice that one may even find certificates being issued under contracts which do not provide for their issue. It should therefore be noted that a certificate is merely a manifestation of the parties' private agreement and its effect is no more than the parties to the contract have agreed that it shall be.

The duty of issuing certificates is usually given to the architect or engineer in the building contract. In this section such a person is referred to simply as the certifier. In modern building contracts the role of the certifier is invariably to act impartially between the employer and contractor. This is distinct from the other role of the engineer or architect as the employer's agent, when he must act in the best interests of his principal (see p. 69). The fact that the law recognises and requires the independence of a certifier who in other situations is the employer's agent is in some ways remarkable, especially when the certifier may even be an employee of the building owner. This is frequently the case where building work is being done for local authorities or large public companies. The fact that this type of contract has continued in use for so long is a tribute to the professions whose members perform such offices.

The function of the certifier, and of the certificate, depends upon the provisions of the contract. In the great majority of building contracts the function is to record the certifier's satisfaction that the work complies with the contract. But in some cases he can impose his own standard, *e.g.* where particular items of work are required to be "to the approval of the engineer." Where the certifier is required to state his satisfaction or approval, it may be necessary to decide whether this can supersede the contract requirements.

Whether or not a certificate is conclusive as to what it purports to certify is again a matter of construction of the contract but subject also to the possibility of avoiding the certificate (see below). A further requirement for any certificate is that it must be properly made in order to have its effect as provided in the contract. Thus, a certificate which is not in the correct form or which is given by the wrong person is invalid. Subject to this the courts will uphold the parties' agreement as to the effect of a certificate. Thus under the JCT form the House of Lords have held that the courts are bound by a final certificate which is to be conclusive evidence that the work has been properly carried out: *Kaye* v. *Hosier & Dickinson* (1972). In this case the architect gave his final certificate during the course of proceedings in court concerning defects. The effect of the certificate was that the employer was no longer entitled to contend that the work was defective.

Types of cerificate

Certificates may be of many kinds; they are usually categorised into three types. First, interim or progress certificates are those which are issued periodically during the course of the work to ascertain the amount of work carried out and the payment to the contractor. The most usual contractual provision is for monthly interim certificates and such payments form a vital part of the economics of contracting. An interim certificate, properly given, creates a debt due from the employer. In a series of cases starting with *Dawnays* v. *Minter* (1971) the Court of Appeal held that the employer must pay the contractor the amount due on an interim certificate without any set off save for liquidated or established claims. The contractor must similarly pay his sub-contractor. These cases were disapproved by the House of Lords in *Gilbert Ash* v. *Modern Engineering* (1973) which held that the general right of set-off was available against sums certified in favour of the contractor or a sub-contractor. Thus, where there has been delay or defective work, the employer may generally withhold the amount of his cross-claim from certified sums due to the contractor, and the contractor may similarly withhold from a sub-contractor. In addition to a set-off, the employer is entitled to challenge the certificate, *e.g.* if the work has been over-valued.

The second type of certificate is the final certificate which may be issued after completion of the works. A final certificate may fulfil either or both of two functions: it may state what is finally payable to the contractor and it may certify approval of the works. The final certificate issued under the JCT form (clause 30) fulfils both functions; under the ICE conditions, the final certificate is merely a document of account (clause 60(3)) and the maintenance certificate signifies final completion of the work (clause 61).

The third type of certificate is that which records some event for the purposes of the contract. Examples of this type are certificates of substantial completion (clause 48 ICE) or practical completion (clause 15 JCT) of the works; and a certificate that the works ought reasonably to have been completed by the date for completion (clause 22 JCT). An extension of time given by the architect or engineer, although not so called, is a form of certificate given under the contract.

Recovery without a certificate

Much of the case law concerning certificates relates to recovery of sums of money for which a certificate is required, where no certificate has been given. This situation properly arises only when, on construction of the contract, the certificate is a condition precedent to recovery. An arbitration clause in the contract may have the effect of removing a condition precedent, and permitting recovery without a certificate, if the matter in issue is within the arbitrator's jurisdiction. The question whether an interim certificate, under the common forms of contract, is a condition precedent to recovery of payment has not been finally settled. Expert views are divided. But it is thought the better view is that a certificate is necessary to recovery. If the certificate is a condition precedent, then the contractor may nevertheless recover without a certificate if he can show that the certifier or the employer has acted improperly.

What constitutes behaviour sufficiently improper to dispense with the requirements of a certificate is illustrated by the following examples. First, fraud or collusion will disqualify the certifier and permit recovery of sums without a certificate. As a principle of civil law it is generally true that a defendant can never rely upon his own wrongful act. Secondly, a certificate may be dispensed with where the certifier has acted without fraud but improperly in some other way. Such improper conduct may consist in a failure to act independently. Thus, where an architect acceded to the employer's instructions not to issue further certificates, it was held that the contractor could recover the sums in question without certificates: *Hickman* v. *Roberts* (1913). It is also improper for the certifier to consider extraneous matters in making a decision. Where the certifier's function was to certify that work was satisfactory, but he refused to issue his certificate until satisfied that the work had also been done economically, it was held that the employer could not rely on the absence of a certificate: *Panamena Europa* v. *Leyland* (1947).

Thirdly, the certifier may be disqualified if there is some interest or other factor which may influence his mind and which is unknown to the contractor. Thus, where an architect, before the signing of the building contract and unknown to the contractor, promised the employer that the cost would not exceed a certain figure, it was held that the architect's decision was not binding and that the court could award sums due to the contractor: *Kemp* v. *Rose* (1858).

Negligent certification

It has long been settled that judges and those performing judicial functions, including arbitrators, are immune from actions in negligence. In the leading case of *Chambers* v. *Goldthorpe* (1901) the Court of Appeal (by a majority) held that an architect giving a final certificate was also immune from liability for giving the certificate negligently. This remained the law until 1974 when *Chambers*' case was over-ruled by the House of Lords in *Sutcliffe* v. *Thackrah*.

In *Sutcliffe*'s case the architect gave an interim certificate, including work not properly done. The builder having been over-paid for the work, became insolvent so that the employer could not recover the loss. The architect contended that, even though negligent, he was immune from action. In holding the architect liable for negligence the court found no inconsistency in owing a duty to the employer to act with due care and skill, while being under a duty to hold the balance fairly between his client (the employer) and the contractor. The rule giving immunity applied only where there was a dispute which called for a judicial decision. Such immunity is not confined to formal arbitration proceedings, and may extend, *e.g.* to the position of the engineer under clause 66 of the ICE conditions, when he is required to adjudicate on a dispute.

ENGINEERS AND ARCHITECTS

One of the most novel features of building contracts is the position in law of the engineer or architect. This varies according to the function being performed. It is important therefore for him, and for those affected by his decsions, to know what is his status. The engineer or architect may perform functions as the agent of, or as the independent contractor of the employer, or as an impartial certifier; he may also do things which incur a duty under the law of tort to other persons. The position of the certifier (see above), and the relationship between principal and agent generally (see p. 68) have already been discussed. In this section the specific duties and liabilities to the employer and to others are considered.

Duties to the employer

The scope of the work normally performed by the engineer or architect is considered comprehensively in the standard works. They may be divided broadly into pre-contract duties and duties which arise under or by virtue of the building contract. In the pre-contract stage, the basic duty is to prepare skilful and economic designs for the works, acting as an independent contractor for the employer (unless the designer happens to be the employee of the building owner). When the work is in progress, the duties arising under or by virtue of the contract are to supervise and administer the carrying out of the works in the best interests of the employer. Such functions will generally be performed as the agent of the employer. In each case the duty is owed in contract and the common law requires such duties to be exercised with a reasonable degree of skill and care. Whether particular conduct will incur liability for its consequences depends primarily upon established practice, that is, whether or not others would do the same. This is ultimately a question for the judge to decide. But in practice unless the failure is gross and obvious it is usually necessary to call a person practising in the same technical field to give expert evidence as to the breach of duty complained of.

There may, however, be occasions on which the court will find that the parties intended a different standard of duty. Where the engineer or architect is employed as an expert in some field, the court may impose a lighter duty. In *Greaves Contractors* v. *Baynham Meikle* (1975) an engineer was employed to design the structure of a building known to be subject to vibrating loads. The floors were not adequately designed to resist the vibrations. The court accepted that the engineer had not failed to exercise reasonable skill and care, but found there to be an implied term of his engagement that the building would be fit for its purpose. The engineer was therefore held liable.

Design

What constitutes reasonable skill and care in the design of work depends upon the circumstances of each case. The duty may normally be discharged by following established practice, but there is no rule that doing what others do cannot give rise to liability. There may be situations where there is no established practice, *e.g.*, where a new construction technique is used. In such cases the duty of reasonable skill and care may be discharged by taking the best advice available and by warning the employer of any risks involved. In *Turner* v. *Garland & Christopher* (1853) the employer instructed his architect to use a new patent concrete roofing which proved to be a failure. It was held that where an untried process was used, failure might still be consistent with reasonable skill. But whenever money may be saved by taking a risk it is the employer who must decide which course to adopt, and he must be given all the necessary information to enable him to reach a decision.

When dealing with the liabilities of the parties and with insurances, the standard forms of contract often use the criterion of whether or not some fault or mishap is caused by the design of the works; see, *e.g.* clause 20 ICE and clause 19 JCT forms. Such a criterion does not necessarily coincide with that of whether the designer has exercised sufficient skill and care. Thus, in *Queensland Railways* v. *Manufacturers Insurance* (1969) a river bridge failed during erection because the piers were subjected to forces beyond those which could be predicted by existing knowledge. It was held that the failure was in fact due to faulty design, although there might be no fault attributable by the employer to the designer.

There may be many situations where design work is undertaken by persons other than the engineer or architect named in the building contract. Problems may then arise as to who can be sued for a design defect, liability arises generally under contract. Therefore, if the employer directly employs a consultant, or even the contractor, to do design work, he will have a remedy for design defects, depending upon the terms of the contract. Where the engineer or architect himself delegates design work, the problem is more difficult because there is then no contract between the employer and the designer. As a general rule the engineer or architect will remain liable for the design unless the employer concurs in a delegation of responsibility. Thus, where an architect delegated a structural design to the contractor, and the design proved to be defective, it was held that the architect was liable. If the architect was not able to carry out certain design work he should either (i) decline the work, or (ii) request the employer to engage a consultant, or (iii) himself employ a consultant, to whom he could look for indemnity: *Moresk Cleaners* v. *Hicks* (1966).

The employer may be in similar difficulties if design work is done by a nominated sub-contractor. The employer may protect himself in such a case by obtaining a direct (or collateral) warranty from the sub-contractor. This is in effect a separate contract under which the sub-contractor warrants his work, usually in consideration of his nomination by the employer. It is thus essential that the warranty is obtained before the sub-contract is entered into, otherwise there is no consideration for the warranty and it is unenforceable. This principle was first applied to a building contract in the case of *Shanklin Pier* v. *Detel Products* (1951). In this case a supplier warranted to the employer that his paint had a life of 7 to 10 years. He was nominated by the employer and entered into a sub-contract with the main contractor. When the paint proved defective it was held that the employer was entitled to sue the supplier for breach of warranty.

The consideration for a warranty is not confined to the nomination. A fee paid to the sub-contractor for his design work is equally effective to make any warranty enforceable. For standard forms of warranty issued by the RIBA, see Chapter 9.

Supervision and administration

The duties of supervision and adminstration arise under or by virtue of the building contract. The purpose of supervision is to ensure that the works are carried out by the contractor in accordance with the requirements of the contract; and the engineer or architect must provide reasonable supervision to achieve this. The amount of supervision required depends on the nature of the works. The building of a house may require visits every two weeks; while engineering operations may require constant attention from a resident staff. But whatever the frequency of inspections, they must be sufficient to check important items, especially those which will be covered up by later work. Thus, where the architect made weekly visits to a house under construction but failed to inspect the bottoming of floors, which was defective, it was held that he was liable to the employer: *Jameson* v. *Simon* (1899).

The term administration is here used compendiously to describe the various functions which the engineer or architect may or must perform under a building contract. The most important of these functions are issuing certificates and ordering variations, which are considered above; and issuing instructions and drawings. In each case the scope of the particular powers or duties depends on the express or implied terms of the contract.

In the absence of express terms (see clause 7 ICE, and clause 3 JCT forms) the contractor is entitled to have instructions and drawing supplied in reasonable time. Whether the express or impled obligation has been complied with is often difficult to determine, *e.g.* when instructions are needed to enable a sub-contract to be placed so as to permit completion on time. This is often a source of contention between contractor and employer. But under the standard forms the contractor is usually required to give notice of any instruction which he considers necessary.

During the course of carrying out construction work the engineer or architect may sometimes issue instructions permitting a deviation from the contract to assist the contractor, when strictly the employer is entitled to rely upon the contract. In such a case the instruction should be carefully distinguished from a true variation order. In *Simplex* v. *St. Pancras B.C.* (1958), the contractor undertook to install piles of specified capacity. This proved impracticable and the contractor offered alternative, differently priced, schemes. The architect accepted one of these "in accordance with quotations submitted." It was held that although the contractor would have been liable for the failure of the first scheme, the architect's acceptance of the alternative amounted to a variation. The contractor was therefore entitled to be paid the price of the alternative scheme and not the (lower) price originally tendered. One way of avoiding such a problem is to add to the instruction words to the effect "provided this is at no extra cost."

Quantity surveyors

The duties of a quantity surveyor may include taking off quantities from drawings, preparing bills of quantities and measuring the works. The quantity surveyor is named in the JCT forms of contract, where he is engaged by the employer. In the ICE form such duties are placed on the engineer, but in practice are usually carried out by the quantity surveyors employed by the engineer. On most construction works of any substance there will, in addition to those employed by or on behalf of the employer, be quantity surveyors employed by the contractor.

In some building contracts, usually smaller ones, a surveyor alone may be appointed as certifier, and may also be given the functions of supervising and administering the contract. The position of the surveyor will then correspond to that of the engineer or architect under larger building contracts.

Liability in tort

The duties of engineers and architects to the employer arise principally in contract. Acts performed for or on behalf of the employer may, however, at the same time give rise to duties and liabilities to other persons. This may arise by virtue of the position as agent for the employer, when there may be personal liability on a contract or liability for acting without authority (see p. 68). There may also be a wider area of liability arising under the law of tort, for negligence. Subject to the general rules as to tortious liability (see p. 173) duties may be owed to the contractor, or sub-contractors, to workmen on the site and possibly to a subsequent purchaser of the building. In addition, architects and engineers are subject to the Defective Premises Act 1972. Under section 1, they owe a duty to any present or future owner of a dwelling, to see that their work is done in a professional manner.

The duty in tort will necessarily be narrower than that owed to the employer. It will generally be a duty to avoid either foreseeable injury to another or to avoid negligent misstatements on which the other person is likely to rely. Thus, where an architect failed to examine a dangerous wall and allowed it to remain in the belief that it was safe, it was held that he was liable in negligence to a workman who was injured when the wall collapsed; the contractor who employed the man and the demolition contractor were also liable: *Clay* v. *Crump* (1963).

It has recently been suggested, in the case of *Esso Petroleum* v. *Mardon* (1976), that duties owed by architects to their clients are not limited to those arising under contract, but also encompass duties in tort. This principle awaits further consideration by the courts. If followed, it will have far-reaching effects, one of which will be that the period of potential liability will be without limit. In contract the period of limitation begins when the breach (*e.g.* negligent design work) occurs. In tort, the cause of action arises and the period of limitation begins only when damage occurs. It was further held, in regard to a defective dwelling, that the cause of action does not arise until the defects are apparent: *Anns* v. *London Borough of Merton* (1977). These principles may greatly enlarge the potential area of liability of architects and engineers.

COMPLETION

This covers the time period within which the work must be carried out and the consequences of delay; what is necessary to achieve completion of the work; and the effect of maintenance or defects liability clauses. Generally building contracts do not require the contractor to carry out individual items of work at particular times, and a programme of work is rarely made a term of the contract. Consequently the contractor will not be in breach by reason of delay during the course of the work (save possibly under terms requiring "due diligence," etc.). Similarly the contractor is not generally in breach by reason only of defective work, provided he can complete in accordance with the contract. Conversely when defects appear within the maintenance period, although the contractor has the duty and right to make good, he is nevertheless in breach so that the employer may sue for damages, *e.g.* through being deprived of use of the work.

Time for completion

The time within which the work is to be performed is a matter of economic importance both to employer and contractor. In most contracts dates will be specified for the start and completion of the work (in the ICE form the period of the work is specified, to run from the engineer's order to commence the work). The contractor is bound to do the work within the period set, and will be liable in damages if he fails to complete, subject to entitlement to extensions of time. He is also entitled so to carry out the work. Thus, if the employer prevents completion, *e.g.* by failing to give possession of the site, he will be liable in damages to the contractor. Where no time period is specified, the same principles apply, save that the contractor is obliged and entitled to complete within a reasonable time.

Damages recoverable by the employer for delay are usually limited to "liquidated damages" (see JCT clause 22, ICE clause 47). When the delay is caused partly by the employer's default, it has been held that no liquidated damages may be recovered unless the contract allows an extension of time to be granted on the ground of the default, and such extension is granted. Thus in *Peak* v. *McKinney* (1970) building works were suspended after the discovery of defective piles, for which the contractor was responsible. The employer caused further delay before work restarted. The contract did not provide for an extension of time for the employer's default. It was held that no liquidated damages could be recovered for any of the delay. The grounds of this decision were that liquidated damages may be recovered only from a date fixed under the contract. If no date can be fixed, time is "at large." For this purpose the liquidated damages and extension of time clauses are regarded as being for the employer's benefit and are construed against him, so that general words cannot be relied on. However, this appears to ignore the fact that pre-determined damages are as likely to benefit the contractor as the employer. If damages for delay are not "liquidated," the employer may sue for his actual loss.

Extension of time

Building contracts usually provide for extensions of time to be granted by the architect or engineer on a variety of specified grounds: see JCT form clause 23, and ICE form clause 44. Where the ground of extension would otherwise be the contractor's risk, the extension is purely a concession; *e.g.* for inclement weather. Where the extension is based on some act or default of the employer, *e.g.* ordering variations or giving late instructions, the contractor may also be entitled to extra payment. For this reason, the contractor may seek to attribute the actual delay to grounds carrying reimbursement in respect of the period granted: see, *e.g.* clauses 23, 24(1) and 11(6) JCT form.

While the employer may not be entitled to rely on general words to protect his right to liquidated damages, such words will benefit the contractor. See, *e.g.* clause 44(1) ICE conditions, where the contractor is entitled to an extension on the ground of "other special circumstances of any kind whatsoever."

Meaning of completion

Generally, full and complete performance is required to discharge contractual obligations. However in building contracts the purpose of signifying completion is not to release the contractor, but to allow him to leave the site so that the employer may take possession of the works. Contracts therefore use terms such as practical completion (JCT clause 15(1)) and substantial completion (ICE clause 48(1)). While such terms do not permit the contractor to achieve completion without finishing the whole of the work (save for permitted exceptions: see ICE clause 48(1)), it is thought they allow completion to be certified despite the existence of non-material departures from the contract.

Completion is not prevented by the existence of latent defects. If defects are discovered after apparent completion (whether during or after the maintenance period) the employer is entitled to sue for damages, including damages for loss of use of the works.

Maintenance clauses

These oblige the contractor to rectify faults appearing within a specified period, often 6 or 12 months, following completion. They may also oblige the contractor to maintain the works and to put right defects not due to his default, the latter at the employer's expense, (compare JCT clause 15 and ICE clause 49).

When a default is due to the contractor's failure to comply with the contract, he is in breach. The maintenance clause permits the contractor to mitigate the effect of the breach by carrying out rectification himself, but he may further be liable to the employer for damage for loss of use of the works, which will not be limited by any stipulation for liquidated damages.

A provision which entitles the employer to have defects rectified within a specified period does not absolve the contractor from liability for defects appearing after the expiry of the period. Clear words are required to make a maintenance clause operate also as an exclusion clause. For an example of a limited exclusion clause see the NHBC form of agreement, Chapter 9, where the purchaser is obliged first to pursue other remedies in respect of defects appearing after an initial guarantee (or maintenance) period.

Further Reading

Keating, *Building Contracts* (4th ed., 1978).
Hudson, *Building and Engineering Contracts* (10th ed., 1970), Wallace.

CHAPTER 8

VICARIOUS PERFORMANCE AND INSOLVENCY

Chapter 7 deals with the operation of building and engineering contracts (the term building contract is used here to cover both) and the parties' rights arising from the contract. This Chapter covers a number of matters outside the contract itself which may affect the parties' rights. Vicarious performance refers to the carrying out of contractual obligations by a person not party to the contract. This may be either by sub-contract or assignment. Sub-contracts are found in most construction work, since very few contractors have the resources to carry out the whole of a project themselves. Particular problems arise when the sub-contractor is nominated. Assignment is the means by which a party may transfer to another the whole or part of his rights or duties under a contract. When the contractor assigns part of his obligation to perform the work, the effect is similar to a sub-contractor save that the assignee is in direct contact with the employer. Finally insolvency and bonds deals with the rights of the parties when one of them becomes unable to perform the contract by reason of financial difficulties.

SUB-CONTRACTS

In the traditional system of contracting in the construction industy the whole of the works is initially let to the main contractor. Subject to the provisions of the main contract, the contractor is entitled to sub-let portions of the work, save where the contract is let by reason of some special skill or quality of the contractor. Thus a contract, for example, for specialist site-investigation work is likely to be one which may not be sub-let without consent of the employer. However, performance by a sub-contractor constitutes vicarious performance on behalf of the contractor, who remains fully responsible for the work, save where the main contract provides otherwise.

The standard forms usually contain terms restricting the right of sub-letting. The JCT form prohibits sub-letting without the architect's consent, which is not to be unreasonably withheld (clause 17). The withholding of consent may be referred to arbitration, if considered unreasonable. Under the ICE form sub-letting is merely prohibited without consent (clause 4). The withholding of consent may not be challenged. If sub-letting occurs without any necessary consent, the contract may provide express remedies, *e.g.* determination. The employer may waive his right to object, *e.g.* by making payment for the sub-contracted work. If there has been no waiver, the employer may call on the contractor to resume performance of the work.

In engineering contracts sub-contractors tend often to be specialists who carry out limited parts of the works, such as piling. In building, it is not uncommon for the majority of the work on a substantial contract to be carried out by a large number of different sub-contractors. In recent years a novel form of main contract has been developed under which it is intended that the whole of the work is sub-contracted, the contractor's role being that of project manager. These are known as "fee contracts" since the employer pays only for the actual cost of the work (the prime cost) plus a fee retained by the contractor.

Work which is intended to be sub-contracted is commonly described in bills of quantities as a prime cost (P.C.) or provisional sum item. A P.C. item usually denotes specific work, the cost of which will depend upon the sub-contractor's price. A provisional sum usually represents work the scope of which is not entirely foreseen. The payment which the contractor is entitled to receive for a P.C. or provisional sum item is generally the actual cost plus a small percentage.

A sub-contract creates no privity of contract between the sub-contractor and the employer. Therefore the sub-contractor can sue only the main contractor for the price of the sub-contract work. The advantage of this system to the employer is that while the work may actually be performed by various specialists, the main contractor alone remains responsible for the whole operation and, perhaps most important, for the co-ordination of his own work and that of sub-contractors. It is common for the employer to fortify his position by retaining the right to decide who will do certain work or supply certain materials. Such sub-contractors or suppliers are usually termed "nominated."

A common feature of main contracts is for the employer to retain the right to make direct payments to a nominated sub-contractor. See, under the JCT form, clauses 27(*c*) and 25(3) (*b*); and ICE form clause 59C. These provisions recognise that payments due to a nominated sub-contractor are generally fixed by the architect or engineer, so that the contractor acts merely as a channel for payment in this regard. However, neither nomination nor direct payment to sub-contractors gives a sub-contractor the right to sue the employer; and no privity of contract is created. The only exception to this principle is where the employer obtains a collateral warranty from the sub-contractor (see p. 97). The warranty itself gives the sub-contractor no right to sue for payment. The RIBA forms of warranty (see p. 126) oblige the employer to operate the direct payment provisions; but such rights are generally subject to any cross-claim against the contractor which the employer may have.

One problem arising out of sub-contracts is that of incorporation of the terms of the main contract. This is often done in an attempt to pass on the contractor's obligations to the sub-contractor. A common device adopted is a general incorporation clause such as "the sub-contractor shall perform all obligations of the main contract." But this is often inadequate and may produce complete ambiguity. For example, in the above clause, is the sub-contractor bound to perform the obligations of the contractor or those of the sub-contractor set out in the main contract? And if the former, do these include the obligations of the contractor to the sub-contractor? Such clauses may not be susceptible of any rational construction and to avoid such problems it is advisable to set out precisely what the sub-contractor's obligations are intended to be.

Nomination

The usual procedure for letting a nominated sub-contract is for the architect or engineer to obtain quotations for the work in question direct from prospective sub-contractors, and to instruct the contractor to place an order with the chosen tenderer. The terms of the sub-contract will largely be settled before the nomination, but both contractor and sub-contractor may seek to amend or alter the terms. The main contract usually gives the contractor some protection by entitling him to object to a nomination which does not contain certain beneficial terms: see ICE form clause 59A(1) and JCT form clause 27(*a*).

One of the difficult legal problems relating to sub-contracts is that of determining the obligations of the main contractor in respect of materials and work of nominated sub-contractors, and thus determining the rights of the employer in the event of default by a nominated sub-contractor. There is generally no problem in regard to the express description of the work. This often becomes incorporated in the main contract only by virtue of the nomination. The problem arises when the sub-contractor's work, while complying with the express terms of main and sub-contract, is not of good quality or is not fit for its purpose.

Generally the main contractor remains liable for the quality of the sub-contractor's work and materials. It has been held, however, that such terms may be excluded if the contractor is compelled to enter a sub-contract under which the sub-contractor does not assume such liability: see *Young & Martin* v. *McManus Childs* and *Gloucester C.C.* v. *Richardson* (both 1969). Further, where the architect or engineer specifies the materials to be supplied, so that there is no reliance on the contractor's skill and judgment, he will generally not be responsible for their suitability.

A further difficult problem arises if a nominated sub-contractor repudiates. Is the contractor himself obliged to complete the work at his own expense, so far as this exceeds the agreed sub-contract price, or must the employer pay the additional cost of finding an alternative sub-contractor? In *N.W. Metropolitan Hospital Board* v. *Bickerton* (1970) it was held that under the JCT form the architect was obliged to re-nominate, so that the employer must generally bear the loss. The decision was based on the fact that the contract contemplated that prime cost work would be carried out only by a nominated sub-contractor. The decision may therefore apply to other forms of main contract, *e.g.*, to the ICE 4th edition. The ICE 5th edition, however, contains extensive provisions dealing with the parties' rights upon the default of a nominated sub-contractor, so that there is very little application for the *Bickerton* principle.

If a nominated sub-contractor causes delay, without repudiating, the contractor generally remains liable, and may pass on the employer's claim to the sub-contractor in default. However the JCT form provides expressly for an extension of time on the grounds of delay by a nominated sub-contractor (clause 23(*g*)). It should be noted that this effectively deprives the employer of remedy, save under any direct warranty. Under the JCT form it may be necessary to decide whether defects discovered after apparent completion can constitute delay by a nominated sub-contractor. In *Jarvis* v. *Westminster Corpn.* (1969) it was held that when the sub-contractor achieved apparent completion (although subject to latent defects), further delay caused when defects were discovered was not delay on the part of the sub-contractor, so that the employer was not deprived of remedy against the contractor.

ASSIGNMENT

An assignment is a transfer, recognised by the law, of a right or obligation of one person to another. Most rights and obligations are capable of assignment. This may be achieved in a number of ways.

Assignments are sometimes brought about by operation of law. This section is concerned primarily with assignment of rights and obligations under building contracts, but the principles involved cover many other things.

It should be noted that an assignment (in common with other legal transactions) is distinct from a contract to make an assignment. An assignment does not generally require consideration (see p. 45). But a contract to assign, in order to be enforceable, must comply with the same requirements as any other contract, including the need for consideration. An assignment of a right or obligation arising under a contract is a further exception to the doctrine of privity (see p. 53) in that rights or burdens are conferred upon persons who are not party to the contract.

Assignments not permitted

Building contracts and sub-contracts often contain terms restricting or prohibiting assignments; see, *e.g.*, JCT form clause 17, ICE clause 3. Such terms have the effect of making any purported assignment invalid as against the other party to the contract. However the right to prevent an assignment may be lost by waiver; *e.g.*, if the contractor assigns his right to receive payment the employer will waive his right to object if payment is made to the assignee.

There are certain rights which may not be assigned. Debts may be assigned; indeed most assignments are of money due. But a right to sue for damages in respect of a past breach of contract or tort may not be assigned. If the right is merely incidental to a right in property the assignment may be valid. Thus the sale of a building together with the right to sue under a lease for dilapidations may be valid. Under building contracts the contractor may not assign the burden, *i.e.* the obligation to do the work, without the consent of the employer.

Methods of assignment

A legal assignment is one which complies with section 136 of the Law of Property Act 1925. This requires that the assignment is in writing, is absolute, and that notice in writing is given to the other party. No particular form is needed and the document need not be under seal. An assignment which is conditional, *e.g.* until a loan is repaid, is not absolute. The assignment takes effect and becomes enforceable against the other party only on receipt of notice.

A transfer which does not comply with the requirements of a legal assignment, *e.g.* one made orally, may be enforceable as an equitable assignment. But an equitable assignment will require to be evidenced in writing, *e.g.* if it relates to an interest in land (see p. 49).

In either type of assignment it is necessary to draw a distinction between a benefit and a burden. In a building contract the benefit to the contractor is the right to be paid and the burden is the obligation to do the work. A benefit may be assigned irrespective of the wishes of the other party (subject to rights under the contract). The burden may be assigned only with the consent of the other party. Thus the contractor may not assign the obligation to carry out the work without the employer's consent; and the employer may not assign the duty to make payments without the contractor's consent.

Apart from the above methods, the assignment of certain rights are governed by statutory provision. These include transfers of shares and debentures in companies, and assignment of life insurance policies. In addition to transfers brought about by act of the parties some assignments take place by operation of law. Thus on death, the rights of the deceased person vest generally in his personal representative. In a less extreme case, upon bankruptcy, the rights of the bankrupt vest in the official receiver and, upon appointment, in his trustee in bankruptcy.

Effects of assignment

Upon a valid assignment, the assignor loses his rights in the things assigned. The assignee acquires the right to sue, *e.g.* for the debt in his own name. However, if the assignment is equitable, the assignor may need to be made a party to the action. The right acquired is subject to any rights of the other party against the assignor, including the right of set-off. Thus if a contractor assigns money payable under a certificate, the employer may set off against the assignee any claim for defects or delay. He cannot counterclaim. but the set off may reduce or extinguish the debt.

Assignment does not generally discharge the party assigning from his own contractual obligation. Thus when a lease is assigned the landlord is entitled to look to the assignee or to the original tenant for payment of rent. Similarly if the contractor assigns the obligation to carry out work, he may still be liable to the employer for breaches, *e.g.* defective work. From the contractor's point of view, a more satisfactory arrangement is that there should be a substitution of the new contractor. This is referred to as a novation. Where both the benefit and the burden of a contract are assigned, the latter requiring express consent, this may operate as a novation. Where a new contractor is substituted in the course of a building contract, difficulties may arise as to existing matters which may later give rise to disputes, *e.g.* where the work is behind programme or there are grounds for a claim. These matters are best dealt with by express agreement.

INSOLVENCY

Insolvency is not a term of art, but means, in practical terms, inability to pay debts. The effects of this depend on whether the debtor is an individual or a company; but in either case the consequences are severe, both for the debtor and for the creditor who is unpaid. The laws of bankruptcy and of winding up companies provide for the realisation and distribution of assets, with certain debts having priority for payment. In building contracts the insolvency of one party will usually bring the work to an end.

The fact that an individual or a company is insolvent does not mean that there will be a bankruptcy or winding up. This depends on the action of the creditors (and of the debtor). The creditors may simply defer the enforcement of their rights; or they may agree to a formal arrangement by which the debtor attempts to pay off or reduce the debts. This shows that the concept of insolvency is rather uncertain. Insolvency is often brought about not by the loss of assets but by the loss of credit facilities or, particularly in the building industry, an exotic condition known as "adverse cash-flow."

Bankruptcy proceedings

The bankruptcy laws apply to individuals and not to incorporated companies. Bankruptcy is a statutory process under which possession of the debtor's property is taken for the benefit of his creditors. The debtor obtains release from his debts and liabilities, but is subject to certain restrictions. The law is contained principally in the Bankruptcy Act 1914 and the bankruptcy rules made thereunder.

Bankruptcy proceedings are set in train by a bankruptcy petition. This requires that the debtor has committed a statutory act of bankruptcy, *e.g.* failure to comply with a bankruptcy notice served by a judgment debtor. The debtor may himself present a petition. On the petition the court appoints the official receiver to be receiver of the debtor's property. The creditors then consider in general meeting whether to agree to a composition (part payment of debts) or a scheme of arrangement. If they do not, the debtor will be adjudicated bankrupt and may be subjected to a public examination. The property of the debtor, on adjudication, passes to a trustee in bankruptcy. The trustee in bankruptcy has the duty of realising the assets and distributing them between creditors. He has powers to carry on the business of the bankrupt and to bring and defend actions. An important power is the right to disclaim unprofitable contracts (Bankruptcy Act 1914, section 54). This right (and a similar right vested in a liquidator) may create difficulties when building contracts are terminated through insolvency (see below). The bankrupt's property is distributed between the creditors subject to certain priorities. Administrative costs, rates and taxes, and wages of employees are paid first. The balance is then distributed proportionately between ordinary creditors.

Assets available to trustee

The assets available for realisation include all property belonging to the bankrupt or acquired by him before his discharge. This may include part of the bankrupt's income from employment. The trustee may take proceedings on behalf of the bankrupt, *e.g.* to recover damages or debts. The bankrupt may, however, retain limited personal property comprising the tools of his trade, clothes and bedding.

The trustee may also take goods in the possession of the bankrupt in his trade or business where he is the reputed owner. Where the bankrupt is a contractor, this may allow the trustee to acquire unfixed materials or goods and construction plant. Generally materials on site are not in the contractor's reputed ownership, but plant may be. Materials in the contractor's own premises will generally be in his reputed ownership, so that provisions in a building contract for payment for materials not yet delivered to the site must ensure the employer's security (see, *e.g.* JCT clause 30(2A) and ICE clause 54).

An important class of assets not available to the trustee is property used to secure debts or loans. The security may be a mortgage or a charge. The secured creditor is entitled to exercise various powers arising under statute or under the mortgage or charge instrument, including powers of sale. The more the debtor has used his property as security the less will be available to satisfy unsecured creditors.

Winding up companies

Winding up procedure is dealt with in Chapter 3 above. This

section deals with the principal ways in which winding up differs from bankruptcy, and its effects on building contracts.

While bankruptcy is always conducted through the courts, winding up may be initiated by the company itself resolving to wind up. The company may then appoint its own liquidator. If the company is insolvent, the winding up will be controlled by the creditors who may have their own liquidator appointed. The winding up may also be made subject to the court's supervision. But in most cases, winding up on the grounds of insolvency will be ordered and conducted by the court on the petition of creditors. In winding up by the court the official receiver initially acts as liquidator, and continues unless replaced by order of the court.

The liquidator's duty is to collect in the assets and apply them in discharge of the company's liabilities. Unlike the trustee in bankruptcy, the assets do not vest in the liquidator, unless by specific order of the court. The liquidator has powers to carry on the company's business, to sell the assets and to compromise claims. A winding up order operates to discharge all the directors and employees of the company, so that only the liquidator retains the power to act for the company. The distribution of assets and the priority of claims follows the bankruptcy rules.

Assets available to liquidator

The liquidator must collect all assets belonging to the company, which includes contributions due from members on shares which are not fully paid-up. Since the winding up is followed by dissolution, no assets are retained by the company (unlike a bankrupt individual). The doctrine of reputed ownership does not apply to liquidation. A liquidator is given power to disclaim unprofitable contracts (Companies Act 1948, section 323). As in bankruptcy, an important limitation on the company's assets arises when they are used as security. The mortgagee or debenture holder may exercise his security, and may prove in the winding up for any unsatisfied balance, including unpaid interest.

Receivers

A receiver is a person appointed to collect and preserve property. The courts have wide jurisdiction to appoint receivers, *e.g.* in pending actions to protect the subject matter of the dispute. However, this section is concerned with a receiver appointed by a party under an instrument, *e.g.* a mortgage or debenture. The receiver's duty in such a case is to take possession of the assets mortgaged or charged in order to protect and realise the security. Such an appointment is usually indicative of the debtor's insolvency or financial difficulty. The appointment and exercise of the receiver's powers may have an important effect on the debtor's ability to perform a subsisting contract.

Receivers appointed under mortgages or charges may exercise certain powers under statute (Law of Property Act 1925, sections 101, 109). But these are invariably enlarged by the terms of the instrument itself. This may provide, *e.g* for powers of management and for the receiver to be the agent of the debtor company. The instrument under which the receiver is appointed will also specify when the right to appoint arises. When the company is being wound up, a receiver may be appointed either before or after the appointment of a liquidator.

When a liquidator is appointed after a receiver, any powers as agent of the company will be terminated since the liquidator takes precedence in managing and winding up the company. But in other matters concerning the right to the company's assets, the liquidator and the receiver may be in conflict.

Effects of insolvency on building contracts

The first is usually that the work is brought to a stop by the inability of the builder to continue financing the work, if he is the insolvent party. If the employer is the insolvent party, his inability to meet interim payments will stop the work. This invariably produces a serious financial loss for the innocent party, which will not be satisfied by the insolvent party. Such loss may be reduced or even avoided by an employer appropriating retention money or the contractor's plant and goods or by enforcing a bond. A contractor is likely to fare less well. His work and materials, whether or not paid for, pass to the employer and to his trustee or liquidator on insolvency, when they become attached to the land. Thereafter they cannot be removed.

The parties' rights are usually regulated by provisions of the contract which operate upon various events indicative of insolvency. When one party intimates that he cannot continue with a contract by reason of insolvency, he will repudiate the contract and the other party has no real choice but to accept. However, standard forms of contract usually provide that the innocent party may terminate the contractor's employment without ending the contract, so that advantage may be taken of contractual terms applying after such termination, *e.g.* as to rights in goods and plant, and claims.

The ICE form does not give the contractor any right of determination under the contract for insolvency, so that he must rely on common law repudiation as above. The employer is given the right to terminate the contractor's employment in the event (*inter alia*) of the contractor becoming bankrupt or having a receiving order made against him or going into liquidation. The employer then has the right to complete the contract by other contractors and to claim or set off the additional cost of completion (clause 63). To fortify these rights the contractor's plant and unfixed goods and materials are deemed to be the property of the employer when brought to site, so that these are available as security in the event of determination (clause 53).

The JCT form gives rights of determination to both employer and contractor. The contractor may determine for non-payment of certificates (whether or not due to insolvency) or if the employer (*inter alia*) becomes bankrupt or is wound up or has a receiver of his business appointed (clause 26). The contractor may then claim his loss from the employer. But such claim is not secured, since goods and materials, when paid for, become the employer's property (clause 14). The employer has similar rights if the contractor (*inter alia*) becomes bankrupt or has a winding up order made or a receiver of his business appointed. In such cases the contractor's employment is automatically ended, subject to reinstatement. The employer may claim the additional costs of completion from the contractor (clause 25), but the only security for such claim is the retention money and any performance bond (see below).

All the above provisions take effect subject to the laws of insolvency. The principles which may conflict with such contractual rights are: first, that provisions which vest the debtor's property, upon insolvency, in a particular creditor may be void; secondly, the statutory right of disclaimer of a trustee in bankruptcy or liquidator cannot be excluded; and thirdly the doctrine of reputed ownership in bankruptcy.

Clause 53 of the ICE form vests the contractor's property in the employer when brought to site, and it is thought this remains enforceable on determination for insolvency, subject possibly to the doctrine of reputed ownership. As to the validity of determination upon insolvency, this is not contrary to the insolvency laws; and it is thought that a determination correctly carried under the above clauses cannot be challenged. But doubt has been expressed as to the validity of such determination where the trustee or liquidator seeks to complete the contract. It is thought that the provisions entitling the employer to claim his loss would not be enforceable where the trustee or liquidator seeks to exercise the right of disclaimer.

BONDS

When the contractor fails to complete the contract, whether by reason of his own default or the employer's determination, and the employer is unable to recover his loss from the contractor, the employer may have some further protection if the contractor has provided a bond.

A bond is an undertaking by a surety to make payment upon the contractor's default. The usual form of bond guarantees the contractor's performance of the contract with an undertaking to be bound in a specified sum until (and unless) such performance is achieved. Upon the contractor's failure to perform in full, the employer is entitled to call on the surety (or bondholder) to make good the loss, up to the maximum amount of the bond. Since a bond is a contract of guarantee, it requires to be evidenced in writing. Further, since the employer gives no consideration (save that the contractor must include the cost of the bond in his price for the work) the bond must be under seal.

Subject to the terms of the bond, a surety may be discharged from liability by a material alteration in the contractor's obligation which has been guaranteed, *e.g.*, extra works being ordered or an extension of the contract period being granted. The employer is also under a duty to mitigate his loss, since otherwise it may be said the loss is not caused by the contractor's non-performance. The ICE form of contract incorporates a form of bond which provides that "no alteration in the terms of the contract ... or in the extent or nature of the works ... and no allowance of time ... nor any forebearance or forgiveness ... on the part of the employer or the said engineer shall in any way release the surety from any liability under the above-written bond." These provisions overcome the above difficulties.

The ICE conditions (clause 10) and tender provide that the contractor may be required to obtain a bond in a specified sum, not exceeding 10 per cent of the tender total. The JCT form does not provide expressly for a bond, but this may be incorporated into the tender documents. The provision of a bond may be made a condition precedent to the execution of the contract or to the contractor's right to payment. If a bond is provided the employer, whether directly or indirectly, must usually pay for it. For this reason, many private employers do not require contracts to be bonded. But local authorities are usually bound by their standing orders to require a bond, where the contract sum exceeds a particular figure. The contractor may similarly require the employer to provide a bond or guarantee for payments under the contract. This is not dealt with in the standard forms.

Further Reading

Keating, *Building Contracts* (4th ed., 1978).
Hudson, *Building and Civil Engineering Contracts* (10th ed., 1970),
   Wallace.

CHAPTER 9

STANDARD CONDITIONS OF CONTRACT

THE law of England provides a very wide measure of freedom of contract so that parties are generally free to choose their own terms. But in practice parties to an aggrement rarely have either the desire or the ability to work out all the terms which are required to govern their contract. If certain provisions are not specified there may be a case for terms to be implied, but this can lead to uncertainty and disputes, and a much more convenient course is to use a set of standard conditions of contract.

Some transactions are governed entirely by predetermined standard conditions. This may be the case, *e.g.* when a journey is made by bus or when clothes are left at the laundry. In the construction industry, contracts almost invariably contain a set of standard conditions, but in addition many other contractual provisions must be specially formulated. The works to be carried out will usually be particularised in drawings, and a bill of quantities or a specification, or both. Other matters, such as the contract price and the time during which the work is to be carried out, will be agreed between the parties. In its final legal form a building or engineering contract usually consists of a complex combination of standard conditions and specially prepared terms. In this chapter some features of common standard forms used in the construction industry are discussed.

The widespread use of standard conditions in the construction industry is partly accounted for by the practical impossibility of writing new conditions for each contract. The complexity of modern construction work and the multitude of legal problems involved necessitate complicated contractual provisions. It is essential that their effect should be understood by the parties, and the only practical way of achieving this is to use a set of standard conditions, so that those professionally involved can acquire experience of the provisions in practice. In 1964 the Banwell Report (H.M. Stationery Office) recommended that a single standard form of contract for the whole construction industry was both desirable and practicable, and that standardisation of sub-contract conditions should follow. Unfortunately these admirable objectives have not been achieved; nor does there at present appear any serious prospect of their being achieved in the foreseeable future, unless by statute. There are those in the industry who daily find themselves dealing with the different provisions of two or more sets of main contract conditions, plus several forms of sub-contract. However, the situation could certainly be worse; without the guidance of the various professional and trade bodies who are concerned in the preparation of the standard forms there could be many more sets than are in fact issued.

One of the great merits of the standard forms is that most of them are drawn up and evolved by groups of independent bodies who together represent the interests of all sides of the industry. As a result of this, the tenor of the conditions tends to be very different from that of the forms drawn up, *e.g.* by hire-purchase companies, who wish primarily to protect their own interests. Further, if a loophole appears in a hire-purchase form the draftsmen will usually have no difficulty in filling it. With the standard forms in the construction industry it is not always so simple. If it is desired to change a clause to remove an ambiguity, the difficulty may be for the various parties to agree how the ambiguity should be resolved. This may explain why anomalies and obscurities tend to remain in standard forms, despite their existence being well known.

The use of a standard form of contract does not, of course, affect the fundamental principle that parties are in general free to contract on whatever terms they agree. Accordingly, it is always open to the parties to agree to modify a standard form and this is frequently done in practice (as to construction, see p. 81). It should, however, be remembered that many parts of the standard forms are interdependent, so that to alter a provision in one clause but not in another upon which it depends is likely to produce ambiguities, and may defeat the object of the alteration. It is therefore most important to consider the whole contract when planning a modification, and it is usually advisable to take expert advice. Alternatively, some forms make it clear that certain provisions are drafted so as to be optional, *e.g.* fluctuations clauses. Such provisions may be left in or struck out of the contract without requiring any consequential amendments.

Of the various sets of standard conditions in common use, those most frequently encountered are the JCT Standard Form of Building Contract and the ICE Conditions of Contract, which are intended for use in building and civil engineering contracts respectively. They are here referred to as the JCT form and the ICE form. Reference is made in other parts of this book to certain provisions of these two forms; and the following two chapters contain an outline commentary on their principal features. The following sections of this chapter contain a brief review of other standard forms likely to be encountered. In some cases further information may be found in the standard works, and copies of the forms themselves may be obtained from the issuing bodies.

FORMS OF MAIN CONTRACT

For an outline commentary on the JCT form of contract and on the ICE conditions of contract see chapters 10 and 11. In addition to these forms, the government publishes its own form of contract known as GC/Works/1; a form of main contract is issued for civil engineering works where tenders are invited on an international basis; and on a smaller scale, many prospective owners of new houses enter into NHBC forms of contract. These are considered below.

Form GC/Works/1

This form is published by H.M. Stationery Office and has the full title General Conditions of Government Contracts for Building and Civil Engineering Works. It is extensively used by all central government departments. These notes are based on Edition 2 of September 1977.

One notable feature of the form is the very wide powers given to the "Superintending Officer" (S.O.), to whose satisfaction the work must be carried out. He is empowered to give instructions in regard to variations, discrepancies between contract documents, removal and replacement of work or materials, the order of execution of the works, hours of working, suspension of work, replacement of workmen, opening up the work, making good defects after completion, emergency work, use of materials excavated from the site, and "any other matter as to which it is necessary or expedient for the S.O. to issue instructions, directions or explanations" (clause 7(1)). Other powers are exercisable directly by the employer ("the authority"). Thus the authority may employ other contractors should the contractor fail to comply with an instruction of the S.O. (clause 8); and may determine the contract in case of various defaults or insolvency (clause 45) or corruption (clause 55) or without default at any time on notice (clause 44). The authority is also given certain powers normally exercisable only by an architect or engineer. These include the power to give extensions of time (clause 28), to give direction as to prime cost items (clause 38(4)), to decide sums to be paid to the contractor (clause 41(1)) and to determine any dispute as to interim certificates (clause 42(3)). As to the latter provision, the authority will be a party to the dispute.

The contract includes the tender and acceptance, the conditions, specification, bills of quantities and drawings: "all of these documents taken together shall be deemed to form one contract" (clause 1(1)). But in case of discrepancy, the conditions are to prevail (clause 4). The contract will usually operate as a lump sum contract, with errors of description or quantity in the bills being dealt with as variations (clause 5(2)). Where the contract is based on provisional bills or bills of approximate quantities or a schedule of rates, it operates as a re-measurement contract (clause 10).

The contractor is entitled to monthly interim payments of 97 per cent. of the value of works executed and materials delivered. The balance of 3 per cent. is held as a "reserve." On larger contracts the contractor is entitled to further advance payments between monthly certificates (clause 40). Additional claims may be made for expense in complying with the S.O.'s instructions, other than a variation order (clause 9(2)); and for expense arising from disruption or prolongation of the progress of the works due to various causes, including S.O.'s instructions, and delay in work to be done by the authority (clause 53).

Disputes are to be referred to arbitration. In default of agreement as to the arbitrator, the authority may select (from a list of presidents of appropriate bodies) the person who is to make the nomination. The clause does not permit arbitration on any matter "as to which the decision or report of the authority or of any other person is by the contract expressed to be final and conclusive." Whether the courts would hold themselves bound by a decision of the authority under the contract is open to considerable doubt.

International (FIDIC) Conditions of Contract

There has been in existence since 1956 a form of contract based on the ICE conditions, for use in contracts having an international element. The third edition of the form was issued in March 1977. The form is prepared by the International Federation of Consulting Engineers (FIDIC) and the European International Federation of Construction (FIEC). The current form is further approved by bodies representing construction interests in most industrialised nations of the western world.

The third edition of the conditions remains based upon the ICE conditions, 5th edition. Much of the wording follows the ICE conditions and the clause numbering (and subject) is substantially the same. The printed document contains forms of tender and agreement, together with an index. The conditions are presented in three parts. Part I follows substantially the ICE conditions; Part II consists of notes for the preparation of special clauses covering matters arising out of Part I which are to be specifically agreed, *e.g.* the law governing the contract; Part III contains conditions of particular application to dredging and reclamation work. The following notes relate to Part I only. For brevity, comment is limited to those features which depart from the ICE conditions. These notes should therefore be read with the commentary on the ICE form, Chapter 11.

Clause 2(1) recognises that the independent function of the engineer may not be compatible with the intentions of some clients. It provides that if by the terms of his appointment the engineer is required to obtain the employers' approval for the performance of his duties, this is to be set out in Part II. Under clause 4, the engineer's consent to sub-letting is not to be unreasonably withheld. Clause 5, in addition to making the contract documents mutually explanatory, provides that Parts I and II of the conditions are to prevail. This clause also requires to be specified in Part II, the language in which the contract documents are to be drawn up and the national law by which the contract is to be construed. If the documents are in more than one language, there is to be a "ruling language."

Clause 11 now requires the employer to provide with the tender documents all available data on hydrological and sub-surface conditions. Clause 13 follows the 4th (and not the 5th) edition of the ICE conditions. The engineer has almost unlimited power to give instructions, but there is no specific provision for claims based thereon. Other instances where the conditions have not followed changes brought in by the ICE 5th edition are in clauses 13 and 14, which contain very limited express powers of control over the contractor's methods of operation; clause 44, where the provisions for extension of time contain no power to give interim decisions; and clause 47, where there are no provisions for application of liquidated damages to sections of the work.

Under clause 52(3) an additional claim may be made where the value of variations exceeds 10 per cent. of the net contract sum. Plant and materials brought to site do not vest in the employer but are deemed to be exclusively intended for the execution of the works. Provisions governing nominated sub-contracts are considerably more concise than under the ICE 5th edition. The contract does not make use of prime costs items. Clause 58 defines a "provisional sum" and permits the engineer to use such sums to order work to be done by the contractor or by a nominated sub-contractor. Clause 59 defines nominated sub-contractors in very wide terms and stipulates minimum terms which the contractor is entitled to. The fact of nomination does not limit the contractor's liability for the work in question, it is submitted.

Clause 60 contemplates monthly payments, but the contractor's entitlement is to be specified in Part II. A further matter to be dealt with here is payment in foreign currency (*i.e.* of a country other than that in which the works are situated). The maintenance certificate under clause 62 does not terminate the parties' rights under the contract; but the employer is not to be liable for any claim unless made in writing before the issue of the maintenance certificate. Clause 65 provides for the consequences of a variety of special risks including war and hostilities. The arbitration clause (67) provides for disputes to be settled by the engineer. His decision may then be challenged under the Rules of Conciliation and Arbitration of the International Chamber of Commerce.

The conditions contain further clauses not based on the ICE conditions, which give the contractor the right to terminate his employment in the event of specified defaults by the employer (clause 69); and which deal with currency restrictions and variations in rates of exchange (Clauses 71, 72).

House Purchaser's Agreement

The functions of the National House-Building Council (NHBC) are referred to in Chapter 5. In this section the main features of the forms of agreement issued by the NHBC are reviewed. The conditions (11 in number) are extremely brief when considered against their importance to millions of home-owners, and further create a number of complex problems of interpretation. The conditions contain an arbitration clause (clause 11) which, in practice, is very frequently invoked (the NHBC pay a proportion of the arbitrator's fees). The form has thus very rarely been before the courts.

The essential feature of the form is that the vendor warrants that the dwelling has been built or will be built (1) in an efficient and workmanlike manner and of proper materials and so as to be fit for habitation, (2) so as to comply with the NHBC's requirements, and (3) so as to qualify for the NHBC 10-year certificate (clause 3). The NHBC requirements consist of a detailed specification of workmanship, materials and performance which amplifies (and also incorporates) the Building Regulations. The 10-year certificate is a condition precedent to certain rights assumed by the NHBC. If defects occur, the vendor undertakes (and is entitled) to rectify them within two years from the 10-year certificate (clause 6). By clause 8(a) the NHBC undertakes to perform obligations set out in the First Schedule. These include an obligation to put right (or pay the cost of putting right) a major defect in the structure of the dwelling, appearing more than two years after the 10-year certificate. If a major defect in the structure appears in the first two years, the vendor only is liable. If the defect is less serious the vendor remains liable after the first two years. Where the NHBC may be liable clause 8(b) requires the purchaser, before pursuing any claim against the vendor, first to pursue his remedy against the NHBC and to give credit for any relief obtained. It is not clear whether this prevents the purchaser issuing proceedings before his action against the NHBC is concluded.

The term "purchaser" is defined as including successors in title. This may give a subsequent owner the right to enforce certain covenants given by the vendor. However, the form contemplates that the benefit of the agreement will be expressly assigned to any purchaser, who will then be entitled to enforce the agreement (see p. 106). A problem may arise if defects appear before sale of the dwelling. The agreement requires defects to be reported in writing as soon as practicable. If defects appear which are not so reported then a subsequent purchaser may fail to acquire rights in respect of such defects. In this regard it was held in *Marchant* v. *Caswell & Redgrave* (1976) that notice of the first manifestation of a defect, *e.g.* a hair-line crack, was sufficient notice of the underlying defect. Thus notice of minor cracking given within the first two years rendered the vendor liable, even though after the expiry of two years the cracks were found to be due to a major defect in the structure. If, after obtaining an award or judgment against the vendor, it cannot be enforced, *e.g.* because the vendor is insolvent, the NHBC (through insurance arrangements) undertake to compensate the purchaser up to a specified limit.

Note that both the wording of the agreement and certain clause numberings have undergone periodic changes.

FORMS OF SUB-CONTRACT

Many contractors impose their own standard terms on subcontractors. These often contain one-sided provisions which place the sub-contractors at a disadvantage in a dispute. Conversely some specialists and suppliers impose their own terms on main contractors. A fairer balance may be achieved by using one of the standard forms of sub-contract designed for use with the standard main forms.

NFBTE-FASS form of sub-contract

A form of sub-contract is issued by the National Federation of

Building Trades Employers (NFBTE) and the Federation of Associations of Specialists and Sub-contractors (FASS) for use in nominated sub-contracts under the JCT form of main contract. The document is popularly known as the "green form" and is widely used in all forms of building work.

The form is drafted specifically to complement clause 27 of the JCT form, and contains the specified terms without which the contractor is entitled to reject a nomination (clause 27(a)). The form contains a recital of the parties and of the main contract, and contains seven appendices. These provide *inter alia* for completion period(s), the value of the work and retention money.

In the conditions the sub-contractor undertakes to comply with the main contract so far as relates to the sub-contract works (clause 3(a)) and gives wide indemnities to the contractor in respect of liability under the main contract and third party claims (clause 3(b)). The sub-contractor must comply with architect's instructions which the contractor issues to the sub-contractor in writing (clause 7). The contractor has no specific power to give instructions. The contractor must apply for the sub-contractor's work to be included in interim certificates. The sums so certified must be paid to the sub-contractor whether or not the contractor has received payment (clause 11). Thus if the employer exercises a right of set-off not connected with the sub-contract, the contractor must himself pay the sub-contractor.

The subcontractor undertakes to complete his work within the period(s) specified. The contractor may grant extensions of time but only with the architect's consent; under clause 23(g) of the main contract the contractor is not liable for the sub-contractor's delay. If the sub-contractor fails to complete by the specified or extended date for completion, the contractor may claim any loss caused by the delay. But the contractor's right to claim or set-off such loss is dependent on the architect certifying that the sub-contractor ought reasonably to have completed the work (clause 8). After completion the sub-contractor must make good any defects in accordance with instructions given by the architect under the defects liability provisions in the main contract (clause 9). The sub-contractor is given a number of rights to obtain the benefit of, or to pursue disputes under the main contract (clauses 7(2), 8(b), (c), 9(a), 10(d), 12). The extent to which some of these provisions are enforceable or practicable is a matter of doubt. Disputes under the sub-contract are to be referred to arbitration. If the dispute is substantially the same as a dispute under the main contract, it is to be referred to an arbitrator appointed under the main contract (although not so expressed, this will require the consent of the employer and the arbitrator). An important qualification is that any decision of the architect which is binding on the contractor (*e.g.* the final certificate) is to be binding on the sub-contractor (clause 24).

ICE Form of Sub-Contract

This document was issued by the Federation of Civil Engineering Contractors for use in conjunction with the ICE General Conditions of Contract 4th edition (1955). It remains in current use, unamended, with the ICE conditions, 5th edition. Being drawn up by one body only, the form is a model of clarity, avoiding the obscurities of the main forms of contract.

The form contains a short recital for the parties' names, and 5 schedules. These are to contain *inter alia* particulars of the main contract, further documents to be incorporated, a description of the sub-contract works, the contract price and the completion period. The sub-contractor undertakes (save where the sub-contract otherwise requires) to perform the obligations of the contractor under the main contract in relation to the sub-contract works (clause 3(2)), and to indemnify the contractor against liability incurred by reason of any breach of the sub-contract (clause 3(3)).

The sub-contractor's obligations are not tied directly to the operations of the main contract. Thus, extensions of time may be granted without reference to the engineer; save that where the delaying event entitles the contractor to an extension, the sub-contractors' extension is not to exceed the extension under the main contract (clause 6). Instructions and variations ordered under the main contract do not bind the sub-contractor, unless the engineer's order is confirmed in writing by the contractor (clauses 7, 8). The contractor further has the same general powers to give instructions under the sub-contract as the engineer has under the main contract, and the sub-contractor has the same rights in relation thereto (clause 7(2)). There is therefore very wide scope both for the exercise of such powers by the contractor and for making claims by the sub-contractors (see, *e.g.* clause 13(1), (3) ICE main contract). The sub-contract also provides for vesting of the plant and materials in the contractor, so that these may vest in the employer under the main contract (clause 11: see also clause 53 ICE main contract).

After completion, the sub-contractor is required to maintain his work until completion of the main works and further to maintain them throughout the maintenance period of the main contract (clause 14). The sub-contractor's right to interim payments is dependent upon the contractor having received from the employer an amount in respect of the sub-contract works (clause 15). The contractor may determine the sub-contractor's employment if the main contract is determined (clause 16) or if the sub-contractor commits specified defaults corresponding broadly to some of those under clause 63 of the ICE main contract. Disputes are to be referred directly to arbitration without the intervention of the engineer: the sub-contract does not provide for the consequences of the engineer's decision under the main contract (see clause 66 ICE main contract). If there is a dispute under the main contract concerning the sub-contract works, and if an arbitrator has been appointed under the main contract, the contractor may require the sub-contract dispute to be referred to him; or if there are proceedings in court under the main contract, the contractor may avoid the arbitration clause and bring the sub-contractor into those proceedings (clause 18).

The form is not specifically designated for use with nominated sub-contractors. It contains provisions broadly in accordance with the minimum requirements for a nominated sub-contract (see clause 59A(1) ICE main contract). The form may therefore be used for any type of sub-contract.

OTHER STANDARD FORMS

The forms dealt with above, together with the JCT and ICE forms of main contract are those likely to be encountered most often in practice. Mention should also be made of other forms which are in general use.

Building Contracts

The Joint Contracts Tribunal which is responsible for the JCT form also issues other forms including a fixed fee form of prime cost contract and a form for minor building works. The fixed fee form provides for the contractor to be paid the prime cost of the work carried out, plus a fixed fee. This form is most appropriate where the nature or extent of the work is uncertain at the time of contracting. However, the architect's powers to vary the works are severely restricted. Many of the provisions in the contract are similar to those in the JCT form, such as the contractor's right to retain a discount from his nominated sub-contractors and suppliers. This latter provision means that the contractor's true profit will in fact exceed the fee stated. The conditions of contract are followed by a number of schedules which set out, *inter alia*, the definition of prime cost sums and the fixed fee.

The form of contract for minor building works, in keeping with its subject matter, is short. A large part of the form is concerned with liability for, and insurance against, various risks. This is necessary since the consequential losses which may arise out of building works may bear no relation to the scale of the works. The form contains many of the provisions of the standard JCT form. For example, the architect may vary the works, and if the job takes more than two months the contractor is entitled to interim payments.

In addition to the standard form of sub-contract referred to above the NFBTE and FASS issue a form of sub-contract for use when the sub-contractor is not nominated. This has many features in common with the green form. But the contractor's actions are not subject to the architect, nor is the right to payment tied to certificates under the main contract. The arbitration clause does, however, allow for joint arbitration with the employer.

Forms of Warranty

This refers to a direct warranty given by a sub-contractor to the employer, which is discussed above p. 97. The RIBA have for some years published two such forms. The form known as the Employer/ Sub-contractor form of agreement is intended for use with nominated sub-contracts under the JCT forms of main contract. The sub-contractor gives warranties of reasonable skill and care in regard to any design work undertaken, and in regard to delay in the sub-contract works. The employer gives warranties as to the operation of the direct payment provisions.

A second form of warranty exists for nominated suppliers. The supplier gives a warranty of skill and care in regard to design and a further (unqualified) warranty that goods shall comply with any performance specification. There are further warranties as to delay. The employer gives no cross-warranty.

Each of these forms is expressed to be subject to the employer's nomination. With suitable modification they may be made to operate in respect of any type of sub-contract, and with any form of main contract.

Conditions of Engagement

Architects and engineers usually employ standard conditions when they accept engagements. These invariably lay down in precise terms the fee-scale to be payable. This operates as a percentage of the value of the work. The conditions may also contain terms defining or limiting the scope of duties to be undertaken, and may therefore become important in a dispute.

The RIBA publish, and periodically revise, Conditions of Engagement for architects. These provide that, where independent consultants are engaged by the client (*e.g.* a structural engineer), the architect is responsible for the direction and integration of their work, but not for the detailed design. In regard to supervision of construction work, the architect is to make periodic visits, but he is not to be responsible for failure by the contractor to perform his contract. When visiting the site the architect is to endeavour to guard the employer against deficiencies in the work, but he is not to be required to make exhaustive inspection. These provisions will be material to any charge of negligent supervision brought against an architect.

Civil engineers are usually engaged under the Association of Consulting Engineers (ACE) Conditions of Engagement. Engineers are required to work in a wide range of situations, and this is reflected in the provision of five forms of engagement, referred to as Schedules 1 to 5. When the engineer is required only to prepare advice and a report, Schedule 1 is appropriate. Schedules 2, 3 and 4 apply to work in the design and supervision of construction. Schedule 2 is appropriate when the engineer has control of the project (*e.g.* under an ICE contract); Schedule 3 applies when the project is in control of an architect (*e.g.* under a JCT contract); Schedule 4 is appropriate to the design and supervision of engineering systems in buildings. When the client enters into a design and build (or "turnkey") contract, Schedule 5 is appropriate if he wishes to employ a structural engineer for advice and checking.

In each case, the Schedule contains a form of agreement and conditions. These define *inter alia* the normal services to be provided and the additional services which the engineer will provide if required, at additional cost. Both the ACE conditions and the RIBA conditions of engagement, above, contain arbitration clauses.

Further Reading

Duncan Wallace, *Building and Civil Engineering Standard Forms* (1969).

CHAPTER 10

THE STANDARD FORM OF
BUILDING CONTRACT

The standard form of building contract is often referred to as the RIBA form because of its long association with that Institute. The form is intended for use with all types of building work. It is issued by the Joint Contracts Tribunal (JCT) under the sanction of the RIBA, the RICS, the National Federation of Building Trades Employers, and bodies representing local authorities and contractors. It is more correctly called the JCT form, and for brevity this title is used below.

The last edition of the form was issued in 1963. It exists in four versions: for a private employer, or for a local authority; and with or without quantities, giving four combinations. The different versions contain variations in detail rather than substance. The commentary which follows is based upon the local authorities' edition with quantities, but most of the provisions are common to all the forms. The issuing body makes periodic revisions of the forms which are published either as amendments or as revisions of the complete forms. The following discussion refers to the revision of July 1977. In the local authority forms "architect" becomes "architect/supervising officer," as it is contemplated that this office may be filled by an employee of the authority who may not be a qualified architect.

The published form contains articles of agreement, which may be executed under seal, an appendix, the conditions of contract, and a supplemental agreement on VAT. The conditions create a "lump-sum" contract, *i.e.* the contractor undertakes to carry out the work described and measured in the bills, for a stated sum of money.

This is subject, however, to many possible alterations, on account, *inter alia*, of variations, price fluctuations and claims.

The conditions contemplate that the work will be carried out under the supervision of the architect/supervising officer (for brevity he will be referred to simply as "the architect"). Under the contract the architect is given powers and duties which are wide and important, but which are also limited in their scope. The powers of the architect are considerably less than those of the engineer under the ICE conditions (see Chapter 11) reflecting the less hazardous nature of building work compared to civil engineering construction.

This chapter is not a full commentary on the JCT form. It is intended as an introduction to the basic working provisions of the form. The most important clauses or sub-clauses are printed, with brief notes as to their effect. Other clauses are referred to where appropriate. Some clauses are omitted altogether as being not essential to the basic scheme of the form. These clauses may, of course, be of vital significance to any particular issue or dispute. For a full exposition on the form reference must be made to the document itself and to one of the standard works noted at the end of the chapter.

THE CONTRACT

The form contemplates that a contract will be made by the parties executing the articles of agreement. This is not essential. The conditions of contract may be incorporated by reference in any other document of agreement. But the articles provide, in the recitals, for specifying the names of the parties, a brief description of the works and a list of contract drawings.

The articles themselves state:

NOW IT IS HEREBY AGREED AS FOLLOWS:

1   For the consideration hereinafter mentioned the Contractor will upon and subject to the Conditions annexed hereto carry out and complete the Works shown upon the Contract Drawings and described by or referred to in the Contract Bills and in the said Conditions.

2   The Employer will pay to the Contractor the sum of
(£   ) (hereinafter referred to as "the Contract Sum") or such other sum as shall become payable hereunder at the times and in the manner specified in the said Conditions.

In articles 3 and 4 the architect and quantity surveyor are named.

By clause 1(1) the contractor is required to carry out the work "shown upon the contract drawings and described by or referred to in the contract bills and in the articles of agreement and these conditions." The relative effect of these contract documents is provided as follows:

12   (1) The quality and quantity of the work included in the Contract Sum shall be deemed to be that which is set out in the Contract Bills which Bills unless otherwise expressly stated in respect of any specified item or items shall be deemed to have been prepared in accordance with the principles of the Standard Method of Measurement of Building Works 5th edition Imperial, revised March 1964/5th edition Metric by the Royal Institution of Chartered Surveyors and the National Federation

of Building Trades Employers, but save as aforesaid nothing contained
in the Contract Bills shall override, modify, or affect in any way whatsoever the application or interpretation of that which is contained in
these Conditions.

(2) Any error in description or in quantity in or omission of items from
the Contract Bills shall not vitiate this Contract but shall be corrected
and deemed to be a variation required by the Architect.

The effect of this clause is that, save for questions of the quality
or quantity of the work, the conditions override the contract bills.
A provision intended to amend the conditions (*e.g.* for sectional
completion) may therefore be ineffective if placed in the bills. The
bills will override the contract drawings. In a contract of any size
there is likely also to be a specification or descriptive schedule. This,
however, is not a contract document. The architect is given the
power and duty to supply such further details as are necessary:

3   (3) So soon as is possible after the execution of this Contract the
Architect without charge to the Contractor shall furnish him (unless he
shall have been previously furnished) with two copies of the descriptive
schedules or other like document necessary for use in carrying out the
Works. Provided that nothing contained in the said descriptive schedules
or other documents shall impose any obligation beyond those imposed by
the Contract Documents.

(4) As and when from time to time may be necessary the Architect
without charge to the Contractor shall furnish him with two copies of
such drawings or details as are reasonably necessary either to explain
and amplify the Contract Drawings or to enable the Contractor to
carry out and complete the Works in accordance with these Conditions.

The architect is further required to provide drawings for setting out
the work:

5   The Architect shall determine any levels which may be required for the
execution of the Works, and shall furnish to the Contractor by way
of accurately dimensioned drawings such information as shall enable
the Contractor to set out the Works at ground level. Unless the
Architect shall otherwise instruct, in which case the Contract Sum shall
be adjusted accordingly, the Contractor shall be responsible for and shall
entirely at his own cost amend any errors arising from his own inaccurate
setting out.

Control of the Work

The conditions envisage that the work will be under the general
supervision of the architect. The RIBA conditions of engagement,

used by many architects, provide for periodic but not constant supervision. Day to day site supervision is therefore left to the contractor and to the employer:

8 The Contractor shall constantly keep upon the Works a competent foreman-in-charge and any instructions given to him by the Architect shall be deemed to have been issued to the Contractor.

10 The Employer shall be entitled to appoint a clerk of works whose duty shall be to act solely as inspector on behalf of the Employer under the directions of the Architect and the Contractor shall afford every reasonable facility for the performance of that duty. If any directions are given to the Contractor or to his foreman upon the Works by the clerk of works the same shall be of no effect unless given in regard to a matter in respect of which the Architect is expressly empowered by these Conditions to issue instructions and unless confirmed in writing by the Architect within two working days of their being given. If any such directions are so given and confirmed then as from the date of confirmation they shall be deemed to be Architect's instructions.

On larger projects the architect and employer may agree to employ a resident architect on the works. The contractor is required, by clause 9, to give the architect access to places where work is being prepared for the contract.

GENERAL OBLIGATION OF THE CONTRACTOR

The contractor's basic obligations are to comply with the contract documents, which define the work and the time within which it is to be done, and to comply with proper instructions of the architect.

1 (1) The Contractor shall upon and subject to these Conditions carry out and complete the Works shown upon the Contract Drawings and described by or referred to in the Contract Bills and in the Articles of Agreement and these Conditions (which Drawings, Bills, Articles of Agreement and Conditions are hereinafter called "the Contract Documents") in compliance therewith, using materials and workmanship of the quality and standards therein specified, provided that where and to the extent that approval of the quality of materials or of the standards of workmanship is a matter for the opinion of the Architect, such quality and standards shall be to the reasonable satisfaction of the Architect.

Clause 1(2) requires the contractor to give notice of any discrepancy or divergence between the drawings, the bills, and the architect's instructions, and for the architect to issue instructions in regard thereto.

Clause 1(1) emphasises that, under the conditions, the architect has no general power of approval or control. Where work or materials are required by the bills to be, *e.g.* "to the approval of the architect," sub-clause (1) means that the item is required only to meet the architect's "reasonable satisfaction" (since by clause 12(1) the conditions override the bills). Where there is no stipulation for the architect's approval, his function is to ensure compliance with the contract documents.

2 (1) The Contractor shall (subject to sub-clauses (2) and (3) of this Condition) forthwith comply with all instructions issued to him by the Architect in regard to any matter in respect of which the Architect is expressly empowered by these Conditions to issue instructions. If within seven days after receipt of a written notice from the Architect requiring compliance with an instruction the Contractor does not comply therewith, then the Employer may employ and pay other persons to execute any work whatsoever which may be necessary to give effect to such instruction and all cost incurred in connection with such employment shall be recoverable from the Contractor by the Employer as a debt or may be deducted by him from any monies due or to become due to the Contractor under this Contract.

This provision makes it clear that the architect's powers are limited to those expressly contained in the contract. The machinery entitling the employer to bring in another contractor in the event of non-compliance with an architect's instruction is a valuable sanction. Sub-clause (2) allows the contractor to challenge an instruction by asking under what power it is given. If dissatisfied, the contractor may seek immediate arbitration (clause 35(2)). Clause 2(3) requires instructions to be given in writing and allows either the contractor or the architect to confirm oral instructions in writing.

Apportionment of various risks arising out of the work and requirements as to insurances are dealt with in clauses 18 to 20:

18 (1) The Contractor shall be liable for, and shall indemnify the Employer against, any liability, loss, claim or proceedings whatsover arising under any statute or at common law in respect of personal injury to or the death of any person whomsoever arising out of or in the course of or caused by the carrying out of the Works, unless due to any act or neglect of the Employer or of any person for whom the Employer is responsible.

(2) Except for such loss or damage as is at the risk of the Employer under clause 20[B] or clause 20[C] of these Conditions (if applicable) the Contractor shall be liable for, and shall indemnify the Employer against, any expense, liability, loss, claim or proceedings in respect of any injury or damage whatsoever to any property real or personal in so far as such injury or damage arises out of or in the course of or

by reason of the carrying out of the Works, and provided always that the same is due to any negligence, omission or default of the Contractor, his servants or agents or of any sub-contractor his servants or agents.

Clause 18(1) renders the contractor liable for third party claims in respect of personal injury, unless due to any act or neglect of the employer. Clause 18(2) renders the contractor liable for third party claims in respect of damage to property only when the contractor is at fault. The words "any property" include the works themselves. However, the duty to carry out and complete the works, under clause 1 means that the contractor is generally liable for damage to the works, unless due to the employer's default.

Clause 19(1) requires the contractor to maintain insurance against his own liability under clause 18. Clause 19(2) requires insurance, in the joint names of the contractor and the employer, against claims for damage to property caused (broadly) by the carrying out of the works. Clause 20 sets out three alternative provisions as to liability for loss or damage to the works (including unfixed materials and goods) by various perils including fire storm and flood. The conditions contain a footnote to the effect that Clause 20A is applicable to the erection of a new building if the Contractor is required to insure against loss or damage by fire, etc. Clause 20B is applicable to the erection of a new building if the Employer is to bear such risks and clause 20C is applicable to alterations of or extensions to an existing building. The latter clause places the risk of loss or damage to the works and to the existing building and contents on the employer and requires him to insure.

The contractor is solely responsible for his methods of work and for any temporary works (*e.g.* scaffolding) plant and equipment. The architect is given no powers either of control or approval.

Workmanship and materials

6 (1) All materials, goods and workmanship shall so far as procurable be of the respective kinds and standards described in the Contract Bills.

(2) The Contractor shall upon the request of the Architect furnish him with vouchers to prove that the materials and goods comply with sub-clause (1) of this Condition.

(3) The Architect may issue instructions requiring the Contractor to open up for inspection any work covered up or to arrange for or carry out any test of any materials or goods (whether or not already incorporated in the Works) or of any executed work, and the cost of such opening up or testing (together with the cost of making good in

consequence thereof) shall be added to the Contract Sum unless provided for in the Contract Bills or unless the inspection or test shows that the work, materials or goods are not in accordance with this Contract.

(4) The Architect may issue instructions in regard to the removal from the site of any work, materials or goods which are not in accordance with this Contract.

(5) The Architect may (but not unreasonably or vexatiously) issue instructions requiring the dismissal from the Works of any person employed thereon.

Sub-clause (1) must be read with the general obligations of clause 1(1). The power to order removal of work, etc., under clause 6(4) is a valuable but limited power. The architect cannot for example under this power, order work, etc., to replace that removed, or order the contractor not to obtain further materials from a particular source. When defective work, etc., is removed, the contractor must replace it in order to comply with his obligation to complete the works, under clause 1(1). If the contractor fails to comply with an instruction under clause 6(4) the architect may invoke clause 2(1). Alternatively the failure may give the employer grounds for determination under clause 25(1)(c).

Completion and Maintenance

The contractor's obligations fall into two separate periods: the period up to the certificate of practical completion, when the work is carried out; and the defects liability period, during which the contractor must make good any defects. These are dealt with as follows:

15 (1) When in the opinion of the Architect the Works are practically completed, he shall forthwith issue a certificate to that effect and Practical Completion of the Works shall be deemed for all the purposes of this Contract to have taken place on the day named in such certificate.

(2) Any defects, shrinkages or other faults which shall appear within the Defects Liability Period stated in the appendix to these Conditions and which are due to materials or workmanship not in accordance with this Contract or to frost occurring before Practical Completion of the Works, shall be specified by the Architect in a Schedule of Defects which he shall deliver to the Contractor not later than 14 days after the expiration of the said Defects Liability Period, and within a reasonable time after receipt of such Schedule the defects, shrinkages, and other faults therein specified shall be made good by the Contractor

and (unless the Architect shall otherwise instruct, in which case the Contract Sum shall be adjusted accordingly) entirely at his own cost.

(3) Notwithstanding sub-clause (2) of this Condition the Architect may whenever he considers it necessary so to do, issue instructions requiring any defect, shrinkage or other fault which shall appear within the Defects Liability Period named in the Appendix to these Conditions and which is due to materials or workmanship not in accordance with this Contract or to frost occurring before Practical Completion of the Works, to be made good, and the Contractor shall within a reasonable time after receipt of such instructions comply with the same and (unless the Architect shall otherwise instruct, in which case the Contract Sum shall be adjusted accordingly) entirely at his own cost. Provided that no such instructions shall be issued after delivery of a Schedule of Defects or after 14 days from the expiration of the said Defects Liability Period.

(4) When in the opinion of the Architect any defects, shrinkages or other faults which he may have required to be made good under sub-clauses (2) and (3) of this Condition shall have been made good he shall issue a certificate to that effect, and completion of making good defects shall be deemed for all the purposes of this Contract to have taken place on the day named in such certificate.

(5) In no case shall the Contractor be required to make good at his own cost any damage by frost which may appear after Practical Completion of the Works, unless the Architect shall certify that such damage is due to injury which took place before Practical Completion of the Works.

The contractor's obligation in making good defects is limited to those which are "due to materials or workmanship not in accordance with the contract or to frost." If defects become manifest due to some other cause, *e.g.* unsuitability of the design, the contractor is not obliged to carry out rectification; nor can the architect exercise his power to order a variation after practical completion. The contractor becomes entitled to payment of the retention money, half on the certificate of practical completion and the remainder on the certificate of making good, (clause 30(4)).

Clause 16 provides for the consequences of the employer (with the contractor's consent) taking possession of any completed part of the works before completion of the whole. This stipulates for a separate defects liability period in respect of the part, starting when possession is taken; and for proportional reductions in the value of the works to be insured, in liquidated damages and in retention money.

Time

The speed with which the Contractor carries out the work is likely to be an important element in the performance of the contract. The contract stipulates, in the appendix, for fixed possession and completion dates, but the period of the work may become extended under the contract.

21 (1) On the Date for Possession stated in the Appendix to these Conditions possession of the site shall be given to the Contractor who shall thereupon begin the Works and regularly and diligently proceed with the same, and who shall complete the same on or before the Date for Completion stated in the said Appendix subject nevertheless to the provisions for extension of time contained in clauses 23 and 33(1)(c) of these Conditions.

(2) The Architect may issue instructions in regard to the postponement of any work to be executed under the provisions of this Contract.

Failure to proceed regularly and diligently may lead to determination under clause 25(1)(*b*). Completion of the works refers to "practical completion" under clause 15(1). The works may be deemed completed although they contain defects which come to light later (see p. 101).

22 If the Contractor fails to complete the Works by the Date for Completion stated in the Appendix to these Conditions or within any extended time fixed under clause 23 or clause 33 (1)(c) of these Conditions and the Architect certifies in writing that in his opinion the same ought reasonably so to have been completed, then the Contractor shall pay or allow to the Employer a sum calculated at the rate stated in the said Appendix as Liquidated and Ascertained Damages for the period during which the Works shall so remain or have remained incomplete, and the Employer may deduct such sum from any monies due or to become due to the Contractor under this Contract.

The list of grounds entitling the contractor to an extension of time are set out in clause 23. If the work is delayed by a default on the part of the employer which does not permit an extension of time, the liquidated damages clause becomes unenforceable (see p. 101).

23 Upon it becoming reasonably apparent that the progress of the Works is delayed, the Contractor shall forthwith give written notice of the cause of the delay to the Architect and if in the opinion of the Architect the completion of the Works is likely to be or has been delayed beyond the Date for Completion stated in the Appendix to these Conditions or beyond any extended time previously fixed under either this clause or clause 33(1)(c) of these Conditions.

(a) by *force majeure*, or

(b) by reason of any exceptionally inclement weather, or

(c) by reason of loss or damage occasioned by any one or more of the contingencies referred to in clause 20[A], [B] or [C] of these Conditions, or

(d) by reason of civil commotion, local combination of workmen, strike or lockout affecting any of the trades employed upon the Works or any of the trades engaged in the preparation manufacture or transportation of any of the goods or materials required for the Works, or

(e) by reason of Architect's instructions issued under clauses 1 (2), 11 (1) or 21 (2) of these Conditions, or

(f) by reason of the Contractor not having received in due time necessary instructions, drawings, details or levels from the Architect for which he specifically applied in writing on a date which having regard to the Date for Completion stated in the Appendix to these Conditions or to any extension of time then fixed under this clause or clause 33(1)(c) of these Conditions was neither unreasonably distant from nor unreasonably close to the date on which it was necessary for him to receive the same, or

(g) by delay on the part of nominated sub-contractors or nominated suppliers which the Contractor has taken all practicable steps to avoid or reduce, or

(h) by delay on the part of artists tradesmen or others engaged by the Employer in executing work not forming part of this Contract, or

(i) by reason of the opening up for inspection of any work covered up or of the testing of any of the work materials or goods in accordance with clause 6 (3) of these Conditions (including making good in consequence of such opening up or testing), unless the inspection or test showed that the work materials or goods were not in accordance with this Contract, or

(j) (i) by the Contractor's inability for reasons beyond his control and which he could not reasonably have foreseen at the date of this Contract to secure such labour as is essential to the proper carrying out of the Works, or

    (ii) by the Contractor's inability for reasons beyond his control and which he could not reasonably have foreseen at the date of this Contract to secure such goods and/or materials as are essential to the proper carrying out of the Works, or

  (k) by reason of compliance with the provisions of clause 34 of these Conditions or with Architect's instructions issued thereunder, or

  (l) by a local authority or statutory undertaker in carrying out work in pursuance of its statutory obligations in relation to the Works, or in failing to carry out such work.

Then the Architect shall so soon as he is able to estimate the length of the delay beyond the date or time aforesaid make in writing a fair and reasonable extension of time for completion of the Works. Provided always that the Contractor shall use constantly his best endeavours to prevent delay and shall do all that may reasonably be required to the satisfaction of the Architect to proceed with the Works.

Failure to give notice of delay does not disentitle the contractor to an extension to which he is otherwise entitled, it is submitted. In making application for an extension, the contractor need specify only the "cause of the delay". He need not claim any specific period, or state under which provision it is claimed. The contractor is, however, concerned with which paragraph an extension is granted under. Extensions under clause 21 (*e*) (*f*) (*h*) or (*i*) may ground a claim for additional payment under clause 24(1).

POWERS AND REMEDIES

The limitations of the architect's powers are commented on above. Specific powers already referred to are those under clause 6(3) to order opening up of work; under clause 6(4) to order removal of improper work; under clause 6(5) to order removal of workmen; under clause 15(2) and (3) to require defects to be made good; and under clause 21(2) to order postponement of work.

Instructions must normally be in writing. Clause 2(3) lays down an elaborate provision for dealing with oral instructions.

2 (3) All instructions issued by the Architect shall be issued in writing. Any instruction issued orally shall be of no immediate effect, but shall be confirmed in writing by the Contractor to the Architect within seven days, and if not dissented from in writing by the Architect to the Contractor within seven days from receipt of the Contractor's confirmation shall take effect as from the expiration of the latter said seven days. Provided always:
  (a) That if the Architect within seven days of giving such an oral instruction shall himself confirm the same in writing, then the Contractor shall not be obliged to confirm as aforesaid, and the said instruction shall take effect as from the date of the Architect's confirmation, and

(b) That if neither the Contractor nor the Architect shall confirm such an oral instruction in the manner and at the time aforesaid but the Contractor shall nevertheless comply with the same, then the Architect may confirm the same in writing at any time prior to the issue of the Final Certificate, and the said instruction shall thereupon be deemed to have taken effect on the date on which it was issued.

The widest power given to the architect is to order variations to the works:

11 (1) The Architect may issue instructions requiring a variation and he may sanction in writing any variation made by the Contractor otherwise than pursuant to an instruction of the Architect. No variation required by the Architect or subsequently by him shall vitiate this Contract.

(2) The term "variation" as used in these Conditions means the alteration or modification of the design, quality or quantity of the Works as shown upon the Contract Drawings and described by or referred to in the Contract Bills, and includes the addition, omission or substitution of any work, the alteration of the kind or standard of any of the materials or goods to be used in the Works, and the removal from the site of any work materials or goods executed or brought thereon by the Contractor for the purposes of the Works other than work materials or goods which are not in accordance with this Contract.

(3) The Architect shall issue instructions in regard to the expenditure of prime cost and provisional sums included in the Contract Bills and of prime cost sums which arise as a result of instructions issued in regard to the expenditure of provisional sums.

The employer will be bound by any variation order given by the architect. However, the architect must ensure that he has authority to order the variation, otherwise he may be liable to the employer for its cost. The effect of clause 2(3) is that a variation order must normally be in writing. Although clause 11(1) contemplates that the power to give variations is unlimited, there will be some implied limit, beyond which the contractor may say that the contract has ceased to apply, and that he is entitled to re-price the work.

Sub-contractors

It is very rare in practice for the contractor to perform the whole of the work himself. Clause 17 provides that the contractor shall not sub-let portions of the works without the architect's consent, which is not to be unreasonably withheld. However, substantial sections of work are frequently required to be sub-let to nominated sub-contractors or suppliers. Such work is designated in the bills as prime cost or provisional sums. The parties' rights are set out in clauses 27 and 28.

Clause 27 governs nominated sub-contracts and provides for the following:

(a) A cash discount of $2\frac{1}{2}$ per cent. to the contractor, which is in effect a profit on the sub-contract work. The contractor is further entitled to have specified terms included in the sub-contract. These include undertakings to comply with the main contract and to give indemnities, and provisions governing time, payment and retention. The specified terms are embodied in a standard form of sub-contract issued by the National Federation of Building Trades Employers and the Federation of Associations of Specialist and Sub-contractors (see above p. 122).

(b) Separate valuations of the work of each nominated sub-contractor in an interim certificate.

(c) Direct payments by the employer to a nominated sub-contractor if the contractor has failed to discharge previous sums due.

(d) Extensions of time to be granted to a nominated sub-contractor, with the architect's consent.

(e) Final payment to a nominated sub-contractor before completion of the whole of the works.

(f) Exclusion of liability of the employer to a nominated sub-contractor (this would probably be the position in any event).

(g) Tendering by the contractor for prime cost work where his business ordinarily includes such work.

Clause 28 governs nominated suppliers, *i.e.* those who supply goods or materials to be fixed by the contractor. This clause provides for the following:

(a) A cash discount of 5 per cent. to the contractor.

(b) Terms to be included in the contract of sale. These include provisions that the goods shall be to the reasonable satisfaction of the architect, liability for replacement of defective materials, and times of delivery.

(c) Payment to the supplier, which is to be in full, without deduction of retention. Note that the employer will hold a retention on the value of the goods, until completion of the main contract works, but this may not exceed 5 per cent. (clause 30(3)).

(d) Limitation of the contractor's liability to the extent the architect approves any limitation or exclusion of liability in the sub-contract of sale. This provision recognises that many suppliers will contract only upon their own terms, which frequently limit their liability; c.f. the contractor's right, in a nominated sub-contract, to comply with the main contract.

In respect both of nominated suppliers and sub-contractors the contractor's liability for the suitability of the work is likely to be excluded by the architect's selection of materials (see p. 105). Further, by virtue of clause 23(g), the contractor is not liable for delay by nominated sub-contractors or suppliers.

Default by the contractor

In the event of the contractor failing to comply with the contract, the employer has a number of remedies. In respect of defective work or work suspected to be defective, the architect may order the removal of the work or opening up or testing under clause 6 (see above). If the contractor fails to complete by the date for completion the employer is entitled to deduct liquidated damages. Note that the work cannot be complete if it contains material patent defects.

If the contractor's default is more serious or if he becomes unable to perform the contract, the employer may become entitled to determine the contractor's employment:

25 (1) Without prejudice to any other rights or remedies which the Employer may possess, if the Contractor shall make default in any one or more of the following respects, that is to say:
  (a) If he without reasonable cause wholly suspends the carrying out of the Works before completion thereof, or
  (b) If he fails to proceed regularly and diligently with the Works, or
  (c) If he refuses or persistently neglects to comply with a written notice from the Architect requiring him to remove defective work or improper materials or goods and by such refusal or neglect the Works are materially affected, or
  (d) If he fails to comply with the provisions of either clause 17 or clause 17A of these Conditions, then the Architect may give to him a notice by registered post or recorded delivery specifying the default, and if the Contractor either shall continue such default for fourteen days after receipt of such notice or shall at any time thereafter repeat such default (whether previously repeated or not), then the Employer may within ten days after such continuance or repetition by notice by registered post or recorded delivery forthwith determine the employment of the Contractor under this Contract, provided that such notice shall not be given unreasonably or vexatiously
  (2) In the event of the Contractor becoming bankrupt or making a

composition or arrangement with his creditors or having a winding up order made or (except for purposes of reconstruction) a resolution for voluntary winding up passed or a provisional liquidator receiver or manager of his business or undertaking duly appointed, or possession taken, by or on behalf of the holders of any debentures secured by a floating charge, of any property comprised in or subject to the floating charge, the employment of the Contractor under this Contract shall be forthwith automatically determined but the said employment may be reinstated and continued if the Employer and the Contractor his trustee in bankruptcy liquidator provisional liquidator receiver or manager as the case may be shall so agree.

The operation of this clause does not terminate the contract; the parties remain bound by its terms. After determination, clause 25(4) entitles the employer to complete the work by other contractors, and to claim from the contractor any additional cost so incurred. Clause 25(3) gives the employer a further right of determination if the contractor or any employee of his gives or offers any gift or consideration as an inducement.

Clause 26(1) gives the contractor a right to determine the contract, which is exercisable in the following events:

(a) Non-payment of a certificate after notice.
(b) Interference by the employer with the issue of any certificate.
(c) Suspension of the work due to various causes (these correspond broadly to some of the grounds for extension listed in clause 23).

Upon determination, clause 26(2) entitles the contractor to be paid the value of all work done and materials supplied, the cost of removal and any loss caused to him.

The right to determine under clauses 25 and 26 should be exercised with caution. Determination which does not comply with the requirements of the contract is likely to constitute a repudiation, entitling the other party to damages. Determination normally involves a substantial loss and frequently leads to a dispute.

CERTIFICATION AND PAYMENT

The sums payable to the contractor may be subject to many alterations, which are discussed below. The contract sum is not, however, to be altered on account of any error:

13 The Contract Sum shall not be adjusted or altered in any way whatsoever otherwise than in accordance with the express provisions of these Conditions, and subject to clause 12(2) of these Conditions any error whether of arithmetic or not in the computation of the Contract Sum shall be deemed to have been accepted by the parties hereto.

The Contract contains extensive provisions for payment as the work proceeds, which are vital to the contractor. He will often, during the course of a contract, have a cash turnover exceeding the value of his assets, so that lack of interim payments will create great difficulties. Cash flow has been referred to by the courts as the life-blood of the industry. The issuing of interim certificates is dealt with as follows:

30 (1) Interim valuations shall be made whenever the Architect considers them to be necessary for the purpose of ascertaining the amount to be stated as due in an Interim Certificate. The Architect shall from time to time as provided in this sub-clause issue Interim Certificates stating the amount due to the Contractor from the Employer, and the Contractor shall be entitled to payment therefor within 14 days from the issue of that Certificate. Before the issue of the Certificate of Practical Completion, Interim Certificates shall be issued at the Period of Interim Certificates specified in the Appendix to these Conditions. After the issue of the Certificate of Practical Completion, Interim Certificates shall be issued as and when further amounts are due to the Contractor from the Employer provided always that the Architect shall not be required to issue an Interim Certificate within one calendar month of having issued a previous Interim Certificate.

(2) The amount stated as due in an Interim Certificate shall, subject to any agreement between the parties as to stage payments, be the total value of the work properly executed and of the materials and goods delivered to or adjacent to the Works for use thereon up to and including a date not more than seven days before the date of the said certificate less any amount which may be retained by the Employer (as provided in sub-clause (3) of this Condition) and less any instalments previously paid under this Condition. Provided that such certificate shall only include the value of the said materials and goods as and from such times as they are reasonably, properly and not prematurely brought to or placed adjacent to the Works and then only if adequately protected against weather or other casualties.

Clause 14(1) provides that where materials or goods, in accordance with clause 30(2), are included in an interim certificate under which the contractor has received payment, the materials or goods become the property of the employer. Clause 30(2)A gives the architect a discretion to include payment for materials or goods before delivery to the site, provided specified conditions are met. Clause 14(2) provides similarly for such materials or goods to become the employer's property when paid for.

Clause 30(3) provides for the employer to hold a retention of 5 per cent. or any lower rate agreed. The retention money is to be paid to the contractor, half on the certificate of practical completion and the remainder on the expiry of the defects liability period or on completion of making good defects (clause 30(4)).

In calculating the sum due in interim certificates the architect is required to include sums due in respect of variations and other claims. Clause 11(4) lays down the procedure for valuing variations. Such work is to be valued at the prices in the contract bills if similar work is priced, otherwise such prices are to be the basis of valuation, failing which a fair valuation is to be made. Where work cannot properly be measured and valued the contractor is to be paid at daywork rates. The contractor may claim payment arising out of a variation:

11   (6) If upon written application being made to him by the Contractor, the Architect is of the opinion that a variation or the execution by the Contractor of work for which a provisional sum is included in the Contract Bills (other than work for which a tender made under clause 27(g) of these Conditions has been accepted) has involved the contractor in direct loss and/or under expense for which he would not be reimbursed by payment in respect of a valuation made in accordance with the rules contained in sub-clause (4) of this Condition and if the said application is made within a reasonable time of the loss or expense having been incurred, then the Architect shall either himself ascertain or shall instruct the Quantity Surveyor to ascertain the amount of such loss or expense. Any amount from time to time so ascertained shall be added to the Contract Sum, and if an Interim Certificate is issued after the date of ascertainment any such amount shall be added to the amount which would otherwise be stated as due in such Certificate.

This provision enables the contractor to claim compensation, *e.g.* for the disruptive effect of a variation on other work, which cannot be claimed under clause 11(4). Similar provisions are contained in clause 24(1) which enable the contractor to claim compensation in respect of other disrupting events:

24   (1) If upon written application being made to him by the Contractor the Architect is of the opinion that the Contractor has been involved in direct loss and/or expense for which he would not be reimbursed by a payment made under any other provision in this Contract by reason of the regular progress of the Works or of any part thereof having been materially affected by:

(a) The Contractor not having received in due time necessary instructions, drawings, details or levels from the Architect for which he specifically applied in writing on a date which having regard to the Date for Completion stated in the Appendix to these Conditions or to any extension of time then fixed under clause 23 or clause 33(1) (c) of these Conditions was neither unreasonably distant from nor unreasonably close to the date on which it was necessary for him to receive the same; or

(b) The opening up for inspection of any work covered up or the testing of any of the work materials or goods in accordance with clause 6(3) of these Conditions (including making good in consequence of such opening up or testing), unless the inspection or test showed that the work, materials or goods were not in accordance with this Contract; or

(c) Any discrepancy in or divergence between the Contract Drawings and/or the Contract Bills; or

(d) Delay on the part of artists tradesmen or others engaged by the Employer in executing work not forming part of this Contract; or

(e) Architect's instructions issued in regard to the postponement of any work to be executed under the provisions of this Contract;

and if the written application is made within a reasonable time of it becoming apparent that the progress of the Works or of any part thereof has been affected as aforesaid, then the Architect shall either himself ascertain or shall instruct the Quantity Surveyor to ascertain the amount of such loss and/or expense. Any amount from time to time so ascertained shall be added to the Contract Sum, and if an Interim Certificate is issued after the date of ascertainment any such amount shall be added to the amount which would otherwise be stated as due in such Certificate.

(2) The provisions of this Condition are without prejudice to any other rights and remedies which the Contractor may possess.

The grounds on which the contractor may claim payment correspond broadly to the grounds for extension of time under clause 23(e) (f) (h) and (i). Both under this clause and under clause 11(6), written application within a reasonable time of the event is a condition precedent to the contractor's entitlement to payment. However, alternative claims may often be framed in breach of contract, e.g. for failure to give necessary instructions. Such a claim will not require notice, but there is no entitlement to have the loss included in a certificate.

Final Accounting

During the period following practical completion the architect is required to undertake the final measurement and valuation of the work, (clause 30(5)). By virtue of clause 12 (see above) the quantities of work are deemed to be those set out in the contract bills. However, if there is any error in the bill either party may ask for re-measurement. The difference in quantity is to be valued as a variation (clause 12(2)).

After the defects liability period or making good of defects, the architect is required, within a specified period, to issue the final certificate. This states merely the adjusted contract sum, the sums paid on account and the difference expressed as a balance due to (or from) the contractor. The certificate may, however, assume an importance beyond the value of the money certified:

30 (7) (a) Except as provided in paragraphs (b) and (c) of this sub-clause (and save in respect of fraud), the Final Certificate shall have effect in any proceedings arising out of or in connection with this Contract (whether by arbitration under clause 35 of these Conditions or otherwise) as
  (i) conclusive evidence that where the quality of materials or the standards of workmanship are to be to the reasonable satisfaction of the Architect the same are to such satisfaction, and
  (ii) conclusive evidence that any necessary effect has been given to all the terms of this Contract which require an adjustment to be made of the Contract Sum save where there has been any accidental inclusion or exclusion of any work, materials, goods or figure in any computation or any arithmetical error in any computation, in which event the Final Certificate shall have effect as conclusive evidence as to all other computations.
  (b) If any arbitration or other proceedings have been commenced by either party before the Final Certificate has been issued the Final Certificate shall have effect as conclusive evidence as provided in paragraph (a) of this sub-clause after either
  (i) such proceedings have been concluded, whereupon the Final Certificate shall be subject to the terms of any award or judgment in or settlement of such proceedings, or
  (ii) a period of twelve months during which neither party has taken any further step in such proceedings, whereupon the Final Certificate shall be subject to any terms agreed in partial settlement,
  whichever shall be the earlier.
  (c) If any arbitration or other proceedings have been commenced by either party within 14 days after the Final Certificate has been issued, the Final Certificate shall have effect as conclusive evidence as provided in paragraph (a) of this sub-clause save only in respect of all matters to which those proceedings relate.
  (8) Save as aforesaid no certificate of the Architect shall of itself be be conclusive evidence that any works materials or goods to which it relates are in accordance with this Contract.

To the extent the certificate is to be conclusive, it will be binding on any court or arbitrator. Thus the employer will be barred from bringing (or defending) proceedings on the ground that work is defective (within the limited effect of the certificate) and the contractor will be barred from pursuing claims for further payment.

As regards the quality of the work, if there is a term in the bills requiring the whole of the work to be to the satisfaction of the architect, the final certificate may preclude any further complaint as to quality (see clause 1(1) above). Conversely if the quality of the work is described in the bills, the final certificate may have no effect on the employer's continuing rights.

DISPUTES

The contract requires disputes to be settled by arbitration. Note that the right to arbitrate does not arise unless there is a dispute, *i.e.* a claim by one party to the contract which is rejected by the other.

35 (1) Provided always that in case any dispute or difference shall arise between the Employer or the Architect on his behalf and the Contractor, either during the progress or after the completion or abandonment of the Works, as to the construction of this Contract or as to any matter or thing of whatsoever nature arising thereunder or in connection therewith (including any matter or thing left by this Contract to the discretion of the Architect or the withholding by the Architect of any certificate to which the Contractor may claim to be entitled or the measurement and valuation mentioned in clause 30(5) (a) of these Conditions or the rights and liabilities of the parties under clauses 25, 26, 32 or 33 of these Conditions), then such dispute or difference shall be and is hereby referred to the arbitration and final decision of a person to be agreed between the parties, or, failing agreement within 14 days after either party has given to the other a written request to concur in the appointment of an Arbitrator, a person to be appointed on the request of either party by the President or a Vice-President for the time being of the Royal Institute of British Architects.

(2) Such reference, except on article 3 or article 4 of the Articles of Agreement, or on the questions whether or not the issue of an instruction is empowered by these Conditions, whether or not a certificate has been improperly withheld or is not in accordance with these Conditions, or on any dispute or difference under clauses 32 and 33 of these Conditions, shall not be opened until after Practical Completion or alleged Practical Completion of the Works or termination or alleged termination of the Contractor's employment under this Contract or abandonment of the Works, unless with the written consent of the Employer or the Architect on his behalf and the Contractor.

(3) Subject to the provisions of clauses 2(2), 30(7) and 31D(3) of these Conditions the Arbitrator shall, without prejudice to the generality of his powers, have power to direct such measurements and/or valuations as may in his opinion be desirable in order to determine the

rights of the parties and to ascertain and award any sum which ought to have been the subject of or included in any certificate and to open up, review and revise any certificate, opinion, decision, requirement or notice and to determine all matters in dispute which shall be submitted to him in the same manner as if no such certificate, opinion, decision, requirement or notice had been given.

(4) The award of such Arbitrator shall be final and binding on the parties.

(5) Whatever the nationality, residence or domicile of the Employer, the Contractor, any sub-contractor or supplier or the Arbitrator, and wherever the Works, or any part thereof, are situated, the law of England shall be the proper law of this Contract and in particular (but not so as to derogate from the generality of the foregoing) the provisions of the Arbitration Act, 1950 (notwithstanding anything in section 34 thereof) shall apply to any arbitration under this Contract wherever the same, or any part of it, shall be conducted.

The words "any dispute or difference" include claims for breach of contract. The architect has no power to deal with claims for breach under the contract. He may, of course, negotiate such claims on the employer's behalf, if authorised.

The requirement of sub-clause (2) that an arbitration is not to be opened until practical completion is subject to many wide exceptions. Articles 3 and 4 govern the appointment of a new architect or quantity surveyor. Disputes as to architect's instructions and withholding certificates cover a wide range of potential differences. The existence of an arbitration agreement does not prevent either party from issuing proceedings in the courts; but see further p. 25.

Note

The above discussion has omitted any reference to the following clauses, for which reference must be made to the form of contract: 4, statutory obligations; 7, royalties; 13A, VAT; 17A, fair wages; 19A, nuclear perils; 29, artists and tradesmen; 30B, statutory tax deduction; 31A–E, 31F, fluctuations; 32, hostilities; 33, war damage; 34, antiquities.

Some of the clauses printed above are given in part only. The following parts are omitted: articles of agreement 3, 4; clause 1(2); 2(2); 3(1)(2)(5)(8); 11(4), (5); 25(3), (4); 30(2A), (3)–(6);

The following clauses are referred to but not printed in whole or in part: 9, 14, 16, 17, 19, 20A, B, C, 26, 27, 28.

Further Reading

Keating, *Building Contracts* (4th ed., 1978).
Duncan Wallace, *Building and Civil Engineering Standard Forms* (1969).

CHAPTER 11

THE ICE CONDITIONS OF CONTRACT

The Institution of Civil Engineers' (ICE) form of contract is intended for use in connection with works of civil engineering construction. The form is issued by the ICE, the Association of Consulting Engineers and the Federation of Civil Engineering Contractors. The form in current use is the fifth edition, which was published in 1973. The fifth edition follows the clause numbering and much of the style of previous editions. This accounts for the rather archaic tone of much of the wording. The conditions are published together with forms of tender, agreement and bond. Unlike the JCT forms, the ICE form exists in one version only, for use by private or other employers.

The conditions create a "re-measurement" or "measure and value" contract; *i.e.* the contractor is to be paid at the contract rates (which are themselves subject to variation) for the actual quantities of work executed. This is recognised by omission, in the fifth edition, of any reference to a "contract sum." Instead the conditions now refer to the "tender total."

Among other changes brought about by the fifth edition may be mentioned the following: there are new provisions relating to nominated sub-contracts; clause 12 (adverse physical conditions) has been simplified; the provisions dealing with payment are substantially amended; there is a novel procedure for interim extensions of time; the effect of the maintenance certificate is defined; and there is, for the first time, express reference to a final account and final certificate.

Under the conditions, the work is required to be carried out to the satisfaction of the engineer. He is given powers of control and direction which are both extensive and apparently arbitrary; although as agent of the employer, the engineer must act in the best interest of his principal. The conditions also contain wide-ranging provisions under which the sums payable to the contractor are subject to alteration, usually in favour of the contractor.

As with the chapter dealing with the JCT form, this is not a full commentary on the ICE form. It is an introduction to the basic working provisions of the form. The most important clauses or sub-clauses are printed with brief notes as to their effect. Other clauses are referred to where appropriate. For a full exposition of the conditions reference must be made to the form itself and to one of the standard works noted at the end of the chapter.

The Contract

The conditions contemplate that the form of contract will be accompanied by drawings and a specification in which the work is described, and by bills of quantities in which the work is measured and priced. The way in which these documents operate is as follows.

1(1)(e) "Contract" means the Conditions of Contract Specification Drawings Priced Bill of Quantities the Tender the written acceptance thereof and the Contract Agreement (if completed);

By clause 9, the contractor agrees to execute the contract agreement (published with the form) if required. This does not add any further obligation, but it may be under seal.

5. The several documents forming the Contract are to be taken as mutually explanatory of one another and in case of ambiguities or discrepancies the same shall be explained and adjusted by the Engineer who shall thereupon issue to the Contractor appropriate instructions in writing which shall be regarded as instructions issued in accordance with Clause 13.

The engineer's power under this clause is limited to the technical descriptions of the work: he is not empowered to re-write the conditions. The contract documents usually do not contain full working details. The engineer is therefore given both the power and duty to issue such further details as are necessary:

7. (1) The Engineer shall have full power and authority to supply and shall supply to the Contractor from time to time during the progress of the Works such modified or further drawings and instructions as shall in the Engineer's opinion be necessary for the purpose of the proper and adequate construction completion and maintenance of the Works and the Contractor shall carry out and be bound by the same.

Subject to giving notice, clause 7(3) entitles the contractor to claim additional payment if necessary details are issued late.

Control of the work

The conditions envisage that work on site will be given full-time supervision on behalf of the engineer and the contractor:

1(1)(d) "Engineer's Representative" means a person being the resident engineer or assistant of the Engineer or clerk of works appointed from time to time by the Employer or the Engineer and notified in writing to the Contractor by the Engineer to perform the functions set forth in Clause 2(1);

2. (1) The functions of the Engineer's Representative are to watch and supervise the Construction completion and maintenance of the Works. He shall have no authority to relieve the Contractor of any of his duties or obligations under the Contract nor except as expressly provided hereunder to order any work involving delay or any extra payment by the Employer nor to make any variation of or in the Works.

2. (3) The Engineer may from time to time in writing authorise the Engineer's Representative or any other person responsible to the Engineer to act on behalf of the Engineer either generally in respect of the Contract or specifically in respect of particular Clauses of these Conditions of Contract and any act of any such person within the scope of his authority shall for the purposes of the contract constitute an act of the Engineer. Prior notice in writing of any such authorisation shall be given by the Engineer to the Contractor. Such authorisation shall continue in force until such time as the Engineer shall notify the Contractor in writing that the same is determined. Provided that such authorisation shall not be given in respect of any decision to be taken or certificate to be issued under Clauses 12(3), 44, 48, 60(3), 61, 63 and 66.

Sub-clause (2) empowers the engineer or the Engineer's Representative (ER) to appoint assistants. Sub-clause (4) allows the contractor to appeal against instructions given by an assistant or by the ER

15. (2) The Contractor or a competent and authorised agent or representative approved of in writing by the Engineer (which approval may at any time be withdrawn) is to be constantly on the Works and shall give his whole time to the superintendent of the same. Such authorised agent or representative shall be in full charge of the Works and shall receive on behalf of the Contractor directions and instructions from the Engineer or (subject to the limitations of Clause 2) the Engineer's Representative. The Contractor or such authorised agent or representative shall be responsible for the safety of all operations.

The contractor is required to give the engineer opportunity to inspect the work:

37. The Engineer and any person authorised by him shall at all times have access to the Works and to the Site and to all workshops and places where work is being prepared or whence materials manufactured articles and machinery are being obtained for the Works and the Contractor shall afford every facility for and every assistance in or in obtaining the right to such access.

General Obligations of the Contractor

These are contained in a number of clauses, which must be read together.

8. (1) The Contractor shall subject to the provisions of the Contract construct complete and maintain the Works and *provide* all labour materials Constructional Plant Temporary Works transport to and from and in or about the Site and *everything* whether of a temporary or permanent nature required in and for such construction completion and maintenance so far as the *necessity* for providing the same is specified in or reasonably to be inferred from the Contract.

(2) The Contractor shall take full responsibility for the adequacy stability and safety of all site operations and methods of construction provided that the Contractor shall not be responsible for the design or specification of the Permanent Works (except as may be expressly provided in the Contract) or of any Temporary Works designed by the Engineer.

This repeats obligations contained in the tender to "construct and complete the whole of the said works and maintain the permanent works"; and in the form of agreement, to "construct and complete the works and maintain the permanent works." The exception of responsibility for temporary works designed by the engineer is a matter of potential importance.

In addition to his responsibility for the site operations and methods of construction (clause 8(2)) and for the works themselves (clause 20(2); see below) the contractor is required to take the risk of the site and the sub-soil:

11. (1) The Contractor shall be deemed to have inspected and examined the Site and its surroundings and to have satisfied himself before submitting his tender as to the nature of the ground and sub-soil (so far as is practicable and having taken into account any information in connection therewith which may have been provided by or on behalf of the Employer) the form and nature of the Site the extent and nature of the work and materials necessary for the completion of the Works the means of communication with and access to the Site the accommodation he may require and in general to have obtained for himself all necessary information (subject as above-mentioned) as to risks contingencies and all other circumstances influencing or affecting his tender.

(2) The Contractor shall be deemed to have satisfied himself before submitting his tender as to the correctness and sufficiency of the rates and prices stated by him in the Priced Bill of Quantities which shall (except in so far as it is otherwise provided in the Contract) cover all his obligations under the Contract.

The contractor's liability is subject to two exceptions. First clause 11(1) expressly permits the contractor to take account of any sub-soil information provided by the employer, *i.e.* any site investigation data. The effect of this provision is obscure, but it may permit the contractor, *e.g.* to bring proceedings under the Misrepresentation Act 1967 if the data is misleading. Secondly clause 12 may entitle the contractor to additional payment if unforseeable physical conditions or artificial obstructions are encountered in the sub-soil. (see below)

13. (1) Save in so far as it is legally or physically impossible the Contractor shall construct complete and maintain the Works in strict accordance with the Contract to the satisfaction of the Engineer and shall comply with and adhere strictly to the Engineer's instructions and directions on any matter connected therewith (whether mentioned in the Contract or not). The Contractor shall take instructions and directions only from the Engineer or (subject to the limitations referred to in Clause 2) from the Engineer's Representative.

This clause gives the engineer very wide powers to give instructions. This is important in regard to claims, as to which, see clause 13(3) referred to below. The contractor is not obliged to carry out the work to the extent it is legally or physically impossible, nor is the employer obliged to pay for work omitted on this ground.

20. (2) In case any damage loss or injury from any cause whatsoever (save and except the Excepted Risks as defined in sub-clause (3) of this Clause) shall happen to the Works or any part thereof while the Contractor shall be responsible for the care thereof the Contractor shall at his own cost repair and make good the same so that at completion the Permanent Works shall be in good order and condition and in conformity in every respect with the requirements of the Contract and the Engineer's instructions. To the extent that any such damage loss or injury arises from any of the Excepted Risks the Contractor shall if required by the Engineer repair and make good the same as aforesaid at the expense of the Employer. The Contractor shall also be liable for any damage to the Works occasioned by him in the course of any operations carried out by him for the purpose of completing any outstanding work or of complying with his obligations under Clauses 49 and 50.

This renders the contractor responsible for the partially completed work in respect of damage from any cause, including the employer's negligence, save for the excepted risks. These are defined in clause 20(3) and include, besides normal insurance risks (such as riot, war invasion, etc.) damage due to occupation of the works by the employer, and the engineer's design. Clause 20(1) provides that the contractor's responsibility for the works ceases 14 days after the certificate of completion.

Clauses 21 to 25 contain important requirements as to insurance and liability for losses. Clause 21 requires the contractor to insure the works and his materials and plant against loss, from any cause other than the excepted risks, so as to cover his liability under clause 20. This insurance is required to be in the joint names of employer and contractor. Clause 22 apportions liability for third party claims which arise out of or in consequence of the work; and clause 23 requires the contractor to insure his own liability. Clause 24 deals with injuries to workmen. Clause 25 gives the employer the right to effect any insurance which the contractor fails to take out.

The Contractor's methods of work

Prima facie the contractor's methods of carrying out the work are his responsibility and his choice. The contractor is responsible for the works and for their safety (clauses 20 and 8(2)). By clause 1(1) "works means the permanent works together with the temporary works." There is an exception provided in clause 8(2) (see above). However, the engineer is given potentially wide powers to affect the contractor's methods.

13. (2) The whole of the materials plant and labour to be provided by the Contractor under Clause 8 and the mode manner and speed of construction and maintenance of the Works are to be of a kind and conducted in a manner approved of by the Engineer.

14. (3) If requested by the Engineer the Contractor shall submit at such times and in such detail as the Engineer may reasonably require such information pertaining to the methods of construction (including Temporary Works and the use of Constructional Plant) which the Contractor proposes to adopt or use and such calculations of stresses strains and deflections that will arise in the Permanent Works or any parts thereof during construction from the use of such methods as will enable the Engineer to decide whether if these methods are adhered to the Works can be executed in accordance with the Drawings and Specification and without detriment to the Permanent Works when completed.

(4) The Engineer shall inform the Contractor in writing within a reasonable period after receipt of the information submitted in accordance with sub-clause (3) of this Clause either:—

    (a) that the Contractor's proposed methods have the consent of the Engineer; or

    (b) in what respects in the opinion of the Engineer they fail to meet the requirements of the Drawings or Specification or will be detrimental to the Permanent Works.

In the latter event the Contractor shall take such steps or make such changes in the said methods as may be necessary to meet the Engineer's requirements and to obtain his consent. The Contractor shall not change the methods which have received the Engineer's consent without the further consent in writing of the Engineer which shall not be unreasonably withheld.

(5) The Engineer shall provide to the Contractor such design criteria relevant to the Permanent Works or any Temporary Works designed by the Engineer as may be necessary to enable the Contractor to comply with sub-clauses (3) and (4) of this Clause.

Clause 14(6) provides for additional payment to the contractor arising from the operation of clause 14. The engineer also has an express power under clause 51(1) to order a variation in the contractor's method of construction.

Workmanship and materials

The following clauses should be read in the light of the general obligations to comply with the contract (clause 13(1), tender and form of agreement):

36. (1) All materials and workmanship shall be of the respective kinds described in the Contract and in accordance with the Engineer's instructions and shall be subjected from time to time to such tests as the Engineer may direct at the place of manufacture or fabrication or on the Site or such other place or places as may be specified in the Contract. The Contractor shall provide such assistance instruments machines labour and materials as are normally required for examining measuring and testing any work and the quality weight or quantity of any materials used and shall supply samples of materials before incorporation in the Works for testing as may be selected and required by the Engineer.

Clause 36(2) and (3) stipulate how the cost of samples and tests is to be borne between the contractor and employer.

38. (1) No work shall be covered up or put of view without the approval of the Engineer and the Contractor shall afford full opportunity for the Engineer to examine and measure any work which is about to be covered up or put out of view and to examine foundations before permanent work is placed thereon. The Contractor shall give due notice to the Engineer whenever any such work or foundations is or are ready or about to be ready for examination and the Engineer shall without unreasonable delay unless he considers it unnecessary and advises the Contractor accordingly attend for the purpose of examining and measuring such work or of examining such foundations.

Clause 38(2) permits the engineer to order uncovering of work and provides for apportioning the cost.

39. (1) The Engineer shall during the progress of the Works have power to order in writing:—

    (a) the removal from the Site within such time or times as may be specified in the order of any materials which in the opinion of the Engineer are not in accordance with the Contract;

    (b) the substitution of proper and suitable materials; and

    (c) the removal and proper re-execution (notwithstanding any previous test thereof or interim payment therefor) of any work which in respect of materials or workmanship is not in the opinion of the Engineer in accordance with the Contract.

(2) In case of default on the part of the Contractor in carrying out such order the Employer shall be entitled to employ and pay other persons to carry out the same and all expenses consequent thereon or incidental thereto shall be borne by the Contractor and shall be recoverable from him by the Employer or may be deducted by the Employer from any monies due or which may become due to the Contractor.

(3) Failure of the Engineer or any person acting under him pursuant to Clause 2 to disapprove any work or materials shall not prejudice the power of the Engineer or any of them subsequently to disapprove such work or materials.

This clause is of great importance. Without it the engineer's only remedies for defective work would be forfeiture (under clause 63) or refusal to certify payment on completion, the latter carrying the sanction of liquidated damages. Note that work is not in accordance with the contract if it does not comply with the drawings or the specification clause $1(1)(e)$).

Completion and maintenance

The contractor's obligations fall into two separate periods: the period up to the completion certificate, when the work is carried out; and the period of maintenance, during which the contractor must repair any defects and maintain the work for a specified period. These are dealt with as follows:

48. (1) When the Contractor shall consider that the whole of the Works has been substantially completed and has satisfactorily passed any final test that may be prescribed by the Contract he may give a notice to that effect to the Engineer or to the Engineer's Representative accompanied by an undertaking to finish any outstanding work during the Period of Maintenance. Such notice and undertaking shall be in writing and shall be deemed to be a request by the Contractor for the Engineer to issue a Certificate of Completion in respect of the Works and the Engineer shall within 21 days of the date of delivery of such notice either issue to the Contractor (with a copy to the Employer) a Certificate of Completion stating the date on which in his opinion the Works were substantially completed in accordance with the Contract or else give instructions in writing to the Contractor specifying all the work which in the Engineer's opinion requires to be done by the Contractor before the issue of such certificate. If the Engineer shall give such instructions the Contractor shall be entitled to receive such Certificate of Completion within 21 days of completion to the satisfaction of the Engineer of the work specified by the said instructions.

Clause 48(2) and (3) enable the engineer to certify completion of sections (as defined in the appendix) or parts of the works before completion of the whole.

49. (1) In these Conditions the expression "Period of Maintenance" shall mean the period of maintenance named in the Appendix to the Form of Tender calculated from the date of completion of the Works or any Section or part thereof certified by the Engineer in accordance with Clause 48 as the case may be.

(2) To the intent that the Works and each Section and part thereof shall at or as soon as practicable after the expiration of the relevant Period of Maintenance be delivered up to the Employer in the condition required by the Contract (fair wear and tear excepted) to the satisfaction of the Engineer the Contractor shall finish the work (if any) outstanding at the date of completion as certified under Clause 48 as soon as may be practicable after such date and shall execute all such work of repair amendment reconstruction rectification and making good of defects imperfections shrinkages or other faults as may during the Period of Maintenance or within 14 days after its expiration be required of the Contractor in writing by the Engineer as a result of an inspection made by or on behalf of the Engineer prior to its expiration.

Note that the contractor is obliged to put right any defects, whether or not they are due to his failure to comply with contract. Clause 49(3) entitles the contractor to payment if the defect is not due to his default.

Time

The speed with which the contractor carries out the work is an important element in the performance of the contract. The appendix specifies the time for completion, but the contract contains extensive provisions under which the engineer may extend the completion date.

41. The Contractor shall commence the Works on or as soon as is reasonably possible after the Date for Commencement of the Works to be notified by the Engineer in writing which date shall be within a reasonable time after the date of acceptance of the Tender. Thereafter the Contractor shall proceed with the Works with due expedition and without delay in accordance with the Contract.

By clause 42(1) the contractor must be given possession of so much of the site as may be necessary to proceed in accordance with his programme. In default of adequate possession the contractor is entitled to additional payment.

During the course of the work the engineer may order a suspension of any part of the works under clause 40(1). If he is dissatisfied with the rate of progress the engineer may require the contractor to take steps to expedite progress, under clause 46. Repeated failure to proceed at an adequate rate may lead to forfeiture under clause 63.

43. The whole of the Works and any Section required to be completed.

within a particular time as stated in the Appendix to the Form of Tender shall be completed within the time so stated (or such extended time as may be allowed under Clause 44) calculated from the Date for Commencement of the Works notified under Clause 41.

44. (1) Should any variation ordered under Clause 51(1) or increased quantities referred to in Clause 51(3) or any other cause of delay referred to in these Conditions or exceptional adverse weather conditions or other special circumstances of any kind whatsoever which may occur be such as fairly to entitle the Contractor to an extension of time for the completion of the Works or (where different periods for completion of different Sections are provided for in the Appendix to the Form of Tender) of the relevant Section the Contractor shall within 28 days after the cause of the delay has arisen or as soon thereafter as is reasonable in all the circumstances deliver to the Engineer full and detailed particulars of any claim to extension of time to which he may consider himself entitled in order that such claim may be investigated at the time.

(2) The Engineer shall upon receipt of such particulars or if he thinks fit in the absence of any such claim consider all the circumstances known to him at that time and make an assessment of the extension of time (if any) to which he considers the Contractor entitled for the completion of the Works or relevant Section and shall by notice in writing to the Contractor grant such extension of time for completion. In the event that the Contractor shall have made a claim for an extension of time but the Engineer considers the Contractor not entitled thereto the Engineer shall so inform the Contractor.

The extension under clause 44(2) is an interim extension. The engineer is required to review his decisions at the date for completion (sub-clause (3)) and again at the actual completion date (sub-clause (4)). The further grounds which entitle the contractor to extensions are dispersed throughout the conditions. They include adverse conditions (clause 12) instructions under clauses 5 or 13, suspension of work (clause 40) and non-possession of the site (clause 42).

The contractor's failure to complete the work by the date or extended date for completion entitles the employer to deduct liquidated damages specified in the appendix. Clause 47 contains very extensive and difficult provisions governing the deduction of liquidated damages in respect of specified sections of the work which are required to be completed in advance of the whole project. In the event of the work being delayed by a default on the part of the employer which does not permit an extension to be granted, the liquidated damages clause becomes unenforceable. In this regard, the general words of clause 44 "other special circumstances" cannot be relied on (see p. 101).

POWERS AND REMEDIES OF THE ENGINEER AND EMPLOYER

Many of these have already been dealt with. The engineer has a sweeping power under clause 13(1) to give instructions and directions on any matter connected with the works. Under clauses 13(2) and 14(3) and (4) the engineer has powers to control the contractor's methods of work.

The engineer has powers as to the progress of the works under several clauses:

14. (1) Within 21 days after the acceptance of his Tender the Contractor shall submit to the Engineer for his approval a programme showing the order of procedure in which he proposes to carry out the Works and thereafter shall furnish such further details and information as the Engineer may reasonably require in regard thereto. The Contractor shall at the same time also provide in writing for the information of the Engineer a general description of the arrangements and methods of construction which the Contractor proposes to adopt for the carrying out of the Works.

(2) Should it appear to the Engineer at any time that the actual progress of the Works does not conform with the approved programme referred to in sub-clause (1) of this Clause the Engineer shall be entitled to require the Contractor to produce a revised programme showing the modifications to the original programme necessary to ensure completion of the Works or any Section within the time for completion as defined in Clause 43 or extended time granted pursuant to Clause 44(2).

Powers under clause 14 are of limited effect. But under clause 46 the engineer has power to require the contractor to take steps to expedite progress; and under clause 40 the engineer may order suspension of any part of the work.

The engineer's most important express power under the contract is to vary the works:

51. (1) The Engineer shall order any variation to any part of the Works that may in his opinion be necessary for the completion of the Works and shall have power to order any variation that for any other reason shall in his opinion be desirable for the satisfactory completion and functioning of the Works. Such variations may include additions omissions substitutions alterations changes in quality form character kind position dimension level or line and changes in the specified sequence method or timing of construction (if any).

(2) No such variation shall be made by the Contractor without an order by the Engineer. All such orders shall be given in writing provided that if for any reason the Engineer shall find it necessary to give any such order orally in the first instance the Contractor shall comply with such oral order. Such oral order shall be confirmed in writing by the Engineer as soon as is possible in the circumstances. If the contractor shall confirm in

writing to the Engineer any oral order by the Engineer and such confirmation shall not be contradicted in writing by the Engineer forthwith it shall be deemed to be an order in writing by the Engineer. No variation ordered or deemed to be ordered in writing in accordance with sub-clauses (1) and (2) of this Clause shall in any way vitiate or invalidate the Contract but the value (if any) of all such variations shall be taken into account in ascertaining the amount of the Contract Price.

(3) No order in writing shall be required for increase or decrease in the quantity of any work where such increase or decrease is not the result of an order given under this Clause but is the result of the quantities exceeding or being less than those stated in the Bill of Quantities.

Note that the engineer's powers include varying the works and also ordering changes in the specified sequence, method of timing of construction. The engineer is never *bound* to vary the work. The employer will be bound by any variation order given by the engineer; but he should ensure that he has the employer's authority before giving an order. Valuation of variations and of changes in quantities of the work are dealt with in clauses 52 and 56(2).

Sub-contractors

By clause 4, the contractor must obtain the engineer's consent to sublet any part of the works to a sub-contractor of his own choosing. The contractor is to remain fully liable for the sub-contractor.

Where the contract provides for specific work to be carried out by a nominated sub-contractor, clauses 58, 59A and 59B lay down extensive provisions governing the parties' rights, particularly in regard to default by the sub-contractor. Such work will be designated as either a provisional sum or a prime cost item. In regard to these the engineer's powers are as follows:

58. (1) "Provisional Sum" means a sum included in the Contract and so designated for the execution of work or the supply of goods materials or services or for contingencies which sum may be used in whole or in part or not at all at the direction and discretion of the Engineer.

(2) "Prime Cost (PC) Item" means an item in the Contract which contains (either wholly or in part) a sum referred to as Prime Cost (PC) which will be used for the execution of work or for the supply of goods materials or services for the Works.

(4) In respect of every Prime Cost Item the Engineer shall have power to order the Contractor to employ a sub-contractor nominated by the Engineer for the execution of any work or the supply of any goods materials or services included therein. The Engineer shall also have power with the consent of the Contractor to order the Contractor to execute any such work or to supply any such goods materials or services in which event the Contractor shall be paid in accordance with the terms of a quotation submitted by him and accepted by the Engineer or in the absence thereof the

value shall be determined in accordance with Clause 52.

(7) In respect of every Provisional Sum the Engineer shall have power to order either or both of the following:—

    (a) work to be executed or goods materials or services to be supplied by the Contractor the value of such work executed or goods materials or services supplied being determined in accordance with Clause 52 and included in the Contract Price;

    (b) work to be executed or goods materials or services to be supplied by a Nominated Sub-contractor in accordance with Clause 59A.

Clauses 59A and 59B contain provisions in regard to nominated sub-contractors covering the following matters:

(a) terms which the contractor is entitled to have in any nominated sub-contract;

(b) powers available to the engineer if the parties to the sub-contract cannot agree terms;

(c) payments in respect of nominated sub-contract work;

(d) consequences of termination of a nominated sub-contract;

(e) limitation of the contractor's liability in the event of default by a nominated sub-contractor.

Clause 59C entitles the employer to make direct payments to a nominated sub-contractor if the contractor has failed, without reasonable cause, to pay sums previously certified in favour of the sub-contractor.

Default by the contractor

In the event that the contractor fails to comply with the contract, the employer has (in addition to the sanctions discussed below) some degree of security against loss. As to the work done and materials supplied, the employer withholds a percentage of the contract value until completion (see under "Payment" below). The employer also has valuable rights over the contractor's plant and materials on the site:

53. (2) All Plant goods and materials owned by the Contractor or by any company in which the Contractor has a controlling interest shall when on the Site be deemed to be the property of the Employer.

53. (6) No Plant (except hired Plant) goods or materials or any part thereof shall be removed from the Site without the written consent of the Engineer which consent shall not be unreasonably withheld where the same are no longer immediately required for the purposes of the completion of the Works but the Employer will permit the Contractor the exclusive use of all such Plant goods and materials in and for the completion of the Works until the occurrence of any event which gives the Employer the right to exclude the Contractor from the Site and proceed with the completion of the Works.

Some of the sanctions exercisable on the default of the contractor are discussed above. If the contractor does not made adequate progress the engineer may require steps to be taken to expedite progress under clause 46, and require a revised programme under clause 14(2). If the works are not completed by the date or extended date for completion the employer may deduct liquidated damages. Where defective work is done the engineer has important powers under clause 39 to order its removal and proper replacement. In respect of all these powers, the choice remains with the contractor to obey the engineer's instructions or pay for his default.

Where the contractor's default is more serious, or when he becomes unable to perform the contract, the employer may become entitled to determine the contractor's employment.

63. (1) If the Contractor shall become bankrupt or have a receiving order made against him or shall present his petition in bankruptcy or shall make an arrangement with or assignment in favour of his creditors or shall agree to carry out the Contract under a committee of inspection of his creditors or (being a corporation) shall go into liquidation (other than a voluntary liquidation for the purposes of amalgamation or reconstruction) or if the Contractor shall assign the Contract without the consent in writing of the Employer first obtained or shall have an execution levied on his goods or if the Engineer shall certify in writing to the Employer that in his opinion the Contractor:—

    (a) has abandoned the Contract; or

    (b) without reasonable excuse has failed to commence the Works in accordance with Clause 41 or has suspended the progress of the Works for 14 days after receiving from the Engineer written notice to proceed; or

    (c) has failed to remove goods or materials from the Site or to pull down and replace work for 14 days after receiving from the Engineer written notice that the said goods materials or work have been condemned and rejected by the Engineer; or

    (d) despite previous warning by the Engineer in writing is failing to proceed with the Works with due diligence or is otherwise persistently or fundamentally in breach of his obligations under the Contract; or

    (e) has to the detriment of good workmanship or in defiance of the Engineer's instruction to the contrary sub-let any part of the Contract;

then the Employer may after giving 7 days' notice in writing to the Contractor enter upon the Site and the Works and expel the Contractor therefrom without thereby avoiding the Contract or releasing the Contractor from any of his obligations or liabilities under the Contract or affecting the rights and powers conferred on the Employer or the Engineer by the Contract and may himself complete the Works or may employ any other contractor to complete the Works and the Employer or such other contractor may use for such completion so much of the Constructional Plant Temporary Works goods and materials which have been deemed to become the property of the Employer under Clauses 53 and 54 as he or they may think proper and the Employer may at any time sell any of the said Constructional Plant Temporary Works and unused goods and materials and apply the proceeds of sale in or towards the satisfaction of any sums due or which may become due to him from the Contractor under the Contract.

Note that the operation of this clause does not determine the contract. Clause 63(4), which remains binding on the contractor, entitles the employer to be paid the additional costs of completing the work by another contractor.

This clause is, in practice, difficult to operate. If the employer expels the contractor from the site without complying precisely with sub-clause (1), he is likely to have repudiated the contract, rendering himself liable to the contractor in damages. The clause is an example of the unnecessary obscurity which pervades much of the contract. It is not clear to what extent these remedies supersede other remedies based on the same grounds; *e.g.* if the engineer exercises the power under clause 39(2) to bring in another contractor to re-execute defective work (see above) can notice also be given under clause 63(1)(*c*)?

Certification and Payment

These provisions are vital to the contractor, who will often, during the course of the work, lay out sums of money or incur liabilities exceeding the value of his assets. The provisions for interim payment make this possible. Cash flow has been referred to by the courts as the life-blood of the industry.

Clause 60 lays down the basic monthly accounting procedure:

60. (1) The Contractor shall submit to the Engineer after the end of each month a statement (in such form if any as may be prescribed in the Specification) showing:—

    (a) the estimated contract value of the Permanent Works executed up to the end of that month;

    (b) a list of any goods or materials delivered to the Site for but not yet incorporated in the Permanent Works and their value;

    (c) a list of any goods or materials listed in the Appendix to the Form of Tender which have not yet been delivered to the

Site but of which the property has vested in the Employer pursuant to Clause 54 and their values;

(d) the estimated amounts to which the Contractor considers himself entitled in connection with all other matters for which provision is made under the Contract including any Temporary Works or Constructional Plant for which separate amounts are included in the Bill of Quantities;

unless in the opinion of the Contractor such values and amounts together will not justify the issue of an interim certificate.

Amounts payable in respect of Nominated Sub-contractors are to be listed separately.

(2) Within 28 days of the date of delivery to the Engineer or Engineer's Representative in accordance with sub-clause (1) of this Clause of the Contractor's monthly statement the Engineer shall certify and the Employer shall pay to the Contractor (after deducting any previous payments on account):—

(a) the amount which in the opinion of the Engineer on the basis of the monthly statement is due to the Contractor on account of sub-clause (1)(a) and (d) of this Clause less a retention as provided in sub-clause (4) of this Clause;

(b) such amounts (if any) as the Engineer may consider proper (but in no case exceeding the percentage of the value stated in the Appendix to the Form of Tender) in respect of (b) and (c) of sub-clause (1) of this Clause which amounts shall not be subject to a retention under sub-clause (4) of this Clause.

The amounts certified in respect of Nominated Sub-contracts shall be shown separately in the certificate. The Engineer shall not be bound to issue an interim certificate for a sum less than that named in the Appendix to the Form of Tender.

Note that retention is not deducted on the value of unfixed goods. The contractor is entitled only to the percentage of their value specified in the appendix. Clause 54 lays down conditions to be satisfied if the contractor wishes to obtain payment for materials (to be specified in the appendix) before delivery to the site. Such goods must become the property of the employer.

Clause 60(3) deals with the final account and final certificate. Clause 60(4) stipulates the limits of retention, which may not exceed 5 per cent. Clause 60(5) provides for payment of the retention. Subject to reductions for sectional completion, the money is to be paid to the contractor as to half on the certificate of completion of the whole of the works, and half on expiry of the period of maintenance, subject to deduction for outstanding work.

Calculation of the contract value of the work (see clause 60(1)(a)) is governed by clauses 55 and 56.

55. (1) The quantities set out in the Bill of Quantities are the estimated quantities of the work but they are not to be taken as the actual and correct quantities of the Works to be executed by the Contractor in fulfilment of his obligations under the Contract.

(2) Any error in description in the Bill of Quantities or omission therefrom shall not vitiate the Contract nor release the Contractor from the execution of the whole or any part of the Works according to the Drawings and Specification or from any of his obligations or liabilities under the Contract. Any such error or omission shall be corrected by the Engineer and the value of the work actually carried out shall be ascertained in accordance with Clause 52. Provided that there shall be no rectification of any errors omissions or wrong estimates in the descriptions rates and prices inserted by the Contractor in the Bill of Quantities.

56. (1) The Engineer shall except as otherwise stated ascertain and determine by admeasurement the value in accordance with the Contract of the work in accordance with the Contract.

(2) Should the actual quantities executed in respect of any item be greater or less than those stated in the Bill of Quantities and if in the opinion of the Engineer such increase or decrease of itself shall so warrant the Engineer shall after consultation with the Contractor determine an appropriate increase or decrease of any rates or prices rendered unreasonable or inapplicable in consequence thereof and shall notify the Contractor accordingly.

The clauses mean that the Contract is subject to re-measurement; *i.e.* the contractor is to be paid for the actual quantities of work executed at the contract rates, which may themselves be varied under clause 56(2).

The amounts to which the contractor is entitled "in connection with all other matters for which provision is made under the contract" (clause 60(1)(*d*)) depend on many clauses throughout the contract. The most important of these is the provision for valuing variations.

52. (1) The value of all variations ordered by the Engineer in accordance with Clause 51 shall be ascertained by the Engineer after consultation with the Contractor in accordance with the following principles. Where work is of similar character and executed under similar conditions to work priced in the Bill of Quantities it shall be valued at such rates and prices contained therein as may be applicable. Where work is not of a similar character or is not executed under similar conditions the rates and prices in the Bill of Quantities shall be used as the basis for valuation so far as may be reasonable failing which a fair valuation shall be made. Failing agreement between the Engineer and the Contractor as to any rate or price to be applied in the valuation of any variation the Engineer shall determine the rate or price in accordance with the foregoing principles and he shall notify the Contractor accordingly.

(2) Provided that if the nature or amount of any variation relative to the nature or amount of the whole of the contract work or to any part

thereof shall be such that in the opinion of the Engineer or the Contractor any rate or price contained in the Contract for any item of work is by reason of such variation rendered unreasonable or inapplicable either the Engineer shall give to the Contractor or the Contractor shall give to the Engineer notice before the varied work is commenced or as soon thereafter as is reasonable in all the circumstances that such rate or price should be varied and the Engineer shall fix such rate or price as in the circumstances he shall think reasonable and proper.

Note that the engineer's power to vary the contract rates under sub-clause (2) applies to "any rate or price contained in the contract for any item of work" and is not limited to the work which is varied. A claim under clause 52(2) is the nearest equivalent to a claim for loss and/or expense under clause 11(6) of the JCT form.

Clause 52(3) enables the engineer to order additional or substituted work to be executed on a daywork basis, clause 52(4) provides for notices to be given of claims under any clause of the contract.

In addition to sums due for varied work, there are many other provisions which may entitle the contractor to further payment.

Claims

Additional payments which may be due to the contractor under provisions other than those covering valuation of the work done are often referred to as "claims." The term may also include damages for breach of contract; but this section is limited to consideration of sums due under the contract.

The principle claims available to the contractor are the following. Clause 7(3) entitles the contractor to payment in respect of the late issue of drawings or instructions. Clause 12(3) allows the contractor to claim additional payment for work to overcome unforeseen physical conditions or artifical obstructions:

12. (1) If during the execution of the Works the Contractor shall encounter physical conditions (other than weather conditions or conditions due to weather conditions) or artificial obstructions which conditions or obstructions he considers could not reasonably have been foreseen by an experience contractor and the Contractor is of opinion that additional cost will be incurred which would not have been incurred if the physical conditions or artificial obstructions had not been encountered he shall if he intends to make any claim for additional payment give notice to the Engineer pursuant to Clause 52(4) and shall specify in such notice the physical conditions and/or artificial obstructions encountered and with the notice if practicable or as soon as possible thereafter give details of the anticipated effects thereof the measures he is taking or is proposing to take and the extent of the anticipated delay in or interference with the execution of the Works.

(2) Following receipt of a notice under sub-clause (1) of this Clause the Engineer may if he thinks fit *inter alia*:—

(a) require the Contractor to provide an estimate of the cost of the measures he is taking or is proposing to take;

(b) approve in writing such measures with or without modification;

(c) give written instructions as to how the physical conditions or artificial obstructions are to be dealt with;

(d) order a suspension under Clause 40 or a variation under Clause 51.

(3) To the extent that the Engineer shall decide that the whole or some part of the said physical conditions or artificial obstructions could not reasonably have been foreseen by an experienced contractor the Engineer shall take any delay suffered by the Contractor as a result of such conditions or obstructions into account in determining any extension of time to which the Contractor is entitled under Clause 44 and the Contractor shall subject to Clause 52(4) (notwithstanding that the Engineer may not have given any instructions or orders pursuant to sub-clause (2) of this Clause) be paid in accordance with Clause 60 such sum as represents the reasonable cost of carrying out any additional work done and additional Constructional Plant used which would not have been done or used had such conditions or obstructions or such part thereof as the case may be not been encountered together with a reasonable percentage addition thereto in respect of profit and the reasonable costs incurred by the Contractor by reason of any unavoidable delay or disruption of working suffered as a consequence of encountering the said conditions or obstructions or such part thereof.

These provisions are of potentially wide application, and limit the contractor's responsibility for the site and sub-soil under clause 11 (see above).

The widest contractual provision for claims is under clause 13(3):

13. (3) If in pursuance of Clause 5 or sub-clause (1) of this Clause the Engineer shall issue instructions or directions which involve the Contractor in delay or disrupt his arrangements or methods of construction so as to cause him to incur cost beyond that reasonably to have been foreseen by an experienced contractor at the time of tender then the Engineer shall take such delay into account in determining any extension of time to which the Contractor is entitled under Clause 44 and the Contractor shall subject to Clause 52(4) be paid in accordance with Clause 60 the amount of such cost as may be reasonable. If such instructions or directions require any variation to any part of the Works the same shall be deemed to have been given pursuant to Clause 51.

An instruction under clause 5 is one given to explain and adjust an ambiguity in the contract. Clause 13(1) refers to instructions on any matter connected with the works (whether mentioned in the contract or not).

In practice, instructions are often given without specifying any clause. It is thought that an instruction is given in pursuance of clause

13(1) only if it cannot be given under any other clause. But the contrary is arguable, *i.e.* that *any* instruction gives rise to a claim under clause 13(3).

Clause 14(6) allows claims in respect of the engineer's requirements in regard to the methods of construction. Clause 31(2) entitles the contractor to payment in respect of providing facilities for the employer's direct contractors. Under clause 40(1) the contractor is to be paid his extra cost arising from a suspension of the work. Clause 42(1) allows claims for non-possession of the site.

All the above claims (and others) are subject to clause 52(4) which requires the contractor to give notice in writing "as soon as reasonably possible" (stricter notices are required for claims under clauses 52 and 56). The contractor's right to final and interim payments in respect of claims are governed by the following provisions:

52(4)(e) If the Contractor fails to comply with any of the provisions of this Clause in respect of any claim which he shall seek to make then the Contractor shall be entitled to payment in respect thereof only to the extent that the Engineer has not been prevented from or substantially prejudiced by such failure in investigating the said claim.

(f) The Contractor shall be entitled to have included in any interim payment certified by the Engineer pursuant to Clause 60 such amount in respect of any claim as the Engineer may consider due to the Contractor provided that the Contractor shall have supplied sufficient particulars to enable the Engineer to determine the amount due. If such particulars are insufficient to substantiate the whole of the claim the Contractor shall be entitled to payment in respect of such part of the claim as the particulars may substantiate to the satisfaction of the Engineer.

Note that paragraph (*e*) sets no time limit on the engineer's investigation. The contractor may re-submit his claim if further information comes to light.

Final Accounting

After the completion of maintenance the engineer is required to issue a maintenance certificate. This is followed by vetting the contractor's final account and issue of a final certificate.

61. (1) Upon the expiration of the Period of Maintenance or where there is more than one such period upon the expiration of the latest period and when all outstanding work referred to under Clause 48 and all work of repair amendment reconstruction rectification and making good of defects imperfections shrinkages and other faults referred to under Clauses 49 and 50 shall have been completed the Engineer shall issue to the Employer (with a copy to the Contractor) a Maintenance Certificate stating the date on which the Contractor shall have completed his obligations to construct complete and maintain the Works to the Engineer's satisfaction.

(2) The issue of the Maintenance Certificate shall not be taken as relieving either the Contractor or the Employer from any liability the one towards the other arising out of or in any way connected with the performance of their respective obligations under the Contract.

60. (3) Not later than 3 months after the date of the Maintenance Certificate the Contractor shall submit to the Engineer a statement of final account and supporting documentation showing in detail the value in accordance with the Contract of the work done in accordance with the Contract together with all further sums which the Contractor considers to be due to him under the Contract up to the date of the Maintenance Certificate. Within 3 months after receipt of this final account and of all information reasonably required for its verification the Engineer shall issue a final certificate stating the amount which in his opinion is finally due under the Contract up to the date of the Maintenance Certificate and after giving credit to the Employer for all amounts previously paid by the Employer and for all sums to which the Employer is entitled under the Contract up to the date of the Maintenance Certificate the balance if any due from the Employer to the Contractor or from the Contractor to the Employer as the case may be. Such balance shall subject to Clause 47 be paid to or by the Contractor as the case may require within 28 days of the date of the certificate.

Neither the maintenance certificate nor the final certificate constitutes a binding approval of the work. This should be compared to the final certificate under clause 30(7) of the JCT form.

DISPUTES

When a dispute exists clause 66 provides for settlement by a two-tier system. When the dispute concerns a claim by the contractor, the system has three tiers: the claim must be referred to and be rejected by the engineer under the relevant clause before a dispute exists: the dispute must then be referred back to the engineer under clause 66: the engineer's decision may then be the subject of arbitration.

66. (1) If any dispute or difference of any kind whatsoever shall arise between the Employer and the Contractor in connection with or arising out of the Contract or the carrying out of the Works including any dispute as to any decision opinion instruction direction certificate or valuation of the Engineer (whether during the progress of the Works or after their completion and whether before or after the determination abandonment or breach of the Contract) it shall be referred to and settled by the Engineer who shall state his decision in writing and give notice of the same to the Employer and the Contractor. Unless the Contract shall have been already determined or abandoned the Contractor shall in every case continue to proceed with the Works with all due diligence and he shall give effect forthwith to every such decision of the Engineer unless and until the same shall be revised by an arbitrator as hereinafter provided. Such decisions shall be final and binding upon the Contractor and the Employer unless either of them shall require that the matter be referred to arbitration as hereinafter provided. If the Engineer shall fail to give such decision for a period of 3 calendar months after being requested to do so or if either the Employer or the Contractor be dissatisfied with any such decision of the Engineer then and in any such case either the Employer or the Contractor may within 3 calendar months after receiving notice of such decision or within 3 calendar months after the expiration of the said period of 3 months (as the case may be) require that the matter shall be referred to the arbitration of a person to be agreed upon between the parties or (if the parties fail to appoint an arbitrator within one calendar month of either party serving on the other party a written notice to concur in the appointment of an arbitrator) a person to be appointed on the application of either party by the President for the time being of the Institution of Civil Engineers. If an arbitrator declines the appointment or after appointment is removed by order of a competent court or is incapable of acting or dies and the parties do not within one calendar month of the vacancy arising fill the vacancy then the President for the time being of the Institution of Civil Engineers may on the application of either party appoint an arbitrator to fill the vacancy. Any such reference to arbitration shall be deemed to be a submission to arbitration within the meaning of the Arbitration Act 1950 or the Arbitration (Scotland) Act 1894 as the case may be or any statutory re-enactment or amendment thereof for the time being in force. Any such reference to arbitration may be conducted in accordance with the Institution of Civil Engineer's Arbitration Procedure (1973) or any amendment or modification thereof being in force at the time of the appointment of the arbitrator and in cases where the President of the Institution of Civil Engineers is requested to appoint the arbitrator he may direct that the arbitration is conducted in accordance with the aforementioned Procedure or any amendment or modification thereof. Such arbitrator shall have full power to open up review and revise any decision opinion instruction direction certificate or valuation of the Engineer and neither party shall be limited in the proceedings before such arbitrator to the evidence or arguments put before the Engineer for the purpose of obtaining his decision above referred to. The award of the arbitrator shall be final and binding on the parties. Save as provided for in sub-clause (2) of this Clause no steps shall be taken in the reference to the arbitrator until after the completion or alleged completion of the Works unless with the written consent of the Employer and the Contractor. Provided always:—

    (a) that the giving of a Certificate of Completion under Clause 48 shall not be a condition precedent to the taking of any step in such reference;

    (b) that no decision given by the Engineer in accordance with the foregoing provisions shall disqualify him from being called as a witness and giving evidence before the arbitrator on any matter whatsoever relevant to the dispute or difference so referred to the arbitrator as aforesaid.

(2) In the case of any dispute or difference as to any matter arising under Clause 12 or the withholding by the Engineer of any certificate or the withholding of any portion of the retention money under Clause 60 to which the Contractor claims to be entitled or as to the exercise of the Engineer's power to give a certificate under Clause 63(1) the reference to the arbitrator may proceed notwithstanding that the Works shall not then be or be alleged to be complete.

The formula "any dispute or difference" includes claims in breach of contract. These must be referred direct to the engineer under this clause since he has no power to deal with them as claims (nor any power to include the sums due in certificates). If the engineer's decision is not challenged as provided, it becomes binding both on the parties and on the courts. An arbitration cannot be opened, without the parties consent, until completion. But sub-clause (2) provides a significant exception, where the dispute concerns the withholding of *any* certificate. Many disputes may, in practice, be brought within this exception.

In view of the possible binding effect of the engineer's decision under clause 66, the contractor should make it plain whether a claim for payment is being re-submitted under the appropriate clause of the contract or being submitted as a dispute. Further, the engineer should make it quite clear that he is giving a decision under clause 66, if this is the case.

The ICE Arbitration Procedure (1973) does not affect the powers of the arbitrator, and deals mainly with the steps leading up to the hearing. The existence of an arbitration agreement does not prevent either party from issuing proceedings in the courts; but see above p. 25.

Note

The above discussion has omitted any reference to the following clauses, for which reference must be made to the ICE form: 3, assignment; 6, supply of documents; 10, sureties; 16, removal of contractor's employees; 17, setting out; 18, ·bore-holes; 19, safety; 26, giving of notices; 27, Public Utilities, etc., Act; 28, patents; 29, interference with traffic; 30, avoidance of damage to highways; 32, fossils, etc.; 33, clearance of site on completion; 34 and 35, labour; 45, night and Sunday work; 50, contractor to search; 57, method of measurement; 62, urgent repairs; 64, frustration; 65, war clauses; 67, application to Scotland; 68, notices; 69 and 70, tax matters; 71, metrication; 72, special conditions; (unnumbered), contract price fluctuations clauses.

Many of the clauses printed above are printed in part only. The following parts are omitted:

Clause 1(1)(*a*)–(*c*), (*f*)–(*o*), (2), (3), (4), (5); 2(2), (4); 7(2), (3), (4); 12(4); 14(6), (7); 15(1); 20(1), (3); 36(2), (3); 38(2); 44(3), (4); 48(2), (3), (4); 49(3), (4), (5); 52(3), (4)(*a*)–(*d*); 53(1), (3), (4), (5), (7)–(11); 56(3); 58(3), (5), (6); 60(4), (5), (6), (7), (8); 63(2), (3), (4); 66(3).

The following clauses are referred to but not printed in whole or in part: Clause 4, 9, 21–25, 31, 40, 42, 46, 47, 54, 59A, 59B, 59C.

Further Reading

Keating, *Law and Practice of Building Contracts* (4th ed., 1978).
Duncan Wallace, *Building and Civil Engineering Standard Forms* (1969).
Abrahamson, *Engineering Law* (3rd ed.).

CHAPTER 12

TORT

The law of tort is mostly to be found in the common law, but there are some important statutes. It is not easy to give a satisfactory definition of a tort. It can be defined as a civil wrong independent of contract, or as liability arising from breach of a legal duty owed to persons generally. The practical consequences of the law of tort are concerned with the adjustment of losses. Where the elements of fault and damage exist, the law determines who should bear the resulting financial loss.

There is no complete body of general principles which applies to all torts in the way that all contracts are governed by the same general principles. Some jurists view torts as a series of separate civil wrongs. For more practical reasons the torts discussed in this chapter are set out in separate sections. There are, however, some principles common to all or most torts, and these are discussed by way of introduction.

There are, naturally, qualifications to the definitions given above. For example, there are torts which are actionable where there is fault, whether or not the plaintiff suffered damage, such as libel. There may also be an action for damages where there is no fault, but where liability is strict, such as under the rule in *Rylands* v. *Fletcher* (see p. 180). Further, unless an act is recognised as unlawful, no amount of intention, malice or damage can made it actionable.

This chapter covers those specific torts which are most relevant to the construction industry and to those professionally involved in it. Inevitably there are some torts not included which may be of relevance, such as trespass, and others which can be of importance in any sphere of activity, such as defamation. Mention should also be made of a group of torts which, although insignificant in terms of the number of actions brought, is of great importance in the growing field of industrial relations. These include interference with contractual relations, intimidation and conspiracy. For the law on these and other torts, reference should be made to one of the works noted at the end of the chapter.

The same act may be both a tort and a crime; and when this is so the "tortfeasor" is liable to prosecution as well as to a civil action for damages. For example, a motor accident may result in proceedings in tort between the parties, as well as in prosecution of one or more of them. Further, the same act may be both a tort and a breach of contract. It has been held that a plaintiff may obtain judgment both in contract and in tort for the same wrong. In *Batty* v. *Metropolitan Property* (1978) a developer was held liable to the purchaser of a defective house both for breach of a warranty that the house was fit for habitation and for negligence in having the house constructed on unsuitable ground. An action by the client against his architect or engineer will generally be brought in contract. However, an action against a professional person by someone other than the immediate client may be brought in tort (see p. 177). Further, it has been suggested that the duties of an architect to his client are owed both in Contract and in tort: *Esso Petroleum* v. *Mardon* (1976). This may have far-reaching consequences in regard to limitation of liability.

There are some exemptions from liability which apply to torts generally. Thus, there can be no redress for damage which is a necessary consequence of something done under statutory authority (unless the statute provides for compensation). The question in issue is then likely to be whether the damage was a necessary consequence or whether it could have been avoided. Further, where a person consents to run the risk of suffering harm, he may have no remedy for the harm he suffers. This principle used to afford a defence to employers against workmen who suffered injury due to the employer's negligence, but this is no longer the law, and in practice the defence of consent to the risk is always difficult to establish. Even where liability is strict there may be certain defences, such as that the damage was caused by the plaintiff's default, or by act of God. This latter expression, which is often found in insurance policies, means an occurrence which man has no power to foresee or prevent, such as a violent storm.

NEGLIGENCE

Negligence is by far the most important of torts, for several reasons. It forms the cause of action in the majority of cases brought in tort; its scope is very wide; and it may also be an element in liability for other torts such as nuisance. The term negligence is sometimes found in other contexts, such as in an action for breach of contract against an architect for negligent supervision. In such a case, "negligent" means without the degree of care or skill which the contract requires, which is usually a reasonable degree. In its proper tortious context, negligent means without the degree of reasonable care which is owed to persons generally. The most typical and common type of action in negligence heard in the courts is that between two or more drivers involved in a road accident. In such cases it is not infrequent for all parties to be held negligent in some degree.

Element of liability

The plaintiff in an action for negligence must show three things: that the defendant owed him a duty of care; that there was a breach of that duty; and that damage was thereby caused. Considering the first of these elements, it is necessary to decide whether in the particular circumstances one person (the defendant) owed a duty of care to the other (the plaintiff). The most commonly accepted test as to when a duty of care arises is that a duty to take reasonable care is owed to "... persons who are so closely and directly affected by my act that I ought reasonably to have them in contemplation"; *Donoghue* v. *Stevenson* (1932). This test was laid down in a case where a manufacturer of ginger beer was held to owe a duty to the ultimate consumer, who was unfortunate enough to find a decomposing snail in the empty bottle, and thereby suffered damage. The consumer could not sue in contract because the ginger beer had been purchased by a friend, and in any event the default was that of the manufacturer, not the seller.

The total list of instances where one person owed a duty of care to another is very long and is being added to continually. A few common examples are the duty owed between road users, between employer and employee and between a manufacturer and the consumer of his products. Recent cases show that a landowner may be under a duty of care to prevent the spread of fire; in the construction field, a building inspector (and through him the local authority) owes a duty of care when carrying out an inspection of foundations for compliance with the Building Regulations (see p. 200) to the ultimate purchaser of the house: *Anns* v. *London Borough of Merton* (1977). In this case the House of Lords suggested also that a builder owed a duty of care to the ultimate purchaser of a house, to comply with the Building Regulations.

There are situations where, although there would appear to be a duty of care, the law does not recognise its existence. A vendor or lessor of premises is generally not liable in negligence to the purchaser or lessee for a defect in the premises at the time of sale or letting. But a builder may be liable. Thus, where a concrete canopy over the front door of a house fell upon and injured one of the occupants due to the builder's negligent work, the builder was held liable: *Sharpe* v. *Sweeting* (1963), although the landlord could not be sued. Under the Defective Premises Act 1972 a person taking on work in connection with the provision of a dwelling (whether by erection or conversion) will generally become liable for not doing the work in a proper manner. The duty applies both to builders and to professional persons, including architects, and is owed to the first owner and to any other person who acquires an interest in the dwelling. It was suggested in *Dutton* v. *Bognor Regis U.D.C.* (1971) that a builder could be liable in tort for defective building work. These developments, and others in the field of contract (see p. 76) mean that purchasers and lessors of houses are now far from having no redress for defective work to the house.

There is generally no liability in tort for purely economic loss without attendant physical damage (but see below), and only the person having a proprietary or possessory right to property can sue for damage to it. Thus, where a lorry negligently driven knocked down a fire-hydrant and caused the water supply to be cut off to the plaintiff's factory, the factory owner could not recover his loss of production because this was purely economic. There had been no physical damage to any property belonging to the plaintiff: *Electrochrome* v. *Welsh Plastics* (1968). However, it was held in *Dutton's* case, above, that cracks in the structure of a house constituted sufficient physical damage to permit an action in tort against a negligent builder.

Finally, there is normally no duty to act positively for another's benefit, so that if a man is drowning an onlooker is under no duty to rescue him. But if someone does attempt a rescue, and is so careless as to cause some injury, the rescuer may then be liable in negligence.

If a duty of care exists, it is then necessary to establish a breach of that duty. The standard of care required is that of a "reasonable man." This is a legal abstraction which represents a person who weighs up the circumstances, considers the characteristics of the persons endangered, takes greater care where there is greater danger, and never loses his temper. The duty is to guard against probabilities, not bare possibilities. But where the risk is greater *e.g.* where children are involved, reasonable possibilities must be guarded against. The required standard of care thus depends on the circumstances, but in any particular case there is one appropriate standard below which a person is legally negligent. The term "gross negligence" is sometimes used, but the adjective has no legal significance since there is only one appropriate standard of care, any breach of which, gross or slight, incurs liability in law.

Finally, the injury to the plaintiff must have been caused by the defendant's act, and the damage must not be too remote (see p. 184). If the plaintiff succeeds in his action in negligence but the loss was caused partly by his own default, the court will reduce the damages recovered in proportion to his share of responsibility. This principle is known as contributory negligence, but it applies also to breaches of statutory duty, such as the employer's duty under the Construction Regulations (see p. 207).

NEGLIGENT MISSTATEMENT

The rule excluding liability for purely economic loss formerly meant that professional men could not usually be sued for negligent statements by anyone other than their immediate client, whose right of action was in contract. However, the law underwent a radical development when, in 1963, the House of Lords held that a bank could be liable for negligent misstatement to a person who was not a client but who relied upon their statement. The bank was in fact protected because the information was, in that case, given "without liability": *Hedley Byrne* v. *Heller*. Thus professional men such as architects and engineers may now be liable to persons other than their employers who suffer loss, whether financial or otherwise, through reliance upon their statements. This area of law was further developed in the case of *Esso Petroleum* v. *Mardon* (1976). M had taken a lease of a garage after relying on the plaintiff's statements as to the likely return from the site. The statements were over-optimistic; M lost money on the venture. The Court of Appeal held that M could sue on the pre-contract statements, despite the existence of a contract between the same parties. The result of this case may be that professional persons such as architects can be liable to their clients in tort as well as contract.

While a duty of care for negligent acts can be owed to the whole world, liability for negligent words must necessarily be more limited. The full effect of the above developments in the law is as yet uncertain because there are few decided cases. But liability probably arises only where the plaintiff relied on the special skill and judgment of the defendant, who knew or ought to have known of this reliance. Liability will normally arise only in a business or professional transaction, but a person may be liable for giving advice which he is not qualified to give.

It is possible to exclude liability by a disclaimer of responsibility, as was done in the *Hedley Byrne* case, but this will only be effective if it is brought to the notice of the person who relies on the statement. Most professional persons protect themselves through indemnity insurance.

The liability discussed above is that arising in tort. An architect or engineer owes his primary duty to the client in contract. This is considered in Chapter 7 (see pp. 95–100). However the degree of care required in particular circumstances will often be the same whether arising in tort or under contract.

OTHER ASPECTS OF NEGLIGENCE

Liability of occupiers

Under the Occupiers' Liability Act 1957 an occupier of premises owes a duty of care to all visitors lawfully on the premises. Unless the occupier can and does modify or exclude his obligations by agreement, he owes to any visitor a duty to take reasonable care so that the visitor will be reasonably safe in using the premises for the purposes for which he is permitted to be there. The occupier may escape liability by giving adequate warning of existing dangers, and he may also expect persons such as workmen entering to carry out a job to guard against the special dangers of their trade. Thus, where two chimney sweeps were warned of the danger of fumes and, disregarding the warning, were asphyxiated, the occupier was not liable: *Roles* v. *Nathan* (1963). An occupier is not liable for the faulty work of an independent contractor (see p. 182) unless he is himself in some way to blame. An occupier may avoid such liability if he has taken reasonable steps to ensure that the contractor was competent and the work properly done.

The statute applies to those who occupy land and buildings (including building and construction sites) and any fixed or movable structure such as a vehicle, vessel, lift or scaffolding. An "occupier" need not be the owner of the premises but is merely a person having some degree of control. There may therefore be more than one occupier of the same premises. On a construction site, the contractor or the employer may be an occupier. In *A.M.F.* v. *Magnet Bowling* (1968) both the general contractor and the employer were held to be occupiers with respect to a specialist direct contractor. A subcontractor may also be an occupier of the whole or part of the site.

The Occupiers' Liability Act does not provide any protection for trespassers, and for many years the courts had held that, in general, an occupier owed no duty to a trespasser other than to refrain from causing intentional harm or acting recklessly. The House of Lords reconsidered the law on liability to trespassers in 1972 when it held that a duty of care arises when the occupier knows that a trespasser is likely to come onto his land and knows also of an existing danger. In *Herrington* v. *British Railways Board* (1972), a section of fence bordering onto a railway line was dilapidated, and through it people took a short cut across the line. The Board had knowledge of the state of the fence but did not repair it. A six-year-old girl trespassed on the line and was injured. It was held that there was a duty of care and the Board were in breach of that duty.

It was laid down in *Herrington's* case that while there is no duty to exclude trespassers, nor to make land safe for them, the occupier owes to a trespasser a duty to take such steps as common sense or common humanity dictate, and which are reasonably practicable to the occupier, to reduce or avert the danger. The conditions which imposed liability in this case are frequently found on building and construction sites, so that where there is a likelihood of trespassers, those in occupation must take steps to exclude them, or otherwise to mitigate the risk of injury to trespassers.

The Unfair Contract Terms Act 1977 provides that liability under the occupier's liability Act cannot be excluded by any contract term or notice, in respect of death or personal injury resulting from negligence; and in respect of other loss, liability can be excluded or restricted only so far as is fair and reasonable (see above p. 48). These restrictions apply only to an occupier in the course of business.

Employers' liability

An employer may be liable for injury caused to his employee in three ways. First, if the injury is caused by the negligence of a fellow employee acting in the course of his employment (see p. 182); secondly, if it is caused by the employer's breach of a statutory duty (see p. 207); and thirdly, if it is caused by the employer's negligence. The third possibility is discussed here.

There is no doubt that an employer owes his employees a duty of care; the problem for the common law has been to trace its extent. It has been defined as a threefold duty: "the provision of a competent staff of men, adequate material, and a proper system and effective supervision": *Wilsons* v. *English* (1937). However, the duty can be viewed as a single duty to take reasonable care for the safety of employees in all the circumstances. Thus the duty is not absolute, and an employer is only liable for injury caused by his failure to take sufficient care.

The standard of care that is required varies with the circumstances so that, *e.g.*, where potentially dangerous plant is being used the employer may have to provide safety devices or protective equipment. The employer remains liable for breach of his duty even though he may delegate its performance. Where work is done on another person's premises, the employer's duty may be lower, although he must still use reasonable care. Thus, where a window cleaner was instructed to leave windows which could not safely be cleaned, and was injured as a result of disregarding the instruction, it was held that the employer had taken reasonable care and was not liable: *Wilson* v. *Tyneside* (1958). Where injury is caused by defective equipment the employer may be liable even though the defect is attributable to someone else, such as the manufacturer: Employer's Liability (Defective Equipment) Act 1969.

In addition to the duties laid on the employer, the employee must show regard for his own safety, and if he is injured as a result of his own negligence this may reduce or extinguish the employer's liability. The employee also owes the employer a duty to exercise reasonable skill and care at his work, and may be liable to his employer for causing injury in breach of this duty.

Rylands v. Fletcher liability

When a person keeps on his land some potentially dangerous object or carries on a dangerous operation the ordinary law of negligence may not afford adequate protection. Instead of stretching the duty of care to its limit, the common law has set apart certain things for which liability is strict, without regard to lack of care. A person who deals in such things does to at his peril.

This special liability is known by the name of the celebrated case in which it was first formulated. In *Rylands* v. *Fletcher* (1860) the defendant had a reservoir built on his land by reputable engineers and with the necessary permission. But when the reservoir was filled, the water escaped down through a disused mine shaft and flooded the plaintiff's coal mines on adjoining land. Although the defendant's actions were without any fault, he was held liable for the plaintiff's loss. In addition to reservoirs, strict liability has been attached to colliery spoil heaps, inflammable goods, and vibrations from pile driving. Thus, where a contractor drove a large number of piles into soil and, due to the vibrations produced, caused damage to an old house belonging to the plaintiff, the contractor was held liable, without proof of negligence, *Hoare* v. *McAlpine* (1923). Although vibrations may also constitute a nuisance (see below) it may be a defence to nuisance that the property damaged was unusually frail. Liability in *Rylands* v. *Fletcher* is, however, strict.

To incur liability the object or operation must be non-natural, so that while there is strict liability for a reservoir, the owner of a natural lake can be liable only under the ordinary principles of tort, *e.g.* in negligence or nuisance. To establish strict liability there must also be an "escape" from the plaintiff's land which causes the damage, such as a slide of material from a spoil heap.

Thus, where an explosion in a munitions factory injured a person on the premises there was no such strict liability since the dangerous thing had not escaped from the defendant's land: *Read* v. *Lyons* (1946). Although *Rylands* v. *Fletcher* liability is strict, it is not absolute. The defendant may escape liability if (principally) the escape was due to the plaintiff's default or due to an act of God. However, where these defences preclude strict liability, there may still be liability for ordinary negligence or nuisance, or for other torts.

Nuisance

Private nuisance may be defined as an unlawful interference with the use or enjoyment of another person's land. The interference may result in damage to property, *e.g.* by flooding or vibrations, or it may be only an annoyance, such as excessive noise or dust. There must be a substantial interference. A nuisance is often a continuing state of affairs, although an isolated happening may support an action in nuisance. Neighbours must exercise some give and take, but deliberate acts intended to annoy neighbours can create an actionable nuisance. Persons who live in noisy or industrial neighbourhoods must usually put up with the attendant discomforts, although actual damage to property will be actionable.

Usually the only person who can sue for nuisance is the occupier of the land, although other persons may be able to sue on the same facts, *e.g.* in negligence. The person liable is usually the occupier of the land or premises where the nuisance exists, but the person who created the nuisance may be liable. Thus, prima facie a building or engineering contractor will be liable for interference with adjoining land caused by the construction operations, but the employer may also be liable (see p. 182).

Unlike negligence, liability for nuisance does not depend primarily on the standard of conduct of the defendant. Thus, it is not necessarily a defence to nuisance that reasonable care was taken to avoid it. But in the context of building and construction operations, those carrying out such work are under a duty to take proper precautions to see that nuisance is reduced to a minimum. Thus, where no steps were taken by a demolition contractor to minimise noise and dust near to the plaintiff's hotel, an actionable nuisance was created for which the employer was liable: *Andrea* v. *Selfridge* (1938). Under the Control of Pollution Act 1974 a local authority has powers to control noise on construction sites. They may serve a notice restricting the use of specified plant, restricting hours of work and limiting the level of noise. The act also permits the contractor to obtain the prior consent of the authority to the methods of work proposed (sections 60, 61).

Other nuisances

In addition to interference with land, a nuisance may be committed by interference with certain rights over land, such as a right of support. There is a natural right of support for unweighted land, and a nuisance is committed if subsidence is caused either by removing the lateral support by excavation, or by undermining. Generally it is unimportant how the withdrawal of support occurs, but as an important exception there is no liability for causing subsidence by withdrawal of subterranean percolating water. Thus, where pumping was carried out to keep excavations dry and resulted in lowering of the water table and settlement of buildings on adjacant land, the adjoining owner had no redress: *Langbrook* v. *Surrey C.C.* (1969). The right of support for a building, as opposed to the land on which it stands, is not a natural right and must be acquired as an easement by grant or by useage (see p. 191). Once acquired, the right is usually a right of support both from adjacent land and from adjoining buildings. Other rights which may give rise to an action in nuisance for interference include rights of light and air, water rights and rights of way.

Where an interference is caused to a wider group of persons than the occupier of neighbouring land, such conduct may constitute a public nuisance. This is primarily a crime, but a civil action may be brought in respect of a public nuisance by an individual who has suffered special damage different from that suffered by the public at large. Common examples of public nuisance are obstruction of the highway, and creating dangers upon or near the highway.

VICARIOUS LIABILITY

Vicarious liability in this context means liability for the torts of others. In the construction industry this may arise in two ways. First, the employer may be liable for the torts of the contractor or the contractor may be liable for the torts of his sub-contractors; secondly, any of the parties involved in the work may be liable for the torts of their own individual employees.

As to the first type of vicarious liability, it is a general rule that a person is not liable for torts committed by his independent contractors. Thus, where the negligence of a sub-contractor's workman caused a tool to fall and injure the plaintiff, the main contractor was not liable: *Padbury* v. *Holliday & Greenwood* (1912). However, there are substantial exceptions to the general rule, whereby the employer may be liable for the torts of his contractor. The circumstances in which such liability may arise include: where the liability is strict, such as under the rule in *Rylands* v. *Fletcher*; where work involves danger on or near a highway; and where work will involve danger to other property unless proper care is taken (see above). Even where prima facie the employer is not responsible he may still be liable for his own negligence in employing an incompetent contractor or for failing to give adequate directions to avoid damage to another. The employer will also be liable under the law of agency if he authorises or ratifies his contractor's unlawful act.

Considering the second head of liability, as a general rule a master is vicariously liable for the unauthorised tort of his servant if it is committed within the course of his employment. The master is, of course, liable for torts which he authorises or ratifies. The terms "master" and "servant" have acquired a special meaning in law which is rather wider than employer and employee. A precise definition is difficult to give; but a servant may be defined as a person employed to carry out work not as an independent contractor. The work of the servant is an integral part of the master's business, while an independent contractor undertakes only to produce a given result. The distinction can be of great importance since, as discussed above, the employer is generally not liable for the torts of his independent contractor. Persons are frequently found on construction sites who are technically self-employed, but who may be difficult to categorise as servants or independent contractors.

In addition to deciding who is a servant, it may be necessary to decide who is the master, for example, where a servant is hired by his employer to another employer. It is presumed that the original employer remains liable as the master, unless the right to control the way in which the work was done passes to the temporary employer. Thus, where an employer hired a crane together with its driver to carry out unloading work and the hirer supervised the work but not the management of the crane, the original employer was held to be responsible for the driver's negligence: *Mersey Docks* v. *Coggins & Griffiths* (1947).

The master will be liable for the tort of his servant only if the tort is committed during the course of his employment; that is, it must be a wrongful way of doing that which he is employed to do. Thus, an employer will be liable if the employee carries out his duties negligently or fraudulently. The employer may even be liable if the employee does something which he has expressly been forbidden to do, provided it is within the scape of his employment. But where a driver, employed on a building site to carry only fellow-employees, carried an employee of another firm on the site, this was held to be an act which he was not employed to perform at all. The employer was therefore not liable for the driver's negligence: *Conway* v. *Wimpey* (1951).

Whether or not the master is liable, the servant is generally liable for his own tort and may be sued jointly with the master, or separately. Similarly where an employer is liable for his independent contractor, the contractor may also be sued jointly or separately. The practical importance to a plaintiff of vicarious liability is that one defendant may have more money than another. The damages may only be recovered once, but it is important to ensure that those sued are able to satisfy a judgment.

REMEDIES AND LIMITATION

The remedy claimed in most tort actions is damages. The successful plaintiff in an action for damages will generally be awarded a sum which is intended to compensate for the real loss suffered. The sum awarded must take into account future loss since usually only one action may be brought. Damages may be proportionally reduced if contributory negligence is found against the plaintiff. In certain extreme cases the damages recovered may vary greatly from the actual loss. Thus, in an action where the plaintiff has succeeded in law, the law court may show its disapproval of his conduct by awarding contemptuous damages of perhaps 1p and may deprive the plaintiff of his costs. At the other end of the scale the court may, in very limited circumstances, show its disapproval of the defendant's conduct by awarding exemplary damages to penalise the defendant.

Once liability is established, the question may arise whether the damage claimed is too remote to be recoverable. The general test is that compensation may be recovered for damage which is of a reasonably foreseeable kind. If this is so it does not matter if damage occurred in an unforeseeable manner or to an unforeseeable extent; the defendant will be liable for the whole loss. The rules of remoteness in contract and in tort are not identical. The tortfeasor is liable for loss which is foreseeable as the possible result of his conduct and therefore may bear a heavier burden than the contract breaker, who is liable only for the probable result of his actions (see p. 58).

A defendant sued in tort may be at an advantage over one sued in contract where there are other defendants potentially responsible for the same loss. The court has power under the Law Reform (Married Women and Tortfeasors) Act 1935 to apportion liability between defendants liable for the same damage. This applies whether or not the other persons liable have been sued by the plaintiff. Thus, for example, a builder sued in negligence by the subsequent owner of a house may recover a contribution from the negligent architect. Conversely, in contract there is no such right. The plaintiff may choose which of the persons potentially liable he will sue. If two or more are sued for the same loss the plaintiff may recover judgment for the full loss from each of the defendants, and may then decide against whom to enforce the judgment. There is no right of contribution between several contract breakers.

An alternative remedy to damages, which may be appropriate particularly in cases of nuisance, is an injunction, either to restrain the defendant from doing some act or to compel the performance of an act. An injunction is an equitable remedy and therefore lies in the court's discretion. It will usually be refused where damages would be an adequate remedy, or where to grant it would be in vain. One very valuable feature of this remedy is the power of the courts to issue an interlocutory injunction (until trial) in a proper case. Thus, a temporary relief may sometimes be obtained within days or even hours of a cause of complaint arising. The power to grant an injunction extends to a threatened but unperformed act.

A final consideration in any action must be the period during which the action may be brought, as provided by the Limitation Acts. Generally, no action in tort may be commenced after the expiration of six years from the date on which the cause of action arose. However, there are further limitations, notably that actions in respect of personal injury arising from negligence, nuisance or breach of statutory duty must usually be brought within three years.

The general rule in tort is that the cause of action arises when damage is suffered. In this respect tort differs materially from contract. If a builder negligently erects a chimney stack, a cause of action in contract arises in favour of the employer when the work is done, or when the builder purports to finish it. If the work remains in place and no complaint is made, the right of action will be lost after six years. If, after 10 years, the chimney falls, to injure a passer-by, a right of action in tort then immediately vests in the injured person. In respect of a claim against a local authority for negligent inspection of foundations, the House of Lords held in *Anns* v. *London Borough of Merton* (1977) that the right of action in respect of consequent damage to the structure of the house would not arise until the damage was apparent.

INTERNATIONAL CASES

In Chapter 2 (see p. 20) the effect of a foreign element upon the procedure in a case was considered. In this section it is assumed that the English courts are proceeding to hear a case in tort containing a foreign element. The question then arising is which national law should the court apply.

If a tort is committed in England by or to a foreign party, then any action brought here is tried by English law as an ordinary domestic case. The conflict of law arises only where torts are committed abroad. Despite acceptance in other common law countries, the concept of a "proper law" of tort is not accepted in English courts (see p. 60).

The rule as to which law applies in a tort action is a compromise between the law of the place of commission and English law. The general rule is that in order to found a suit in England for a tort committed abroad, it must be actionable under English law and also actionable as a civil wrong at the place of commission. The defendant's conduct is therefore to be judged by both laws. It seems that such matters as the amount of damages claimable may be determined by English law, while the law of the place of commission may affect, for example, what defences are available to the defendant.

An incidental problem may be to decide where a tort is committed. This may arise, for example, if a fire is negligently started in England and spreads across the border to do damage in Scotland. Although there are at least two possible views on this point, the English rule is generally that a tort is committed where the wrongful act takes place; in this example, in England.

Further Reading

Salmond on Torts (17th ed.), Heuston.
Winfield and Jolowicz on Tort (10th ed.), Jolowicz.
Baker, *Torts* (2nd ed., 1976), (Concise College Texts).

CHAPTER 13

LAW OF PROPERTY

IN England the law relating to land has always been different and distinct from law relating to other property. There are many reasons for this. Perhaps the most obvious is that a piece of land is indestructible and unique; no other land is quite the same. On a practical level, it is common for two or more persons to hold simultaneously different interests in the same land, and this is one of the reasons why a sale of land is more complicated and lengthy than a sale of other property.

Although the expression "land owner" is often encountered it requires some qualification in legal terms. It is not possible to "own" land in the absolute way that other property (such as a motor car) may be owned. Instead, the law speaks of owning an estate or interest in land, which gives the owner certain rights over that land. The largest estate which may be owned is called a fee simple absolute in possession. This is what is commonly known as a "freehold" and for convenience it is so called in this section, although in legal terms an estate lasting only for the life of the holder may be a type of freehold.

Another type of estate in land is a tenancy. This may be created out of the estate of the freeholder or of a superior tenant. The word "tenancy" refers to a right to possession of land for a limited period. This may be for a fixed term of years (when the tenancy must normally be created by a lease) but also includes periodic tenancies such as a weekly or quarterly tenancy. In practice a building owner is likely to be concerned only with long tenancies created by lease.

Interests in land generally indicate something less than an estate; they may be of many kinds. Two of the most important are easements and restrictive covenants, and these are mentioned further below. Another very common interest in land is a mortgage, where the land is used as a security.

Two further provisions may illustrate the special legal status of land. First, an infant (*i.e.* a person under 18 years) cannot own a freehold in land. Secondly, a contract for the sale of land or any interest in land is unenforceable unless evidenced in writing and signed by or on behalf of the party to be charged (Law of Property Act 1925 s. 40).

Throughout its history land law has been profoundly affected by the principles of Equity (see p. 7). The result is that interests in land are for some purposes classified as being either legal or equitable. The practical importance of this distinction is that a legal interest attaches to the land itself and is enforceable against any person. An equitable interest binds only certain persons, and is not enforceable against a bona fide purchaser of the land who has no notice (actual or constructive) of such interest. An equitable interest is therefore less secure. An example of an equitable interest is an agreement for a lease. Practically, this is as good as an actual lease but if another person purchases the land without notice of the agreement, it becomes unenforceable against that person.

Rights of the Owner or Occupier of Land

When a person wishes to build on land there are many factors to be considered. He must obtain a sufficient interest to give him a right of possession; he must consider what restrictions there are as to what may be done with the land; he will also wish to know who is entitled to ownership or use of things on or in the land. These points are considered below. Another factor, which may be of great importance, is the question of rights which other persons hold concurrently over the land. Such rights are considered in the following section.

Types of possession

A right of possession of land is usually obtained by the building developer purchasing the freehold or a tenancy. Where there are existing tenants of the land, whether for residential purposes, or for business, agricultural, or other purposes, they will usually have some statutory protection against eviction even when the fixed term of the tenancy has expired. However, in regard to business tenancies specific provision is made to permit a lessor to gain possession in order to re-develop the site. Under the Landlord and Tenant Act 1954 a business tenant is entitled, at the end of his tenancy, to apply to the court for the grant of a new tenancy. But the application is to be refused if the landlord intends to demolish or re-construct the premises or to carry out substantial work of reconstruction (section 30(1)). This right is available to the landlord only at the end of the tenancy. If possession cannot be obtained by lawfully dispossessing a sitting tenant, possession may be obtained by negotiating an assignment of his tenancy, or a sub-tenancy from the tenant. In the first case the original tenant is supplanted; in the second he becomes an intermediate landlord.

A right to occupation of land which is not sufficient to create a true tenancy is said to create a licence. This is essentially a right to do some act which would otherwise be a trespass. Examples of the operation of licences are a person occupying a cinema seat or an hotel room, and a contractor in possession of a building site. Essentially a licence is a personal arrangement between grantor and grantee which does not bind third parties. There may, however, be circumstances where an interest in the land affecting third parties is created. Thus, where a man allowed his son to build a bungalow on his (the father's) land and then died leaving the land to others, it was held that the son should be allowed to remain in the bungalow as long as he desired: *Inwards* v. *Baker* (1965). It is not to be recommended, however, that building developers should proceed upon such a tenuous interest in the land.

A gratuitous licence merely to enter land may be revoked at any time; while a licence coupled with an interest in the property (such as a right to dig gravel) cannot be revoked. A more usual type of licence in business transactions is one given under a contract. Such a licence will be regarded as part of the contract creating it and its revocation in breach of contract may in some circumstances be resisted by injunction. In a recent case in the Chancery Division, a contractor's employment under a building contract had been terminated by the employer, but the contractor, contending the termination was invalid, refused to leave the site. The employer claimed an injunction to remove him. The injunction was refused; the employer was held to be under an implied obligation not to revoke the contractor's licence except in accordance with the contract: *Hounslow L.B.C.* v. *Twickenham* (1971). This case, however, has been criticised and may not be followed, should similar circumstances arise.

Rights over the land

The question of what the owner or occupier is entitled to do with the land depends upon many factors. It is subject to numerous statutory provisions, such as the Housing Acts and Public Health Acts. Building work itself is closely controlled by regulations and by-laws (see Chapter 14). The occupier of land may become liable to his neighbours in tort, for example by committing a nuisance (see p. 181). Perhaps the most fundamental restriction upon the user of land arises through statutory planning controls (see below). Rather than to say that land is owned subject to restrictions, it is probably more accurate to say that land is held for the benefit both of the owner or occupier and of the community.

As to ownership of things on or in the land (as opposed to "ownership" of the space occupied by the land), it is presumed that the owner of the freehold owns everything upon or below the land. He is generally entitled to everything which is attached to the land. Such items are commonly called fixtures (as opposed to mere fittings) and they will belong, *e.g.* to the freeholder as against a tenant. The question of what attachment is sufficient to make an object a fixture is a matter of degree and purpose. Thus a corrugated iron building bolted to, but not embedded in, a concrete floor was held not to be a fixture although the concrete floor was a fixture: *Webb* v. *Bevis* (1940). Building materials will become the property of the freeholder as soon as they are attached to the land or to the permanent works, whether paid for by the employer or not. As between landlord and tenant there are certain exceptions to the rule, which relate particularly to trade and agricultural fixtures.

Water

A land owner who borders a watercourse is known as a "riparian owner" and he normally owns the land up to the middle of the stream. At common law the riparian owner is entitled to the use of flowing water for ordinary purposes such as domestic use. He may also use the water for an extraordinary purpose such as manufacturing or irrigation, provided the water is returned in the same volume and character to the stream. However, there are very stringent statutory controls on the right to abstract water from any source of supply, whether it be a watercourse or a well or bore-hole, for other than domestic purposes: see Water Resources Act 1963 Part IV.

Another important question is what persons are entitled to put into water. This is also strictly controlled by statute: see Control of Pollution Act 1974 Part II, re-enacting earlier statutes. Under this Act it is an offence, punishable by fines or imprisonment, to cause or knowingly to permit pollution of a river or coastal waters. Where the offender is a corporate body an officer of that body (such as a director or manager) may also be liable. In one case a manufacturer was held liable for causing pollution of a river, even though he had taken elaborate precautions to prevent it and accidental spillage occurred only because of a defect in the apparatus: *Alphacell Ltd.* v. *Woodward* (1972).

RIGHTS OVER LAND OF OTHERS

Of the many types of interest over land belonging to or in the possession of other persons, the most important so far as a building developer is concerned are easements and restrictive covenants. In this context the building developer is seen as the "other person" over whose land rights exist which may affect its use or development. The short account given below describes the nature of these interests; for the much wider topic of their creation, transmission and extinguishment, reference should be made to one of the standard works on the subject.

An *easement* is a right which allows the holder to use, or restrict the use of, the land of another person in some way. Common examples are private rights of way, rights of light and rights of support. An easement can exist only in relation to other land which is nearby, which is said to "benefit" from the easement. A "quasi-easement" (which is referred to in clause 22 of the ICE conditions) is a term used to describe a habitual right exercised by a person over a part of his own land, which would be an easement if the two parts were in different occupation; *e.g.* a right of support between adjoining buildings. A quasi-easement may become a real easement upon a sale of one or both parts of the land.

There are a number of other rights which are similar to, but which do not comprise easements. For example, a profit (or profit à prendre) is a right to take something from the land of another person, such as grass or sand; a licence is a private right to go upon another's land (see p. 189). Either of these rights may exist without the holder owning land which is benefited. An easement of support relates only to a building and is distinct from the natural right to have unweighted land supported by adjoining land (see p. 182).

A contractual provision which seeks to constrain the way in which the holder of land may use it is termed a *restrictive covenant*. An example of the type of covenant which might be relevant to a building developer is one not to build on certain land. As between the original parties a covenant is binding; *e.g.* when the covenantee and convenantor are respectively landlord and tenant. It will also be binding on successors if it constitutes an easement (see above). Otherwise, only in limited circumstances will a restrictive covenant be enforceable by and against successors in title. A plaintiff who wishes to enforce a restrictive covenant must show that he has acquired what is known as the "benefit" of the covenant and that the defendant has acquired the "burden".

An example of the operation of restrictive covenants occurs where an estate is laid out in lots to be sold or leased for building and each purchaser or lessee agrees to restrictive covenants. It is necessary that the area be clearly defined and that restrictions are

imposed by the common vendor or lessor which are consistent with
the general scheme of the development. The covenants must be for
the benefit of all the lots and the sale or leasing must be trans-
acted with this intention. Provided these conditions are satisfied, the
covenants will be enforceable by and against the owners or lessees
for the time being of any plot on the estate. The covenants therefore constitute a local law for the estate.

PLANNING LAW

Planning law is substantially a creature of the twentieth century.
The first attempts at systematic town planning were introduced
in 1909, and since then the scope and complexity of planning law
have widened enormously. The destruction brought about by the
second world war with its consequent opportunities for replanning
has been responsible for much of this development. The principal
enactment is now the Town and Country Planning Act 1971 which
consolidates, with amendments, most of the previous statute law
relating to planning. There are also many other important Acts
together with regulations, rules and orders made under statutory
powers.

The practical effect of modern planning law is that the owner's
rights to use his land are to a large extent subrogated to the good
of the community. In general, a land owner has no right to use
his land for any purpose other than its present use unless he obtains
permission. Further, he may be dispossessed of even its present use
by authorities exercising powers of compulsory acquisition. The
economic importance of planning law to the individual is demon-
strated by the direct effect which planning consent has upon the
value of land.

In origin, planning law is entirely statutory, that is to say, it is
all contained in Acts of Parliament and the delegated legislation
made under the Acts. Most statutes are periodically considered and
interpreted by the courts and this usually makes them easier to
understand. But planning law is brought before the courts on com-
paratively rare occasions. The usual procedure is that planning
decisions are made initially in a purely administrative way, by the
local authority or government department. An appeal is usually
allowed to the Minister, and his function is sometimes described as
quasi-judicial. But in either case the decision is not of legal rights
(as in the case of a decision in the courts) but of the proper administration of planning policy. Thus, in a case which arose under the
New Towns Act 1946, the Minister stated publicly that Stevenage

would be the first new town. He made a draft order to this effect
and an inquiry was held into objections. The Minister then confirmed his order. The court held that there was no judicial duty
upon the Minister, but only a duty to consider the objections:
Franklin v. *Minister of Town and Country Planning* (1948). In this
sense the Minister is the judge in his own cause.

Following the Minister's decision there may be a limited right of
appeal to the courts against the decision, as in the *Franklin* case.
It is only through such appeals that case law precedent is created.
Administrative decisions may serve as guides, for example, to enable
an applicant to assess whether or not planning permission may be
granted, but they are not binding in any way.

Planning authorities and their functions

The administration of planning law at local level is carried out
by the local planning authority. This body will be either a county
council or a district council. The G.L.C. is the local planning
authority for Greater London as a whole but each individual London
Borough Council has very considerable powers within the borough.
The authority responsible for central administration is referred to in
the Acts as the Secretary of State.

In addition to these authorities, there are other bodies which have
specific functions in relation to planning administration. In particular, the Lands Tribunal, among its various functions, has powers
to settle disputes over the valuation of land arising out of planning
decisions.

A primary creative duty of the planning authority is periodically
to produce plans for future development. The development plan is
comprised of two parts. First, the structure plan formulates policy
and general proposals for development and use of land, relating this
to relevant proposals for neighbouring areas. The structure plan is
prepared by the county planning authority, and must indicate any
"action areas" which are selected for imminent development.
Secondly, local plans may be prepared by district planning authorities
to show development proposals in any part of the area. Local plans
must be provided for action areas, but different plans may cover the
same area for different purposes. Both the structure plan and local
plans must be given adequate publicity and inquiries may be held.
The structure plan must be approved by the Secretary of State;
and a local plan must be adopted by the local planning authority,
but the Secretary of State may direct that his approval is required.

The two-tier arrangement of the development plan was introduced
by The Town and Country Planning Act 1968. The 1971 Act con-

tains transitional provisions for the change-over to the new system. The 1968 Act also introduced a wider public involvement in the preparation of structure and local plans, which is continued in the 1971 Act.

The ultimate objective of a planning authority is to see that its development is carried out. Where this can be achieved by planning restrictions the problem is reduced to one of enforcement, but positive development may require more than mere control. One of the most important powers of local authorities in this respect is the power to acquire land compulsorily for planning purposes, with the authorisation of the Secretary of State. The measure of compensation which is payable upon compulsory acquisition is basically the market value, but subject to some statutory modifications. There are also provisions for additional compensation for such matters as disturbance and severance of lands. Local authorities may compulsorily acquire land within their own areas and also in other areas. They may also acquire land by agreement, when the consent of the Secretary of State is generally not required.

Where land has been acquired or appropriated by a local authority for planning purposes, the local authority itself may carry out building or work upon the land; or instead of carrying out development itself the authority may make arrangements with an authorised association to carry out such operations. Alternatively the local authority may dispose of land so as to secure the use or development of the land needed for the proper planning of the area. This latter method has been used to secure the redevelopment of war-damaged land. Where land which was acquired compulsorily is to be disposed of the previous occupants must, so far as is practicable, be afforded an opportunity to return to their land.

Requirement of planning consent

In general any development of land requires a formal application for planning consent to be made to the local planning authority and the development may not be carried out unless such consent is granted. "Development" is defined by the Town and Country Planning Act 1971 as meaning *the carrying out of building, engineering, mining or other operations in, on, over or under land, or the making of any material change in the use of any buildings or other land* (section 22). The Act contains further definitions of many of its terms, such as "building," "land" and "use" (section 290). There are, however, some classes of exceptions under which things may be done to or with land without the necessity of obtaining planning consent.

The first exception is that no planning permission is required if the project is not within the meaning of "development." The Act states that certain operations or uses of land are not to be taken to involve development. These include most works which do not materially affect the external appearance of a building, and highway maintenance. But the division of a dwelling-house into two or more separate units requires planning permission, as does also the extension of a refuse tip, in area or in height, so as to exceed the level of adjoining land (section 22).

Where land is being used for a purpose specified in an order (the Town and Country Planning (Use Classes) Order 1972), the change to another use of the same class does not constitute development. Thus, the change from a grocery shop to a tobacconist does not require planning permission; but the change to a fried fish shop or to an office is a development and requires permission. If there is uncertainty as to whether any project constitutes a development within the meaning of the Act, it may be resolved by application to the local planning authority (section 53) with an appeal to the Secretary of State and a further appeal to the High Court.

Secondly, the Secretary of State has power to make orders known as development orders which may permit either a particular development or some class of development. An order may itself grant planning permission or provide for permission to be granted by the local planning authority. An order may be limited in its area of application and may be subject to conditions. The general order currently applicable to all land in England and Wales is the Town and Country Planning General Development Order 1977. This sets out classes of permitted development for which the order itself constitutes planning permission. The classes include limited additions to a house, fences and walls of limited size, and specified classes of development by local authorities and statutory undertakers. There are also local development orders.

The third exception is that planning permission is not required in some specified cases relating to the resumption of a former use of land, for example, after the expiry of planning permission granted for a limited period (section 23). A fourth exception applies to local authorities and statutory undertakers. Where authorisation is required from a government department for a development, the department may itself grant deemed planning permission (section 40).

Applications for planning consent

If a project requires planning permission to be obtained then the usual course is to make application to the local planning authority. An application must be made in such a manner as is prescribed by regulations, and must be accompanied by plans and other particulars of the project. In some cases the applicant is required to certify that he has given certain notices; for example, where the applicant is not the freeholder or leaseholder of all the land in question, he must take steps to notify the owner of the land of the application. Also, applications relating to certain classes of development must arrange for the local advertisement of the application (section 26–28).

An application may be made for "outline planning permission," in accordance with the provisions of a development order (section 42). Such permission will be subject to subsequent approval of "reserved matters" not particularised in the application. Outline planning permission will only be granted subject to application for approval of reserved matters, and commencement of the development, being made within specified periods. The procedure for outline planning applications may be useful for a prospective developer who does not own the land in question.

The local planning authority must generally give its decision within two months of an application for planning permission. In coming to a decision the authority must have regard to the development plan, and to other material matters. There are provisions requiring various persons and bodies to be consulted. Where applications require local advertisement, the planning authority must take into account representations received. Where the applicant is not the freeholder or leaseholder the representations of owners of the land must be considered (section 29).

Planning permission may be granted or refused or granted subject to conditions, and unless it is granted unconditionally reasons must be given for the decision. The conditions imposed may be permanent or of limited duration, although they must relate to the development. For example, a condition that payment should be made to the local authority does not relate to the development, and is invalid. The planning permission may itself be granted for a limited period, requiring the land to be reinstated at the end of such period (section 30). As an alternative to planning applications being determined by the local planning authority, the Secretary of State may "call in" particular applications or classes of application and himself determine them (section 35). Such applications may also be referred to an *ad hoc* Planning Inquiry Commission for special inquiry and report (section 48).

Once planning permission is obtained it attaches to the land for the benefit of subsequent owners. However, there is generally an implied condition that the development will be begun within five years unless other express time limits are laid down (section 41).

The local planning authority is also given powers to promote timely completion of developments. Thus, the authority may serve a "completion notice" (to be confirmed by the Secretary of State) whereby planning permission will cease to have effect after a specified period in respect of uncompleted work (section 44). The authority also has powers to modify or revoke planning permission, with the confirmation of the Secretary of State (section 45).

An appeal against the local planning authority's decision may be made to the Secretary of State, generally within six months. He will reconsider the whole application, so that an appeal against the conditions imposed with a consent may result in a refusal of consent. If any party wishes to make representations there will be a private hearing before an inspector, or the Secretary of State may direct that a public local inquiry be held (section 36). There is a final appeal from the Minister's decision to the High Court on a point of law. As an alternative, there is provision for an appeal from a decision of the local planning authority relating to the design or external appearance of a building to be heard by an independent tribunal (none have yet been established). Appeals from the local planning authority's decision may also be referred to a Planning Inquiry Commission (section 48).

Powers of control

If a development is carried out without planning consent, or contrary to conditions imposed with such consent, the local planning authority may enforce their control by serving an enforcement notice (section 87). This must specify the matters of complaint, the steps required for their rectification and the period for compliance. The steps required to be taken may include demolition or alteration of buildings or works. Such a notice must be served generally within four years of the offence. A copy must be served on the owner and on the occupier of the land and on any other person having a sufficient interest. The period for compliance must be reasonable, but development may be stopped on three days' notice by an interim "stop notice" (section 90). An appeal against a notice may be made to the Secretary of State and the appeal is deemed also to be an application for planning permission in respect of the offending building or works (section 88). There is a further appeal to the High Court on a point of law. If the enforcement notice takes effect and the required steps are not taken then the local planning authority may itself carry out the work and recover the cost from the land owner. The owner is also liable to a fine of up to £400 on conviction by a magistrates' court and thereafter to a daily fine of up to £50 for non-compliance (section 89).

Compensation

Since permission to develop land has such a direct influence on its value it is obviously right that a measure of redress should be provided for those who suffer loss through planning restrictions (see 1971 Act parts VII, VIII and IX). Redress may be available in one of two ways. First, if planning restrictions prevent or hamper development or cause depreciation in the value of the land, compensation may be payable in a limited number of cases. Such restrictions may take the form of a refusal of planning consent or may arise from the exercise of powers, *e.g.* to revoke or modify an existing consent or to order removal of an existing building (sections 45, 51). Compensation may also be payable where land value drops as a result of the future possibility of compulsory purchase. Where the restriction relates to new development the right of compensation depends on whether there was a claim on the fund created under the Act of 1947.

Secondly, when planning permission is refused, or granted subject to conditions, the owner may in some cases require his land to be purchased by the local authority. But this is possible only if the land is virtually useless in its existing state.

The discussion above had been concerned principally with building and construction works being carried out upon land. The 1971 Act also contains extensive provisions relating to buildings of special architectural or historic interest, trees, advertisements, waste land, industrial development, office development and other matters, for which reference must be made elsewhere.

New town development

The concept of building new towns dates from the end of the Second World War when the policy of rebuilding devastated city centres produced an excess of population which needed to be re-housed. New towns were seen as the only alternative to continued urban sprawl. The main Act currently in force is the New Towns Act 1965. The first step in creating a new town is the designation of the area by the Minister. In some cases this has been virgin land but more usually an existing small town is chosen as a nucleus. Before designating a site the Minister will consult local authorities in the area, and if any person or body objects to the site chosen a public local inquiry must be held. However, after considering the objections, the Minister may properly override them and make his decision on the grounds of policy: see *Franklin's* case, above.

The development of a new town will be undertaken by an *ad hoc* authority called a development corporation. This is a corporate body consisting of a number of persons selected by the Minister, and having statutory objects and powers. The purpose of the corporation is to prepare proposals for the development of the new town and to secure their implementation. The corporation does not displace the local planning authority, but is absolved from the normal requirements for obtaining planning consents.

To achieve their purposes, development corporations are invested with wide powers. These include acquisition of land (by compulsory purchase if necessary), carrying out building or other operations, provision of services, and carrying on any business or undertaking for the purposes of the new town. However, the Minister retains a general power of control over any of the powers of the development corporation. Further, a corporation may not undertake, *inter alia*, the supply of water, electricity or gas without first obtaining specific powers to do so.

A new town development corporation is intended to have a limited life. When the laying out and development of a new town has been substantially achieved the corporation will be wound up and its property transferred to the Commission for New Towns.

Further Reading

Encyclopedia of the Law of Town and Country Planning, Heap.
Heap, *An Outline of Planning Law* (7th ed., 1978).
Megarry, *A Manual of the Law of Real Property* (5th ed., 1975).
Swinfen Green and Henderson, *Land Law* (3rd ed., 1975), (Concise College Text).

CHAPTER 14

STATUTORY PROVISIONS

Contracts under which work is carried out in the construction industry are affected directly by few statutory provisions. However, matters such as the design of the works and the mode of carrying out operations are likely to be subject to many statutory controls. These may impose obligations on one or more of the parties involved. A breach of such an obligation may give rise to statutory penal sanctions and also to consequences at civil law, in tort or for breach of contract (see JCT clause 4 and ICE clause 26).

The more directly relevant statutes which affect the construction industry include the Public Health Acts 1936 and 1961, the Factories Act 1961, which is gradually being supersided by the Health and Safety at Work, etc., Act 1974, the Highways Act 1959, the Water Act 1973, and the various planning Acts mentioned in Chapter 13. There are also a number of statutes which apply only to London, which include the three Acts known as the London Building Acts. Many of the Acts referred to contain powers for the creation of further delegated legislation in the form of regulations or by-laws, which lay down detailed provisions.

In this chapter two groups of statutory provisions are discussed, which are those of greatest importance in relation to new construction work. First, the Building Regulations and the London Building By-laws, which govern the design and construction of building works. Secondly, the regulations and other statutory provisions, as to health and safety which govern the manner in which building and construction work is carried out on sites. For the full text of statutes with annotations, see *Halsbury's Statutes*, 3rd edition. The regulations and by-laws are often amended. Copies of provisions currently in force may be obtained from H.M. Stationery Office. In the following sections references thus: (A10), (2.04) and (23) refer to the regulation or by-law number. Passages in italic type *thus* are quoted directly from the regulation or by-law in question.

THE BUILDING REGULATIONS

Prior to 1965 building work throughout England and Wales was governed by by-laws made by the particular local authority (these should be distinguished from the by-laws which apply still in

London). Latterly the provisions were based upon model by-laws, but there were important variations between different authorities. In 1965 a new set of Building Regulations was made under the Public Health Act 1961 which applied to the whole of England and Wales with the exception of the Inner London Boroughs. The regulations were amended periodically, and have now been further amended and consolidated into the Building Regulations 1976.

The power to made Building Regulations has been amended and extended by Part III of the Health and Safety at Work, etc., Act 1974. This also contains new provisions for administration of the Regulations. Section 70 of the Act contains powers to make building regulations for Inner London, so that eventually a uniform system will be produced.

Content and application of the regulations

The regulations are divided into sections as follows: A, Interpretation and general; B, Materials; C, Preparation of site and resistance to moisture; D, Structural stability; E, Safety in fire; F, Thermal insulation; G, Sound insulation; H, Stairways, ramps, balustrades and vehicle barriers; J, Refuse disposal; K, Open space, ventilation and height of rooms; L, Chimneys flue pipes, hearths and fireplace recesses; M, Heat producing appliances and incinerators; N, Drainage, private sewers and cesspools; P, Sanitary conveniences. These are followed by 12 important schedules.

In view of their length and largely technical content it is not proposed to comment here upon the substantive content of the regulations. Reference will be made only to provisions which are relevant to the way in which the regulations operate. For further information, a copy of the regulations may be obtained from H.M. Stationery Office.

The purpose of the regulations is the protection of public health and safety. This is achieved by providing minimum standards of design in relation to the various matters set out above. The regulations apply, in general, to the erection of a building (A6) including any part of a building, to a structural alteration or extension (A7), to certain works and fittings (A8) and to a building undergoing a material change of use (A9). There are exceptions to which the regulations may not apply (A5); these include buildings belonging to a statutory undertaker, school buildings and buildings erected in connection with a mine or quarry. Schedule 2 defines classes of buildings which are partially exempted from the regulations and sets out the provisions with which compliance is required. Partially exempted buildings include small structures such as a greenhouse or potting shed, contractor's temporary buildings and small detached garages.

In addition to the specified standards, there are set out throughout the regulations many "deemed-to-satisfy" provisions. These are alternative standards for materials or methods of construction compliance with which, while not mandatory (A4(9)), are deemed to comply with the regulations. For example, materials complying to a British Standard or a B.S. Code of Practice are deemed to satisfy regulation B1 (Fitness of Materials) *if the use of that material is appropriate to the purpose for and condition in which it is used* (B2). In relation to structural stability, extensive use is made of Codes of Practice as deeming to satisfy regulations. For example, Foundations may comply with C.P.2004 (D4); Structural Work of steel may comply with B.S. 449 (D8).

Notices and compliance with the regulations

The regulations provide for the giving of written notices to and deposit of plans and particulars with the local authority, in accordance with the relevant rules of Schedule 3 (A10). Thus, a person intending to erect a building which is neither wholly nor partially exempted must submit, with specified particulars, the following: notice of intention to erect a building; particulars so far as necessary to show whether the building complies with the regulations; a block plan and key plan; and a plan of every floor and roof and section of every storey with particulars to show whether the building complies with the regulations (Rule B). The local authority may require certain further drawings and particulars, including specifications of materials, calculations of loading and strength, and details of construction (Rule E). The Public Health Acts provide that the local authority must pass or reject plans within a period of five weeks, which may be extended by agreement to two months. If plans are rejected, the notice must specify the defects by reason of which they are rejected. The Acts also set out the local authority's powers in respect of work which does not conform to the regulations. These powers include ordering demolition or alteration to secure compliance with regulations, and fines, including continuing daily penalties, (Public Health Act 1936 section 65).

In addition to notices to secure building regulation approval, other notices of commencement and completion of certain stages of the work must be given. Thus, a builder must give specified written notice not less than 24 hours before the following: commencement of the operation; the covering up of foundations, etc; and the covering of drains, etc. Notice is also required not more than seven days after certain drain works. In default of giving notice the builder may be required to open up the works. The builder must give further written notices not more than seven days after completion of the works (A11). The local authority's officer must be permitted at all times to take samples of materials to ascertain if they comply with the regulations (A15).

The Public Health Act 1961 section 6, provides powers for dispensing with or relaxing any requirement of the regulations, and for delegation of these powers to the local authority with a right of appeal to the Minister. Powers of dispensation and relaxation are delegated to local authorities (save for their own buildings) in respect of all sections of the regulations except for A (Interpretation and general), D (Structural stability) and part of E (Safety in fire) (A.13). A dispensation or relaxation may be made only where the operation of any requirement *would be unreasonable in relation to the particular case*. Schedule 4 provides forms for applications.

Selected decisions on dispensation with or relaxation of the building regulations are published by H.M. Stationery Office. The decisions are administrative and not judicial, so that a future decision in a similar case will not necessarily be the same. The decisions however may be of guidance to applicants. As an example, the applicant in one case had purchased a second-hand prefab consisting of an asbestos clad steel frame. There was insufficient information to show compliance with part D (Structural stability). The applicant proposed to alter the structure, and argued that compliance with the regulations was unreasonable because the prefab had previously been used with government approval. Dispensation was refused and calculations to show structural stability were required.

Civil liability

The Public Health Acts and Building Regulations are enforced primarily through the criminal law. But the Regulations are frequently incorporated into building contracts so that failure to comply will be a breach by the builder. The NHBC technical requirements incorporate the Building Regulations. The JCT and ICE forms of contract contain general obligations to comply with statutory provisions (see clauses 4 and 26 respectively) which include the Regulations.

In addition, it was held in *Anns* v. *London Borough of Merton* (1977) that an owner of a dwelling could bring an action for breach of statutory duty against a builder failing to comply with the Public Health Acts or Building Regulations. The importance of this decision is that the builder is liable to any subsequent purchaser; and also the period of limitation does not begin to run until the defect is or ought to be discovered. Undetected defects typically affect foundations, so that the builder may now be subject to a virtually unlimited liability. The above principles will apply to liability under the London Building By-laws. Section 71 of the Health and Safety at Work, etc., Act 1974 further provides for the imposition of civil liability for breach of duty imposed by building regulations.

THE LONDON BUILDING BY-LAWS

London has had its own system of building construction control since the last century. The provisions currently in force are the London Building (Constructional) By-laws 1972 which, while replacing the previous by-laws, substituted metric units. While the Building Regulations form a reasonably comprehensive code without reference to the Public Health Acts, the London Building By-laws are not complete without numerous references to the parent legislation. This consists of three Acts: the London Building Act 1930, the London Building Act (Amendment) Act 1935 and the London Building Acts (Amendment) Act 1939, of which the last is the most important. The three Acts are collectively referred to as the London Building Acts, and will here be referred to singly as the 1930 Act, etc.

The area in which the By-laws are in force, and consequently where the Building Regulations are not in force, is the City of London and the twelve inner London Boroughs: Westminster, Camden, Islington, Hackney, Tower Hamlets, Greenwich, Lewisham, Southwark, Lambeth, Wandsworth, Hammersmith, and Kensington and Chelsea. As noted above, powers exist under the Health and Safety at Work, etc., Act 1974 to create a uniform system of building control applying also to Inner London; but this is unlikely to be brought about for some years.

Content and application of the By-laws

The By-laws are divided into sections as follows: I Definitions; II General; III Dead and imposed loads; IV Materials and construction; V Sites of buildings, excavations, foundations, etc.; VI Roofs, external enclosures etc.; VII Walls and piers; VIII The structural use of steel; IX The structural use of reinforced, etc. concrete; X The structural use of timber; XI Fire resistance etc.; XII Flues, chimneys, hearths etc.; XIII Oil burning appliances etc.;

XIV Lighting and ventilation etc. These are followed by three schedules. Again, it is not proposed to comment upon the substantive content of the By-laws. Reference will be made only to provisions which are relevant to the way in which the By-laws are intended to operate. For further information a copy of the By-laws may be obtained from the G.L.C.

The By-laws contain provisions which specify materials and work, and lay down design standards. A central figure in the administration system is the district surveyor, to whom very extensive powers are given. For example, all work affected by the By-laws must be carried out *to the satisfaction of the district surveyor in a proper and workmanlike manner* (2.10). The satisfaction of the district surveyor is used as a criterion for many alternative materials, work and design standards laid down in the By-laws, and in relation to certain matters his approval is obligatory. Thus, piling used in connection with foundations must be *to the satisfaction of the district surveyor* (5.08), and no part of the ground which supports a building must be subjected to pressure *other than such as may be approved by the district surveyor* (5.07). It is evident that in certain matters he is required to be in advance of engineering science. There is generally a right of appeal to the G.L.C. against any decision or requirement of the district surveyor, and a further limited right of appeal to a tribunal of appeal established under the 1939 Act.

In common with the Building Regulations, the By-laws contain numerous references to British Standards and to B.S. Codes of Practice. But the way in which they are used varies. Thus, cement may be in conformity with various B.S. provisions *or* be approved by the district surveyor *as being suitable* (4.04); structural steel must comply with B.S.449 (8.03) as well as with other By-laws; while reinforced, prestressed and precast concrete and structural timber must *comply to the satisfaction of the district surveyor or with* the relevant codes of practice, *i.e.* CP 114, 115, 116 and 112 respectively.

The By-laws apply generally to the *construction of every building or structure* and to the conversion of, addition to or alteration of a building or structure. The 1939 Act, sections 149 to 152, contains provisions for partial or total exemption from the requirements of the Acts and the By-laws. Buildings totally exempt include Crown buildings, and certain special and temporary buildings. Partial and specified exemptions apply to many specific London buildings, engineering structures such as highway bridges and dock works, and other buildings such as greenhouses. Certain classes of buildings are exempt from the provisions of the Acts and By-laws relating to means of escape in case of fire.

On receipt of an application in respect of a particular building, the G.L.C. has power under the 1935 Act, section 9 to modify or waive *the requirements of any* by-law, and may do so subject to any conditions they think fit. Where such a modification or waiver would affect the rights or interests of an adjoining owner, he must be given notice of his right to make representations when the application is considered.

Notices and compliance with the By-laws

The 1939 Act, section 83, provides that a builder must serve building notices on the district surveyor when work is about to begin, when work is about to be resumed after suspension exceeding three months or when the builder has been changed, giving in each case two clear days' notice. Every building notice must give certain particulars including the situation, area, height, number of storeys and proposed use of the building, the proposed work, and an estimate of the cost of the work (section 84). A building notice must generally be accompanied (unless the district surveyor otherwise agrees) by *plans and sections of sufficient detail to show the construction* and by calculations and particulars of materials. The district surveyor may require additional details (2.01). Further notices in writing to the district surveyor are required two clear days before disturbance of support to any superstructure (2.02), or before conversion of a building (2.03).

The district surveyor may require proof by means of samples, tests or otherwise that any materials conform to the by-laws (2.04). He may also require tests to be made on any metal which is used or to be used (2.05).

Where a building notice discloses any infringement of the Acts or By-laws, the district surveyor will serve a "notice of objection" under the 1939 Act (section 87), against which there is an appeal to the Magistrates' Court. If a contravention of the Acts or By-laws occurs during the course of the works, the district surveyor will serve a "notice of irregularity", (section 88). Such a notice may be served after completion of works. The 1939 Act provides a scale of fines for contravention of various provisions (section 148) and also provides for powers of demolition or alteration to secure compliance with the Acts or By-laws (section 104). Any person who contravenes the By-laws or any requirement made thereunder is liable to a fine of £50 and to a daily penalty of £10 (2.11).

It should be noted that while the By-laws contain detailed provisions as to the design and construction of buildings there are other, more general provisions contained in the London Building Acts, under which the By-laws are made, particularly in Part III of the 1939 Act. Part IV of this Act also makes important provisions relating to party walls and foundations where lands belonging to different owners adjoin. The service of notices on adjoining owners is required before carrying out works, and there are provisions for the statutory settlement of differences which arise between adjoining owners.

HEALTH AND SAFETY

Prior to 1974 the health and safety of workpeople was governed by a multiplicity of statutory provisions. In the construction industry, these derived from the Factories Act 1961, and were enforced by the factory inspectors. Since the early days of industrialisation, the law has made great progress in securing compensation for those injured at work. It was however widely thought that the law was not achieving the primary objective of securing the health and safety of workpeople, *i.e.* of preventing accidents. This was the reason for setting up a committee under Lord Robens to inquire into health and safety. The committee reported in 1972 and their recommendations lead to the Health and Safety at Work, etc., Act 1974.

The intention of the Act is to replace existing legislation by a system of regulations and codes of practice to maintain and improve existing standards of health and safety. The Act itself also contains some new and important powers of control. Enforcement of the law is transferred to the new Health and Safety Executive, the functions of former factory inspectors being transferred to health and safety inspectors. The Executive operates under the direction of the new Health and Safety Commission (see section 11), which is charged with the overall duty of achieving the general purposes of Part I of the Act, *i.e.* to secure the health safety and welfare of persons at work (section 1(1)). One of the powers of the Commission is to order investigations or inquiries, *e.g.* into accidents, which may carried out by the Executive or by others. Apart from powers contained in the Act itself, there has been no sudden change in the detailed legislation governing health and safety. Instead the Act is intended to facilitate the progressive replacement of existing provisions. To this end the Act contains sweeping powers to repeal or modify existing statutory provisions, including the Factories Act 1961, (section 15).

Day to day operations in the construction industry, both in building and civil engineering work, are governed by the Construction Regulations of which there are four principle sets. Some of these were made under powers pre-dating the Factories Act 1961, but from 1962 they took effect under that Act. The Regulations have not been amended or repealed under the Health and Safety at Work, etc., Act, but they now take effect under the new Act and must be read in the lights of its provisions. The Construction Regulations will eventually be replaced by new provisions; but at the date of writing no new measures are contemplated.

In the following sections the main provisions and effects of the Act are discussed; this is followed by an outline of the principal features of the Construction Regulations.

Effects of the Health and Safety at Work, etc., Act 1974

The Act creates general duties on employers to ensure, so far as is reasonably practicable, the health safety and welfare at work of employees (section 2). A similar duty is placed on employers and self-employed persons to ensure, so far as reasonably practicable, that other persons are not exposed to risks to health or safety (section 3). Persons having control of premises must ensure, so far as is reasonably practicable, that the premises are safe and without risk to health (section 4).

Enforcement of the Act is placed in the hands of inspectors who are given powers considerably wider than those formerly available under the Factories Acts. Their powers include the right to enter premises, to make examination and investigation, to take samples, to take possession of articles or substances, to require persons to answer questions and to require the production of documents (section 20). Where there is a contravention of certain statutory provisions (including the Act and the Construction Regulations) the inspector may serve an "improvement notice" (section 21); and where the contravention involves a risk of serious personal injury, he may give a "prohibition notice," which may have immediate effect (section 22).

The Act provides penalties for breach of its provisions or other offences such as obstructing an inspector. Fines of up to £400 may be imposed on summary conviction. Certain offences carry higher penalties on indictment; *e.g.* contravention of an improvement notice may lead to an unlimited fine or imprisonment.

Civil Liability

The Health and Safety at Work etc., Act does not itself confer any civil right of action (section 47(1)). However the Act does not affect civil liability under existing provisions (including the Construction Regulations) and the new regulations to be made under the Act will carry civil liability unless they provide otherwise. The rights of individual workmen are therefore, as yet, substantially unaltered by the new Act. Before 1974 the likelihood of civil liability to those injured was probably a greater incentive to safety than was the criminal law.

In order for a workman to succeed in a civil action for breach of a regulation, he must show that four conditions are satisfied. These are that: (i) the regulation was intended to protect a class of which he was a member; (ii) the regulation was broken; (iii) he has suffered damage of a kind against which the regulation was intended to protect; (iv) the damage was caused by the breach.

These requirements may appear self-evident, but their effect in practice may be less than obvious. Thus, in a number of cases it has been held that self-employed workmen were not entitled to the protection of the Construction Regulations. Instead of having a right of action in respect of their injuries, self-employed men may themselves be liable to prosecution for breach of the regulations. However, the Court of Appeal has now laid down that the question whether a man is employed or self-employed is to be approached broadly. The fact that he pays his own income tax is not decisive. If he is in effect an employee, he will be so treated for the purposes of the regulations: *Ferguson* v. *John Dawson & Partners* (1976).

The kinds of damage against which the Construction Regulations are intended to protect cover personal injuries, but would not extend, for example, to loss of earnings due to unsafe scaffolding preventing work. The damage must also be caused by the breach. Thus, where a workman was killed in a fall because he did not wear a safety belt, it was found that the contractor, in breach of regulations, failed to provide belts for the men; but the contractor showed that the deceased would not have worn a belt even if it had been provided, and consequently was not liable in civil law for damages; *Cummings* v. *Arrol* (1962).

Application of the regulations

The main provisions of the four sets of regulations are outlined below. The question when the duty to comply arises must be answered by considering the individual regulations. In general the duties are placed upon *every contractor*, but for certain specified regulations, compliance is not required in respect of any workman if his presence is *not in the course of performing any work on behalf of his employer* and is not authorised. Most of the requirements of the Health and Welfare Regulations may be complied with by arranging for the use of existing facilities, for example those of another contractor on the site.

In respect of injury to a particular workman, liability for breach of regulations may be placed either on his employer, or upon the contractor who performs the operation in question, or who erects or uses the plant or equipment in question. Workmen are themselves required to comply with the regulations, to co-operate in carrying them out and to report any defect in plant or equipment.

Each set of regulations provides that the chief inspector (now appointed by the Health and Safety Executive) may make exemptions from any or all of the regulations. This may done if the chief inspector is *satisfied that the requirements in respect of which the exemption is granted are not necessary for the protection of persons employed or are not reasonably practicable.* Certain exemptions have been made which affect hoists in chimneys, scaffolding to steeples, etc., and lifting operations by a tracked shovel or dragline excavator.

The Construction (General Provision) Regulations 1961

Parts IV and V of these Regulations deal with the safety of excavations, shafts and tunnels, and with cofferdams and caissons. *Adequate* timbering or *other suitable support* must be provided for excavations etc. *as early as is practicable*, unless no fall from a height of more than four feet is liable to occur (8); and inspections and reports are required (9). Special care is necessary where excavation may reduce the stability of any structure (12). A barrier or cover must be provided where a person is liable to fall more than six feet six inches (13). Work on timbering and cofferdams must be supervised and all materials inspected (10, 17). Timbering and support work, cofferdams and caissons must be of *good construction*, of *sound material free from patent defect and of adequate strength* and *properly maintained* (10, 15). Safe egress must be maintained in case of flooding (11, 16). The regulations do not apply to those engaged in inspection of stabilising work, provided that appropriate precautions are taken for their safety (9, 18). There are exemptions from the regulations in respect of *physical conditions* over which the contractor had no control and *against which it was not reasonably practicable* to provide (8, 11, 12, 16).

Other parts of the Regulations cover explosives (VI), dangerous or unhealthy atmospheres (VII), work on or adjacent to water (VIII) and transport (IX). Part X deals with demolition. Where there is a risk of collapse *so as to endanger any person employed*, the work must be closely supervised or carried out by experienced workmen under competent direction. Adequate shoring or other precautions are required to prevent a collapse which *may endanger any person employed*, but the requirement does not apply to those erecting shoring (41). Part XI is concerned with the safety of machinery and general precautions to be observed on construction sites.

The Construction (Lifting Operations) Regulations 1961

Part III of these Regulations applies to lifting appliances, which include a hoist, crane, sheer legs, excavator, dragline and piling frame. Such plant must be of *good mechanical construction, sound material, adequate strength and free from patent defect* and *properly maintained* and subject to regular inspection and report (10). The controls of the machinery must generally facilitate safe operation (16). The driver must be a *trained and competent* person (26) and must be adequately protected at his work (14). Testing and examination is required at certain times, when the safe working loads must be specified (28) and displayed on the machine (29). These loads must not be exceeded, except for testing purposes (31).

Part IV deals with chains, ropes and lifting gear, which must be of *good construction, sound material, adequate strength, suitable quality, and free from patent defect*, and must be tested and examined to determine the safe working load (34). A retest is required after any alteration or repair (35). Special provisions apply to hoists (Part V) and to machinery to carry persons (Part VI). Generally loads must be secured and loose objects prevented from falling out of containers; but the last requirement does not apply to a grab or shovel, provided that effective steps are taken to prevent any person being endangered (49).

The Construction (Working Places) Regulations 1966

These Regulations apply particularly to scaffolding, including working platforms. The general requirements are that every place of work must *so far as is reasonably practicable* be safe and have safe access to and egress from it (6), and that *sufficient and suitable* scaffolding or other support is to be provided where required (7). The scaffolding must be of *good construction, of suitable and sound material and of adequate strength for the purpose for which it is used* (9), and must be supervised and inspected (8, 22) and maintained (11). Some construction requirements are laid down (13) as well as general requirements as to stability: scaffolding must be *rigidly connected with the building* unless independently stable (15). A part of a building used for support must itself be *sufficiently stable* and strong to afford support (18).

There are specific provisions for special types such as slung (16), cantilever (17) and suspended scaffolds (19), and boatswain's chairs, etc. (20). Trestle scaffolds are permitted where a person is not liable to fall more than 15 feet (21). With regard to working platforms, gangways and runs, there are requirements as to span, projection and width in various circumstances (25–27). Platforms, gangways etc. must be kept free from unnecessary obstruction and must not be allowed to remain slippery (30). Where a person is liable to fall more than six feet six inches, guard rails and toe boards must generally be provided (28, 29, 33). There are provisions as to the construction, maintenance (31) and use of ladders (32). A continuous run must normally not exceed thirty feet. Where it is impracticable to comply with certain of the regulations so far as they relate to the falls of persons, the contractor must comply so far as practicable, and in addition should provide safety nets or safety belts (38).

The Construction (Health and Welfare) Regulations 1966

Regulations 5 to 10 deal with health and require various facilities to be provided on sites. These include first-aid boxes, stretchers and a first-aid room, depending on the number of people employed. Regulations 11 to 16 deal with welfare and require the provision on site of *adequate and suitable accommodation* for workmen for shelter, deposit and drying of clothes and taking meals. The contractor must also provide drinking water, facilities for washing, sanitary conveniences and protective clothing.

Further Reading

Building Regulations *Encyclopedia of Public Health, Law and Practice*, Cross.

London Building Acts *Halsbury's Statutes of England* (3rd ed.), vol. 20.

Health and Safety Act and Construction Regulations *Redgrave's Health and Safety in Factories* (1976), Fife and Machin.

GLOSSARY OF LEGAL TERMS

ADJOURN: To put off the hearing of a case or matter to a later date.

AFFIDAVIT: A written statement sworn on oath which may be used in certain cases as evidence.

AGENT: A person with authority to act for another (the principal).

APPELLANT: The party who brings an appeal to a higher court.

APPEARANCE: Acknowledgment, by the *defendant* in a civil action, of the *writ* or *summons*.

ARBITRATION: Proceedings before a private tribunal, to which the parties agree to submit disputes.

ASSETS: Property which is available for paying debts.

ASSIGNMENT: The transmission by agreement of a right or interest to another person.

ATTESTATION: Authentication of a document by the signatures of witnesses.

AWARD: The decision given by an arbitrator.

BAILMENT: Delivery of goods into the possession of a person who is not their owner.

BANKRUPT: A person who cannot pay his debts and who is adjudicated a *bankrupt*.

BAR: The profession of barristers from which practically all judges are recruited.

BREACH: Non-fulfilment of some contractual (or other) obligation.

BY-LAWS: Rules, usually made under statutory authority and having full force of law.

CASE STATED: A statement of facts prepared by a court or arbitrator for the decision of a higher court on a point of law.

CAVEAT EMPTOR: "Let the buyer beware"; a maximum indicating that any risk is upon the buyer and not the seller.

CHANCERY: One of the three divisions of the *High Court*.

CHARGE: An interest, usually over land, given as security.

CHATTELS: Personal property.

CHOSE IN ACTION: An intangible right which can be enforced by action; *e.g.* a debt.

CLAIMANT: The party who initiates *arbitration* proceedings.

COMMERCIAL COURT: A special court in the *Queen's Bench* Division for dealing with commercial actions.

COMMON LAW: Law embodied in case precedent, as opposed to *Statute* law or *Equity*.

CONDITION: An important term of a *contract*.

CONSIDERATION: The bargain or inducement provided by a party to a *contract*.

CONSOLIDATION: Joining of two separate actions so that they may be tried together.

CONTRACT: An agreement which is binding in law.

CONVEYANCE: A written instrument which transfers property (especially land) from one person to another.

COUNTERCLAIM: A cross action brought by the *defendant* against the *plaintiff*, or by the *respondent* against the *claimant*.

COUNTY COURTS: Local courts which deal with smaller civil claims.

COURT OF APPEAL: The court which hears appeals from (*inter alia*) the *High Court* and *county courts*.

COVENANT: An undertaking contained in a document, especially in a *deed* or *lease*.

CROWN COURT: The branch of the *Supreme Court* which deals with criminal trials (and also some civil cases).

DAMAGES: The money award made to a successful party in a civil action.

DEED: A written instrument, signed, *sealed* and delivered.

DEFENCE: A pleading from the *defendant* in answer to the *Statement of Claim*.

DEFENDANT: The person sued in an ordinary civil action.

DETINUE: An action in *tort* for recovery of a specific *chattel*.

DISCOVERY: Disclosure of all the documents relating to a case, before the trial.

DOMICILE: The country or state with which a person or company is most closely connected.

EASEMENT: A right enjoyed over land belonging to another person.

EQUITY: Law based upon discretion and conscience, derived from the old Court of Chancery.

ESTATE: General term for an interest in land.

EX PARTE: by one side only, *e.g.* an application *ex parte* for an *injunction*.

EXECUTION: Methods of enforcement of a *judgment* in an action.

EXHIBIT: A document used in evidence, especially when annexed to an *affidavit*.

FI FA: Abbreviation of *Fieri Facias*; *execution* of a *judgment* by seizing and selling the debtor's goods.

FORCE MAJEURE: Irresistible compulsion; especially such as to cause a breach of *contract*, *e.g.* war or Act of God.

FORFEITURE: A provision, especially in a *contract* or *lease*, enabling one party to strip the other of his whole interest in certain events; *e.g.* determination of a building contract.

FRUSTRATION: Determination of a *contract* by some intervening event, *e.g.* destruction of the subject matter.

GARNISHEE: A person against whom a *judgment* debt is enforced by ordering another (*e.g.* a bank) who owes him a debt to pay it instead to the judgment creditor.

GENERAL DAMAGES: Unascertained *damages*, to be assessed by the judge.

GENERAL INDORSEMENT: A brief description of the plaintiff's claim *indorsed* on the *writ*; a full *statement of claim* must then be served separately.

HEARSAY: Testimony by a witness as to a matter not within his personal knowledge.

HIGH COURT: The principal court in which civil actions are heard at first instance.

HOUSE OF LORDS: The highest court of England and Scotland.

INCORPOREAL: Rights and interests which are intangible are said to be incorporeal, *e.g.* debts or shares in a company.

INDORSEMENT: Something written on the back of a document, such as the claim indorsed on a *writ*.

INJUNCTION: An order of the court which commands a person to do or refrain from doing some act.

INNS OF COURT: The four societies of Inner and Middle Temple, Lincoln's Inn and Gray's Inn. Every barrister must be a member of one of the Inns.

INTERIM: Provisional, until further direction; *e.g.* an *interim* order.

INTERLOCUTORY: A matter dealt with before the trial of an action; *e.g.* an *interlocutory injunction*.

INTERROGATORIES: Questions formally put in writing by one party to another, before the trial of a civil action.

JOINT: Where two or more persons share some right or obligation such that their interest is not severed, each having an interest in the whole; *e.g.* a *joint* tenancy or account.

JUDGMENT: The order given by a court after hearing a case.

JURISDICTION: Authority of a court or arbitrator to hear and determine causes, *e.g.* the *county court jurisdiction* is limited financially and geographically.

KING'S BENCH: A division of the *High Court*, called *Queen's Bench* when the sovereign is female.

LAW REPORTS: Authenticated reports of decided cases in the superior courts.

LAW SOCIETY: The governing body of English solicitors.

LEASE: A letting or demise of land; also the instrument containing the demise and its covenants.

LEGAL AID: A system for providing free or assisted legal advice or representation, for persons of slender means.

LICENCE: An authority, especially to enter land without having exclusive possession.

LIEN: A right to retain possession of some article until a claim by the holder is satisfied.

LIMITATION: Statutory periods within which actions must be commenced.

LIQUIDATED DAMAGES: Ascertained or calculated monetary loss claimed in an action. *Also* a sum provided by a *contract* as payable in the event of breach, which is not deemed to be a *penalty*.

LIQUIDATION: Winding up of a company.

LORD JUSTICE OF APPEAL: Title of a judge of the *Court of Appeal*.

LORD OF APPEAL IN ORDINARY: Title of a judge in the *House of Lords* or *Privy Council*; commonly called a "Law Lord."

MASTER: An official of the *High Court* who decides many *interlocutory* matters.

MITIGATION: Abatement of loss or damage.

MORTGAGE: A *conveyance, assignment* or *lease* of property as security for a loan.

MUTATIS MUTANDIS: With the necessary changes.

NEGLIGENCE: Conduct falling short of the duty of care owed to persons generally.

NUISANCE: Unlawful interference with the use or enjoyment of another person's land.

OBITER DICTUM: Statement of a judge on a point not directly relevant to his decision, and therefore not strictly of authority.

OFFICIAL REFEREE: A judge who tries technical cases which are transferred usually from the *Queen's Bench* Division of the *High Court*.

OFFICIAL SOLICITOR: An officer of the *Supreme Court* who acts for persons under a disability.

PARI PASSU: In proportion: on an equal footing.

PARTICULARS: Details of some allegation pleaded in an action. If a pleading is insufficient the opponent may ask for further and better *Particulars*.

PARTNERSHIP: An unincorporated association of persons in business with a view to profit.

PENALTY: A sum provided by a *contract* as payable in the event of breach, which sum is not deemed to be *liquidated damages*.

PETITION: A document used to begin certain civil actions such as a divorce or a winding-up.

PLAINTIFF: The party who begins an ordinary civil action.

PLEADING: A written statement of a party's case in a civil action.

POINTS OF CLAIM, DEFENCE: The title of pleadings in an *arbitration*.

PRESCRIPTION: A claim to some right, based upon long user.

PRIVY COUNCIL: The judicial committee of the *Privy Council* is the final court of appeal for some Commonwealth countries.

PROFIT A PRENDRE: A right to take something from another person's land.

PUISNE JUDGE: A judge of one of the divisions of the *High Court*, who should be referred to as Mr. Justice ———.

QUEEN'S BENCH: One of the three divisions of the *High Court*.

QUEEN'S COUNSEL: A senior barrister, appointed by the Lord Chancellor. Q.C.s are known colloquially as "silks" because they wear silk gowns.

QUANTUM MERUIT: An action claiming a reasonable price for work or goods.

RATIFICATION: Confirmation, *e.g.* of a *contract*, so as to make it binding.

RATIO DECIDENDI: The relevant part of a judge's decision in a case, which is authoritative.

REAL PROPERTY: Certain interests and rights in land; as opposed to personal property.

RECTIFICATION: Correction by the court of a document so as to express the parties' true intention.

REPLY: A *pleading* from a *plaintiff* in answer to *defendant's defence*.

REPUDIATION: An express or implied refusal by one party to perform his obligation under a *contract*.

RESPONDENT: The *defendant* in certain types of action, *e.g.* an *arbitration*.

RIPARIAN OWNER: An owner of land bordering on a watercourse.

SEAL: An impressed piece of wax attached to a document so as to make it "under seal."

SEQUESTRATION: Order of the *High Court* to seize goods and lands of a *defendant* who is in contempt of court.

SET-OFF: Diminution or extinction of the *plaintiff*'s claim in an action by deducting the *defendant's counterclaim.*

SEVERAL: Where two or more persons share an obligation so that it may be enforced in full against any one of them, independently.

SHERIFF: A local office of great antiquity. The present-day duties of a *Sheriff* in civil cases are principally the *execution* of *judgments.*

SIMPLE CONTRACT: A *contract* not under *seal*, whether oral or in writing.

SPECIAL DAMAGES: Ascertained or calculated monetary loss; as opposed to unascertained or *general damages.*

SPECIAL INDORSEMENT: A full *statement of claim indorsed* on a *writ*; as opposed to a *general indorsement.*

SPECIFIC PERFORMANCE: An equitable remedy whereby a person may be compelled to perform his obligation under a *contract.*

STATEMENT OF CLAIM: The plaintiff's initial *pleading* in an ordinary civil action in the *High Court* (followed by the *defence* and *reply*).

STATUTE: An Act of Parliament.

STATUTORY INSTRUMENT: A form of delegated legislation, which has full force of law.

SUBPOENA: An order requiring a person to appear in court and give evidence or produce documents.

SUBROGATION: The right to bring an action in the name of another person.

SUE: To take legal proceedings for a civil remedy.

SUMMONS: An order to appear before a judge or magistrate. Some civil actions are begun by an originating *summons.*

SUPREME COURT: The *High Court*, the *Court of Appeal* and the *Crown Court* are collectively known as the *Supreme Court* of Judicature.

TAXATION: Settlement by the Taxing *Master* (or in the *County Court*, the Registrar) of the amount payable by one party to the other as costs.

THIRD PARTY: A person not originally a party to an action, but who may be brought in by a *defendant.*

TORT: A civil wrong, independent of *contract* or breach of trust.

TRESPASS: A tortious injury to the person or goods of another, or an unwarrantable entry upon his land.

TRUST: A disposition of property to be held by trustees for the benefit of beneficiaries.

UBERRIMA FIDES: The utmost good faith, required in certain transactions, *e.g.* insurance contracts.

ULTRA VIRES: Beyond their powers; especially of a limited company or statutory body. The opposite of *intra vires*.

UNLIQUIDATED DAMAGES: Damages which cannot be calculated as a monetary loss, and which are assessed by the judge; *e.g.* damages for personal injury.

VACATION: The periods between legal terms, when the superior courts do not sit. There are four vacations in the year.

WARRANTY: A term of a *contract* which is not a *condition*; especially a statement by the vendor as to the quality of goods.

WITHOUT PREJUDICE: Correspondence in connection with a dispute, thus headed, is privileged and cannot be taken as implying any admission by the writer.

WRIT: A document used to begin an ordinary civil action. It must bear a *special* or a *general indorsement* of the *plaintiff*'s claim.

INDEX